GW00649276

Stalag Luft 1

An Official Account of the PoW Camp for Air Force Personnel 1940-1945

Stalag Luft 1

An Official History

Introduced by Mark Hillier

Frontline Books

STALAG LUFT I
An Official Account of the PoW Camp for Air Force Personnel 1940-1945

Published in Great Britain in 2018 by Frontline Books,
an imprint of Pen & Sword Books Ltd, Yorkshire – Philadelphia

Based on file reference WO 208/3282, from a series of records from the
Directorate of Military Intelligence, at The National Archives, Kew and licensed
under the Open Government Licence v3.0.

Introduction Copyright © Mark Hillier, 2018
Text alterations and additions © Frontline Books, 2018
ISBN: 978-1-52670-879-3

No part of this book may be reproduced or transmitted in any form or by any
means, electronic or mechanical including photocopying, recording or by any
information storage and retrieval system, without permission from the Publisher
in writing.

Typeset in 10.5/12.5 Palatino.
Printed and bound by TJ International Ltd, Padstow, Cornwall

Pen & Sword Books Ltd incorporates the imprints of Pen & Sword Archaeology,
Air World Books, Atlas, Aviation, Battleground, Discovery, Family History,
History, Maritime, Military, Naval, Politics, Social History, Transport, True Crime,
Claymore Press, Frontline Books, Praetorian Press, Seaforth Publishing and White
Owl

For a complete list of Pen & Sword titles please contact:

PEN & SWORD BOOKS LTD
47 Church Street, Barnsley, South Yorkshire, S70 2AS, UK.
E-mail: enquiries@pen-and-sword.co.uk
Website: www.pen-and-sword.co.uk
or
PEN AND SWORD BOOKS
1950 Lawrence Roadd, Havertown, PA 19083, USA
E-mail: Uspen-and-sword@casematepublishers.com
Website: www.penandswordbooks.com

Contents

CONTENTS

CONTENTS

CONTENTS

Part III
NCOs' CAMP
October 1942 to November 1943

CONTENTS

Part IV
OFFICERS' CAMP
November 1943 to May 1945

CONTENTS

CONTENTS

Publisher's Note

This 'official history' is reproduced in the form that it was originally written at the end of, or just after, the Second World War. Aside from correcting obvious spelling mistakes or typographical errors, we have strived to keep our edits and alterations to the absolute minimum.

A direct consequence of this policy is that there are inconsistencies in the text. The original manuscript, for example randomly used capitals for Prisoner and Camp. Likewise, the abbreviation for Prisoners of War has been retained as the original P's/W. Many place names should have umlauts; we have retained the spellings used by the original authors.

Introduction

For historians and enthusiasts alike, eye-witness accounts from Second World War aircrew often make for gripping reading. The stories from those who were facing danger every day is also crucial to our understanding of the emotional, psychological, and sometimes immense physical strain put upon those who were in action.

Whilst we are often drawn to the cut and thrust of combat, the missions and the losses, in the midst of all this excitement and drama are the experiences of those who fell into the hands of the enemy to languish in captivity. For these PoWs, their war was just as hard and tough and mentally challenging. Many endured isolation, poor treatment and the risk of execution if caught trying to escape.

During the research for a book on the history of RAF Westhampnett I had the fortune to correspond with a former pilot of 610 (County of Chester) Squadron, who was based at the West Sussex airfield in 1941. In his mid-nineties and living in Canada at the time of our first acquaintance, John Anderson started his letter to me by stating that he didn't feel he had much information to give me as he had only carried out three sorties as a Spitfire pilot prior to being shot down and taken prisoner. Whilst he was certain that I would only want accounts of fighting and victories, I was able to assure him his story was just as important as those of the top-scoring aces.

I am glad that I persisted with John, as his is an amazing story. It is one that highlights the trials and tribulations of many whose final sortie ended in a prisoner of war camp.

On the morning of 10 July 1941, Sergeant John Anderson and his best friend, Horace Blackman, attended a briefing for their third *Circus* operation since arriving at RAF Westhampnett. As part of the Tangmere Wing, 610 Squadron was tasked with escorting bombers to a target at Chocques in France's Pas de Calais.

John was to fly Spitfire P8520. Coded DW-Q, this Mk.IIb was a presentation aircraft named *Mendip Spitfire*, it costs raised through the efforts of the Mendip Spitfire Fund. He was to operate in the 'tail end Charlie' position as a weaver to cover the squadron on its way out across the Channel. Horace flew in DW-K, which has the serial number P8374.

John recalled that he had been somewhat nervous before the mission, but that he had known that once he was airborne he would settle in to the task and focus on looking out as best he could for any signs of being 'bounced' from the rear. The operation was led by Wing Commander Douglas Bader.

Once airborne, hazy cloud forced six of the Spitfires to abort over the French coast, but the rest of Bader's force continued to the target. There were running combats with Messerschmitt Bf 109s on the way in, but up to this point no losses. There was, however, worse to come for on the way out from the target three of 610 Squadron's Spitfires were shot down, including best friends Blackman and John Anderson. Sadly, Blackman was killed aged just twenty-four.

John, who had been injured in the leg by 20mm cannon shell splinters, knew his luck had also run out. With glycol streaming from his Spitfire's engine, and in considerable pain from his injuries, John nursed his damaged fighter back to the coast but with every mile his failing aircraft dropped lower and lower. He knew he was too low to bale out and decided to belly-land his Spitfire on the heaving sea. John put the aircraft down and, amazingly, it stayed afloat long enough for him to get into his dinghy. Shortly after the Spitfire's tail rose in the water and sank to its final resting place beneath the waves.

After several hours afloat John was picked up by a German E-boat. He recalled the captain saying, 'For you the war is over' in heavy accented English, which, despite his injuries, made John chuckle.

John was hospitalised in St Omer and on recovery he volunteered to serve as a hospital orderly in an effort to keep himself out of the inevitable PoW camp. Unfortunately, after a few months John fell out with some of the hospital staff. He was duly transferred to Stalag IXC, an army camp, arriving there in March 1942 with the PoW number #39314.

In May of that year he was transferred to Stalag Luft III at Sagan, followed by a move to Stalag Luft I at Barth in October, where he remained for almost a year.

Though I communicated at length with John about his time as a PoW, learning much of his own personal experiences and recollections, finding out exactly how camps such as Stalag Luft I operated was not always an easy task. This book, however, now uncovers the facts about the camp and I can recommend it to those who want to find out more about what went on 'behind the wire'.

In November 1943 John was moved to Stalag Luft VI at Hyderkrug in Lithuania. This was followed by incarceration at Stalag Luft IV at Gross Tyschow in Poland from July 1944. As the Russians advanced the Germans decided to force the PoWs out of the camps on what became known as the 'long marches'. Ill-clad for the harsh conditions and inadequately fed, John and his comrades were made to walk over 300 miles in the depths of winter to Fallingbostel. Inevitably, many suffered terribly.

This detailed and informative book is a fascinating read and certainly helps one understand what these amazing men went through during their captivity. It details how they overcame the anxiety, boredom and frustration and how they used their ingenuity and intellect to beat the situation and in some cases plot and plan escapes.

The passage of time ensures that every documented record becomes increasingly valuable. Fortunately, this detailed account of prison life at Stalag Luft I was compiled at the end of, or just after, the war with the help of those who endured the agonies of prolonged incarceration. Its publication adds greatly to our understanding of that often-neglected element of the Second World War and, as such, is a vitally important document.

Mark Hillier,
Fontwell, 2018.

List of Abbreviations

2nd Lt.	Second Lieutenant
A.A.C.	Army Air Corps
A.A.F.	Auxiliary Air Force
A.C.1.	Aircraftman First Class
A.C.2.	Aircraftman Second Class
Capt.	Captain
Col.	Colonel
Cpl.	Corporal
F.A.A.	Fleet Air Arm
F/Lt.	Flight Lieutenant
F/O.	Flying Officer
F/Sgt.	Flight Sergeant
G/Capt	Group Captain
I.S.9	Intelligence School 9
L.A.C.	Leading Aircraftman
Lt.	Lieutenant
Lt.(A).	Lieutenant (Aviation)
Lt. Cmdr. (A).	Lieutenant Commander (Aviation)
Lt. Cmdr.	Lieutenant Commander
Maj.	Major
P/O	Pilot Officer
P.O.	Petty Officer
Ps/W	Prisoners of War
P/W	Prisoner of War
R.A.A.F.	Royal Australian Air Fore
R.A.F.	Royal Air Force
R.Bde.	Rifle Brigade
R.C.A.F.	Royal Canadian Air Force
R.H.A.F.	Royal Hellenic Air Force

R.N.	Royal Navy
R.N.A.F.	Royal Norwegian Air Force or Royal Netherlands Air Force
R.N.R.	Royal Naval Reserve
R.N.V.R.	Royal Naval Volunteer Reserve
R.N.Z.A.F.	Royal New Zealand Air Force
S.A.A.F.	South African Air Force
S.A.S.	Special Air Service
Sgt.	Sergeant
S/Ldr.	Squadron Leader
Sub. Lt.	Sub-Lieutenant
U.S.A.A.C.	United States Army Air Corps
W/Cdr.	Wing Commander
W.O.	Warrant Officer

Map showing the location of Stalag Luft I.

Part 1

OFFICERS' COMPOUND
July 1940 to April 1942

Chapter 1

Description of Camp

1. LOCATION AND DESCRIPTION OF CAMP

Stalag Luft I (Barth) was situated one-and-a-quarter miles north-west of the town of Barth and sixteen miles west-north-west of Stralsund, on the western side of a small flat peninsula projecting northward into the large inlet between the Der Darss peninsula and the mainland.

The Camp, which was constructed specially for the accommodation of Air Force personnel, was built on sand. The water level was about 5 feet below the surface.

An aerial photograph of the whole camp, taken in April 1944, is at [Plate 1]. The Compound which is dealt with in the succeeding Chapters of this Part is marked '26', but during the period under review it contained only two barracks at first. In September, 1940, a third barrack was built. The fourth building which appears on the photograph on the west side of the Compound, was built after April, 1942.

2. CAMP CONDITIONS

(a) *Number of P's/W and accommodation.*

The Camp was opened in July, 1940, when a party of twenty-one officers arrived from Dulag Luft (Oberursel). During the next few weeks other parties of officers, including about 40 French Air Force personnel, were transferred from other Camps, i.e. Oflag 1X A/H (Spangenburg) etc. in September, the French Officers were moved to another Camp. From this time until December, 1941, additional parties arrived from Dulag Luft, the total strength then being about two hundred and thirty officers of the R.A.F., R.A.A.F., R.C.A.F., R.N.Z.A.F., S.A.A.F. and Naval Air Arm.

These officers were accommodated in three wooden barracks, each divided into twenty-eight small rooms. Three of these were used as kitchens, lavatory and wash-room. One of the barracks had an extension built on to it which was used as a dining-hall.

3

In early February, 1941, a party of 50 Officers was transferred to Stalag XX A (Thorn). About July, 1941, a further party of 50 officers was transferred to Oflag X C (Lubeck).

In April, 1942, the Camp was evacuated to Stalag Luft III (Sagan) where the officers were accommodated in the East Compound.

(b) *German Administration.*

The Camp was administered by German Air Force personnel, numbering about 200 officers and men. Very few of these had any previous experience of dealing with British P's/W.

The majority of the German Administration Staff remained throughout the period under review, but the Kommandant was changed several times. The guard personnel were changed at irregular intervals.

(c) *P/W Administration.*

The first Senior Officer in the Camp was Lt. (A) Wood R.N. He was responsible for liaison with the Germans. He appointed a small number of officers to assist him in the administration of the Compound. These were in charge of rations, canteen etc.

About three weeks later the position of Senior British Officer was taken over by 28097 S/Ldr. B. Paddon R.A.F., who remained in office with a staff of three officers until his transfer from the Camp on 1st February, 1941. Prior to his departure he handed over his duties to 26165 S/Ldr. G.D. Stephenson R.A.F., who held the position until June, 1941.

At that time a party arrived from Dulag Luft which included 5175 W/Cdr. H.M.A. Day R.A.F., who took over the position of Senior British Officer. He appointed 33120 S/Ldr. A.R.D. Macdonnell R.A.F. as Camp Adjutant. This administration continued until the evacuation of the Camp. Orders were transmitted to the P's/W through the senior officer of each room.

The Senior British Officer was able to make contact with the Camp Kommandant at all times to register protests, make requests, etc.

During the period under review the Germans permitted the P's/W to conduct their own affairs and merely conducted searches, counted the number of P's/W etc.

(d) *Roll Calls.*

There were two roll-calls daily. These were held indoors or outdoors according to the weather. At first, the P's/W were counted and the Germans were satisfied if the total was correct. About November, 1940, following several escapes, the Germans called the name of each officer during roll-calls. This continued until April, 1942.

(e) *Food.*
During the first few months a small number of individually addressed Red Cross parcels arrived in the Camp. About October, 1940, consignments of Red Cross parcels began to arrive, addressed to the Senior British Officer. These were issued to officers in rotation, starting with those who had been P's/W for the longest period. This system was adopted because not enough parcels were received at a time to issue one to each officer. There was a gradual increase in the number of parcels arriving in the Camp and from June 1941, onwards there was a weekly issue of one parcel to each P/W.

During the period when insufficient Red Cross parcels were arriving the German rations were inadequate and most of the P's/W were hungry. It is estimated that the ration was about 1,500 calories daily. After the arrival of the parcels the German rations were reduced.

Limited quantities of fresh vegetables could be purchased through the Canteen during the whole of the period under review. The permissible amount diminished towards the end.

The issue of Red Cross food parcels was controlled by an Air Force officer working under the supervision of several Germans.

No food was reserved for escape purposes until about the middle of 1941. From that time onwards a quantity of German bread, sausage and margarine was available. This was controlled by the Escape Committee.

(f) *Clothing.*
The Germans issued a limited amount of captured uniform, underwear, etc. in necessitous cases. All officers were dependent upon the arrival of their next-of-kin clothing parcels, which began to arrive about six months after capture, though in some cases the period was much longer. Small quantities of blankets, quilts, etc. began to arrive from the International Red Cross Society during the Summer of 1941.

Clothing in connection with escape activities is dealt with [elsewhere in this book].

(g) *Searches.*
All P's/W arriving at the Camp were subjected to a thorough search in a building in the Vorlager before they were permitted to enter the Compound.

During the first six months, searches of the barracks were carried out at irregular and unpredictable intervals by interpreters working under the direction of the German Abwehr (Security) Officer. The searchers appeared to be inexperienced, and comparatively little escape material was discovered by them.

After the discovery of the first tunnel in early January, 1941, a very intensive search was made of the barrack under which the tunnel had started. This lasted for about a week and during that time the occupants were accommodated elsewhere in the Camp. Wallpaper was removed from walls, mattresses were emptied, all P's/W possessions were examined closely and thrown in a heap on the floor.

From then on sporadic surprise searches were carried out in all barracks by a squad of trained Abwehr personnel.

During the months of April and May, 1941 all the P's/W were transferred to the N.C.O's Compound and accommodated in a spare room in the Cookhouse. They were kept there under guard from morning until evening and during that time intensive searches of their barracks were carried out. This occurred about once weekly. In May, 1941, twenty-eight searches of this kind were conducted on successive days. Very little escape material was found by the Germans, mainly because the P's/W had virtually nothing of this kind. As the P's/W were transferred from their own Compound to the N.C.O's Compound they were subjected to a personal search, but after a time these diminished in thoroughness, then ceased.

From June, 1941 until April, 1942, spasmodic searches of individual rooms in barracks took place. On a few occasions the officers were transferred to the N.C.O's Compound and a whole day search carried out.

(h) *German anti-escape measures.*
During the first few months, the German anti-escape measures were very simple. They were as follows: A double barbed-wire fence about eight feet in height with a space of six feet between the fences. This space was filled with a concertina wire to a height of about three feet. There were three sentry towers fitted with searchlights and machine-guns. These were situated at the North-east, South-east and South-west corners of the Compound. Sentries patrolled outside the fence throughout the 24 hours. Arc lights were situated about twenty yards apart along the Compound fence.

A warning wire was situated about three feet inside the main fence and it was a German order that any P/S touching it would be fired upon. This threat was not put into effect. There was no system of passes authorising German personnel to enter or leave the compound, but they were supposed to book-in and book-out at the main guardroom situated in the Vorlager. There was a dog patrol in the compound at night. All vehicles leaving the camp were searched at the gate.

Following an escape over the fence in February, 1941, the Germans concluded that it had been effected during an air-raid warning when

6

all the camp lights had been switched off. Soon afterwards each sentry tower was fitted with a car head-lamp operated by a battery.

About this time the Abwehr Officer was given an establishment of two Luftwaffe personnel. They spent part of their time walking around the compound by day and by night observing the activities of the P's/W. One of them, at least, spoke English and was known to listen at barrack-room windows at night. Gradually these men controlled the searches for contraband material and tunnel sites. Formerly this work had been done by interpreters working under the direction of the Abwehr Officer. After the first few weeks the Abwehr personnel wore dark blue overalls whilst on duty. They were not visibly armed. Because they spent a great deal of time crawling under barracks the P's/W gave them the nickname of "ferrets". In due course their number in this compound was increased to three.

About May, 1941, a trench was dug down to below water level along the North fence between the fence and the warning wire. After a time the sides collapsed and it was filled in.

During the twenty-eight successive days of searches in June, 1941, a system of carbon microphones was installed along the North and West boundary fences of the compound. These were connected to a control room in the German Compound. It was several months later before the P's/W learned that some electrical system of indicating the vibrations caused by tunnelling had been installed. The full details of its operation were not learned during the period under review.

About August, 1941, following a partly successful tunnel which emerged beyond West fence, rows of short stakes were driven into the ground over an area fifteen yards in depth outside the West fence. This was designed to prevent crawling after emerging from a tunnel on that side of the compound.

German workmen entering the compound usually were accompanied by a guard. The Polish chimney sweep entered and left the compound without an escort.

Throughout the period under review all P's/W leaving the compound for recreational purposes, i.e. sea-bathing, walks, etc. were required to sign a parole and were accompanied by armed guards.

All P's/W were photographed and finger-printed on arrival at the Camp and these, together with a full description of each individual, were kept by the Abwehr Department.

From January, 1942, onwards an interpreter was on duty in the guardroom during the hours of daylight to scrutinise all personnel leaving the Camp.

7

All shutters covering the barrack windows were closed, and locked so that they could not be opened from inside, from dusk each evening until 07.00 hours next morning.

About October, 1941, trenches were dug centrally below and along the length of each barrack, also two cross trenches. This was to enable the area beneath each barrack to be searched for tunnel sites.

(i) *Punishment for escape activities, etc.*
At first the usual punishment for escape activities was five days in cells for the first offence, ten days for the second offence, etc. Normal German rations and Red Cross food were permitted. Officially, smoking was forbidden, but this rule was not enforced by the guards.

About June, 1941, sentences were increased to fourteen days in cells for all offences and Red Cross food was disallowed.

With a few exceptions, all P's/W were returned to the compound upon completion of their sentences. The exceptions were transferred direct to Oflag IV C (Colditz).

In one instance, about February, 1942, four officers were sentenced to twenty-eight days in cells – fourteen days for attempting to escape, seven days for damaging German property and seven days for refusing to carry their bedding from the cells to the de-lousing centre in the Vorlager. In addition all four had their hair clipped short.

(j) *Education.*
There were no educational facilities for the first six months. Books, paper, etc. were not available. During the winter of 1940-41 one or two classes were started but there was a lack of material and instructors. In the summer of 1941 an R.A.F. Staff College Preparatory Course was started. It was organised by 32108 S/Ldr. C.E.S. Lockett R.A.F.

At first it was well attended, but after a time interest diminished and it was abandoned.

About September 1941, an Education Section was organised by 70699 F/Lt. F.H. Vivian R.A.F., a former schoolmaster. He selected instructors in various subjects, including modern languages, art, mathematics, etc. These classes, which were held in three rooms in one of the barracks, were well attended. By this time quantities of books of all kinds had been received from the International Red Cross Society and in personal book parcels.

(k) *Library.*
The nucleus of a Library was formed in the Autumn of 1940. The books were contributed by P's/W who had received them in parcels from the

U.K. In early 1941 larger quantities of these parcels arrived, as well as books sent to the Camp by the International Red Cross Society. About this time Continental editions of books, written in English, were acquired through the Camp Canteen.

The Library Officer from April, 1941, was 34205 S/Ldr. D.C. Torrens R.A.F.

All P's/W made extensive use of the library at all times. It was situated in a room in one of the barracks.

(l) *Sports.*

The sports field was in a separate adjacent compound. P's/W were supposed to have access to it for one hour daily, but in actual fact the Germans permitted its use about twice weekly. The reason for this was that they had to provide additional guards.

Prior to July, 1941, very little sport was played, mainly because of the above mentioned restrictions and the shortage of food and sports equipment. From that time onwards the Germans were prevailed upon to allow the Sports Field to be used for one hour daily. Small quantities of equipment arrived from the Young Men's Christian Association about this time and the food situation had improved. The main game was soccer.

During the winter of 1940-41 an ice-skating rink was constructed in the Compound by the P's/W. Four pairs of ice-skates were purchased through the Camp Canteen and issued on loan to the P's/W in rotation. During the winter of 1941-41 ice-skating was better organised, as eighteen pairs of skates had been procured; also ice-hockey equipment. Matches were played against the N.C.O.'s.

Between the Autumn of 1941 and Spring of 1942 a few rugby matches were played between the Officers and N.C.O.'s. These took place on the Sports Field in the N.C.O.'s Compound.

(m) *Amateur theatricals, etc.*

The first entertainment which was attempted was a Pantomime at Christmas, 1940. This took place in the Dining-Hall. Scenery and costumes were made from coloured paper obtained through the Camp Canteen, and cardboard. A stage was made by placing all the tables together. The organiser was 41004 F/Lt. H.E.L. Falkus R.A.F.

From then onwards Plays and Concerts were produced. These were organised by 39175 F/Lt. M.H. Roth R.A.F.

About the Spring of 1941 a number of musical instruments were purchased by individuals through the Camp Canteen. In addition, two pianos were purchased communally. An orchestra was formed by 39629 F/Lt. C.Y. Buckley R.A.F.

After some time this post was taken over by 36103 F/Lt. H.C. Marshall R.A.F., who wrote the musical scores, etc. A large number of band concerts took place and were much appreciated.

There was an interchange of Shows between Officers' and N.C.O.'s Compounds, but parole had to be given. On occasions the Officers were permitted to visit the N.C.O.'s Theatre on parole accompanied by interpreters. No intermingling of Officers and N.C.O.'s was permitted.

On a few occasions the Germans showed news films in the N.C.O.'s Theatre. Officers were taken there to see them, but they were under escort.

(n) *Religion.*
From the opening of the Camp until mid 1941 sporadic Church Services were held in a Common Room in one of the barracks by 40258 F/Lt. J. Plant R.A.F.

About July, 1941, a member of the New Zealand Church Army arrived in the Camp. From then onwards he officiated as a Padre and held Services each Sunday morning in the Dining-Hall. He was Mr Walton R.N.Z.Ch.A.

From the beginning until about the end of 1941 the Germans conducted parties of Roman Catholics to Mass in the town of Barth. These parties, which left the Camp each Sunday morning, were accompanied by an armed guard and an interpreter. Finally the priest refused to officiate and this privilege ceased.

(o) *Shooting incidents.*
Not applicable.

(p) *P/W morale.*
The morale of the P's/W was very high at all times, but towards the end of the period it dropped slightly. This is thought to have been due to the somewhat overcrowded conditions in the barracks and the smallness of the Compound.

The reception of the B.B.C. News Bulletins as described in Chapter VI assisted in the maintenance of morale.

(q) *Medical.*
A Sick Quarters was situated in the Vorlager. It was staffed by a German Medical Officer and German Medical Orderlies. Two R.A.F. N.C.O.'s assisted and lived in the Sick Quarters.

Sick parades were held almost daily. Treatment was reasonably good, but medical supplies were inadequate. Patients requiring hospital treatment were sent to Griefswald Hospital, or to Stralsund Hospital.

At first P's/W requiring dental treatment were taken to a civilian dentist in the town of Barth. At a later date a Luftwaffe dentist visited the Sick Quarters weekly.

(r) *Reprisals.*
The only mass reprisals taken by the Germans were the twenty-eight successive days of searches related in sub-Section (h). During that period no lights were switched on in the barracks at night.

(s) *Finance.*
From the beginning all officers paid a compulsory levy of a percentage of their pay, in Camp money, into a Common Fund. This paid for items obtained through the Canteen for common use; also for providing similar facilities for the N.C.O's Compound and a sum for each N.C.O. and airman.

In addition, individual officers sent sums of Camp money to N.C.O's under private arrangements about repayment.

About July, 1941, this scheme was modified and the sums paid to individual N.C.O's by individual officers were recorded by NZ 40631 F/Lt. R.G. Stark R.N.Z.A.F. This scheme continued until October, 1941, when all officers were invited to contribute to a Fund upon which N.C.O's could draw. Repayment was to be made after the cessation of hostilities. This Fund was administered by Stark.

About the end of 1941 an appeal was received through the Germans from several British Merchant Seaman's Camps requesting financial assistance on repayment. This was given and repayment was made by the seaman's employers direct to the individual officers banking accounts in the U.K. This remained in operation until April, 1942.

Throughout the period under review the Camp Kommandant levied a ten per cent tax on all purchases made through the Canteen. It was stated that this was paid to the German Government as "Canteen Tax". It is estimated that this amounted to about sixteen thousand marks.

Chapter 2

Escape Organisation

3. CONTROL BY CAMP AUTHORITIES

Throughout the period under review all intending escapers were required to inform the Senior British Officer, or his Deputy, of the details of their plans and to obtain his authority for the attempt. During the first year this control was largely nominal and there were instances where individuals making attempts did not obtain authority to do so. About July, 1940, the Senior British Officer, 28097 S/Ldr. B. Paddon R.A.F., appointed an officer to deal with escape matters on his behalf. He was 37467 S/Ldr. K.C. Doran R.A.F.

The Senior British Officer informed all the P's/W that any person wishing to make an attempt to escape must first acquaint this officer of their intentions and receive permission to carry out their plans; also that this officer would render every possible assistance.

During the ensuing months it became apparent that this arrangement was not satisfactory to the majority of those interested in escape and the Senior British Officer decided to modify this scheme. About January, 1941, the occupants of each of the three barracks were asked to elect an Escape Representative. This was done and the elected officers formed an Escape Committee which was responsible to the Senior British Officer. The Escape Representatives were:

> Lt. Cdr.(A) P. Fanshawe R.N.
> 40058 F/Lt. A.R. Mulligan   R.A.F.
> 33331 F/Lt. A.D. Panton   R.A.F.

This Committee functioned for several months in an advisory and co-ordinating capacity.

In early July, 1941, the Senior British Officer at that time, 05175 W/Cdr. H.M.A. Day R.A.F., appointed an officer to the Committee to act as his representative. This officer was Lt. Cdr. (A) J. Buckley R.N.

The functions of the Committee remained unaltered.

In September, 1941, Fanshawe was arrested by the Germans and removed from the Camp. Full details are given [elsewhere in this book].

Fanshawe did not take any further active part in escape activities during the period under review, but his place on the Escape Committee was not filled.

About January, 1942, Mulligan resigned from the Committee and another Escape Representative was elected. He was 37321 F/Lt. R.G. Kerr-Ramsay R.A.F. The Committee continued to co-ordinate escapes, rendering assistance and advice where needed, until the evacuation of the Camp in April, 1942.

4. PLANNING

Throughout the period under review the Escape Committee did not plan any escape attempts. Individuals planned their own schemes and in most cases submitted their ideas to the officer, or officers, responsible for controlling escape attempts as indicated in the preceding Section. If the scheme was approved assistance was rendered. As a rule this took the form of advice; the names of officers who might be willing to help by making clothing, maps, false documents, etc.; the organisation of diversions to distract the attention of guards whilst the attempt was being made, etc.

Intending escapers made all their own preparations with the help of those of their colleagues who were willing to assist them. The Escape Control Officers, or Escape Committee, did not organise the provision of clothing, maps, false documents, etc., but they had control of a small quantity of escape aid maps, compasses and money. The maps were available for copying and compasses and money were provided. From about July, 1941, onwards the Escape Committee also provided a certain amount of food.

5. SECURITY

During the first few months the security of escape activities was organised by the officers engaged in the construction of the first tunnel. The tunnellers themselves took turns to watch the Compound gate to give warning of the approach of Germans. This system operated only when tunnelling, or dispersal of sand, was in progress.

About October, 1940, the Senior British Officer approved of the instruction of a scheme whereby all officers might be called upon to take their turn on watching duties. The Senior British Officers' Escape Representative detailed officers as required.

When the Escape Committee was formed in January, 1941, an officer was appointed to control the gate watching system. He was 37673 F/Lt. E.C.S. Fewtrell R.A.F.

P's/W who were engaged in escape activities informed him when they required a watch to be kept. Fewtrell advised the Barrack Escape Representatives of the number of officers he required from each of their barracks and the times of their periods of duty.

After a short time this scheme was modified because the watchers frequently failed to appear for duty. From then onwards the Barrack Escape Representatives supplied Fewtrell with the names of officers who were next for this duty in each of their barracks. Fewtrell warned them of their times of duty and ensured that they reported punctually.

About this time the Barrack Escape Representatives co-ordinated the times when escape activities were in progress within their barracks. These activities were: Copying of maps, manufacturing of clothing, forging of documents, etc. Whilst work of this type was in progress watchers were on duty to give warning of the approach of Germans. These were detailed for duty by the Barrack Escape Representative.

Those escape aids which were required by the Escape Committee, i.e. maps, compasses and money, were hidden behind concealed wall panels, etc. by the Committee members. This did not present a serious problem as very small quantities were held.

6. CLOTHING
In most cases intending escapers made their own clothing from uniform, dyed blankets, bed sheets, etc. However, a number obtained assistance of fellow P's/W who possessed some tailoring skill and were willing to do such work. The principal officers who helped others in this way were:

	Lt. (A) C.A. Conn	R.N.
41004	F/Lt. H.E.L. Falkus	R.A.F.
	Lt. C.H. Filmer	R.N.
84934	F/Lt. C.R. Hubbard	R.A.F.
40714	F/Lt. K. Jones	R.A.F.

All the above named worked independently for individuals who were preparing to escape. Their work was not organised in any way.

7. FORGERY
(a) *Papers.*
From about October, 1940, until December, 1941, a certain amount of forgery of documents was done under the direction of the Senior British

Officer. These documents were inventions and included rail travel permits, identity cards and letters purporting to be from German concerns introducing a former employee to another firm, or an employee to another branch of the same firm. This work was done by 42102 F/Lt. M.A. Bussey R.A.F.

During this period only a limited number of these forged documents were made and they were not available to the majority of intending escapers. In December, 1941, the Senior British Officers' Escape representative, Lt. Cdr.(A) J. Buckley R.N., organised the nucleus of a Forgery Section. From then onwards Bussey was assisted by:

```
101024 F/Lt. W.J.H. Greenaway  R.A.F.
       Capt. (A) G.B.K. Griffiths  R.M.
43422  F/Lt. F. Hugill           R.A.F.
70699  F/Lt. F.H. Vivian         R.A.F.
```

The documents which were made were inventions and advice on style and language was given by Vivian who did not do any actual forgery. Only a limited number of documents were made and these were not available to all intending escapers.

(b) *Photographs.*
The P's/W were not in possession of a camera, but a German officer was persuaded to take photographs of groups of P's/W from time to time. Intending escapers who were in a position to obtain forged identity cards were included in these groups. When the prints of the photographs were received they were treated in such a way that only the intending escaper was visible, then cut down to the required size.

(c) *Stamps.*
Imitations of the impressions of rubber stamps on forged documents were done by the forgers.

8. FOOD
Intending escapers saved their own food in preparation for their attempts, but from about July, 1941, onwards a certain amount of additional food was available on application to the Escape Committee. This comprised German bread, sausage and margarine.

9. MAPS
The supply of maps to intending escapers was not organised. A small number of maps were held by the various Escape Representatives and

these were available to those who wished to make copies. In most cases
the individuals preparing for escape made their own copies, but in some
cases colleagues did this work for them. The chief helpers in this
connection were:

74666	F/Lt J.C.W. Bushell	R.A.F.
	Lt (A) C.A. Conn	R.N.
41004	F/Lt. H.E.L. Falkus	R.A.F.
	Lt. (A) C.H. Filmer	R.N.
84934	F/Lt. C.R. Hubbard	R.A.F.
43422	F/Lt. F. Hugill	R.A.F.
64926	F/Lt. E.H.L. Shore	R.A.F.
40020	F/Lt. J.W. Stephens	R.A.F.

10. COMPASSES
A number of compasses were held by the Escape Representatives and
these were supplied to intending escapers to the extent of their
availability. When supplies were short, compasses were made by:

42102	F/Lt. M.A. Bussey	R.A.F.
41004	F/Lt. H.E.L. Falkus	R.A.F.
42356	F/Lt. V. Parker	R.A.F.

each of whom supplied several to various colleagues. The usual method
of manufacture was to magnetise sewing needles, or strips of razor
blade, using a magnetic razor and a magnet removed from a German
loudspeaker in the Compound.

11. ESCAPE INTELLIGENCE
Throughout the period under review information which might be of
use to escapers was obtained from the undermentioned sources by the
various Escape Representatives, who made it available to those
preparing to make attempts to escape.

(a) *Contacts.*
The bulk of the escape information which was acquired from Germans
was obtained by those P's/W who were engaged in trading. As a rule
the information was gathered during the course of conversation and
the Germans were unaware that they were being helpful.

(b) *Journeys outside Camp.*
All the P's/W were permitted to leave the Camp at frequent intervals

for walks and sun-bathing. On these occasions parole had to be given and the parties were accompanied by guards, but all those who were interested had the opportunity to study the topography of the area within a few miles of the camp.

Officers who were sent for hospital treatment at Stralsund and Griefswald made a mental note of all interesting features en route and related the details upon their return to the Compound.

(c) *Recaptured escapers.*
All recaptured escapers were interrogated by the various Escape Representatives upon their return to the Compound.

(d) *New P's/W.*
The Escape Representatives had conversations with all new arrivals in the Compound and endeavoured to obtain any information which might be useful to escapers.

(e) *From I.S.9.*
As far as can be ascertained the only information which might be of use to an escaper which was received by code message from I.S.9 was the details of the successful escape from the Camp which was effected by 39177 F/Lt. J.T.L. Shore R.A.F.

The message was received about September, 1941, and all the P's/W in this compound were informed of the details of the route taken by Shore.

12. SUPPLIES
The acquirement of supplies for escape purposes was not organised, with the result that materials of this kind were in short supply throughout the period under review. The details of the various sources of supply are set out below.

(a) *Contacts.*
During the whole of the period under review the acquirement of escape aids from Germans were not satisfactory. This was due to the following three causes:

(i) Lack of control by the various Senior British Officers.
(ii) Lack of discipline among the P's/W; individual P's/W were dealing with the Germans in cigarettes, soap, tea, chocolate, etc. which were given in exchange for such items as eggs, cooking utensils, etc. for the comfort and private use of the individual.

17

These articles being non-contraband, this practice forced up the price of contraband articles and eventually contraband items were unobtainable, owing to the fact that Germans were not willing to take great risks to supply contraband when they could procure all they wanted in the way of luxuries by supplying non-contraband articles.

(iii) The fact that during this period the Germans were not really short of cigarettes, etc. and their morale was fairly high.

However, certain P's/W who were interested in escape induced their 'contacts' to supply articles of use for escape purposes. They were reimbursed from communal supplies. Such items included: maps, pens, inks, dyes, railway time-tables, money, etc. The chief personnel connected with this form of trading were:

73727	F/Lt. P.F. Cazenove	R.A.F.
42699	F/Lt. B.A. Davidson	R.A.F.
37467	S/Ldr. K.C. Doran	R.A.F.
37673	F/Lt. E.C.S. Fewtrell	R.A.F.
70899	S/Ldr. R. Herrick	R.A.F.
43422	F/Lt. F. Hugill	R.A.F.
28097	S/Ldr. B. Paddon	R.A.F.
79220	F/Lt. J.V. Silverstone	R.A.F.
40020	F/Lt. J.W. Stephens	R.A.F.

(b) *Camp resources.*
Personnel who were engaged in escape activities scoured the Compound for materials which could be made to serve some useful purpose, but there was no organisation for the collection of such items.

The materials which came into this category were: bed boards and boards from the lower section of the double floors of barracks, which were used for shoring tunnels. Coal shovels were supplied by the Germans for each stove in the Compound and these were used for digging tunnels. Electric cable was removed from part of the Germans secret microphone system and used to provide electric lighting in the tunnel. Bed sheets were provided for all officers and some of these were used for making certain types of clothing; also the bellows of an air pump installed in a tunnel. Some of the iron tie-bars off the sectional wooden barracks were used for making wire cutters. Iron bars were detached from heating stoves and used as hammers. Table knives were converted into saws and screwdrivers. Tinfoil from cigarette packets was collected and melted down for making German uniform buttons, badges, etc.

In addition to the foregoing, a number of items which were used for escape purposes were obtained from the Canteen. These included: Pens, ink, coloured crayons, water colour paints, artists' brushes and coloured and white paper of various kinds, all of which were used in connection with the forgery of documents. Quantities of wallpaper were purchased and this was used to cover the walls of rooms thereby concealing hiding places in which escape aids were kept. Wallpaper was used to make an airline for a tunnel.

From July, 1941, onwards the Escape Committee controlled all escape aids acquired through semi-official Camp sources.

(c) *New P's/W.*
New arrivals in the Compound were a disappointing source of supplies. A few were able to conceal compass needles, maps and hacksaw blades during the various searches following capture, but in most cases these were regarded as personal property and retained for possible use at some later date. Towards the end of the period the Escape Representatives endeavoured to collect all such items, but this was not wholly successful.

(d) *Parcels from I.S.9.*
The first parcel which was received from I.S.9 arrived in the Camp in May, 1941. From that date until the evacuation of the Camp in April, 1942, about five other parcels were received. All these were games parcels in which maps, money and compasses were concealed. They were addressed to individual code users.

From about July, 1941, onwards the contents of all such parcels were collected by the Escape Committee and held for issue to personnel who were about to make attempts to escape.

13. CARPENTRY
Very little carpentry was done in connection with escape activities. The main project in which timber was used was the first tunnel, which was shored throughout its length. This was done by the tunnelling team.

14. METAL WORK
Several pairs of wire cutters were made for various individuals from the tie-bars off barracks by:

43076	F/Lt. F.A.B. Tams	R.A.F.
78536	F/Lt. J.E. Thompson	R.A.F.

About December, 1941, the manufacture of German uniform badges, buttons and belt buckles was commenced. These items were made from melted tinfoil. Torches of the type carried at night by German guards were made from tin cans. This work was done by P.0554 F/Lt. Z. Gotowski R.A.F. working under the direction of 39103 S/Ldr. T.G. Kirby-Green R.A.F.

15. LEATHER WORK
The only leather work which was undertaken was the manufacture of belts similar to those worn by the Germans. Usually such work was done by the individuals who required these items.

16. TOOLS
Tools of various kinds were acquired from Germans by 'trading' and by stealing them from German workmen engaged on construction or alteration work in the Compound.

17. GADGETS
Two dummy rifles were made by:

88039	F/Lt. P.I. Hall	R.A.F.
64926	F/Lt. E.H.L. Shore	R.A.F.

These were used by S/Ldr's Craig and Turner as related later in this Chapter.
 Air-pumps were made for ventilating tunnels. These were all of the foot-bellows type and were made by the tunnelling teams.

18. TUNNEL CONSTRUCTION
(a) *General.*
Those P's/W who were interested in tunnel construction formed themselves into Groups, selected sites and registered them with the Escape Representatives. The object of this system of registration was to ensure that no two groups began operations from the same location and to settle questions of priority. As a rule the Escape Representatives inspected the proposed sites and if there were no obvious objections gave permission for work to commence.

(b) *Engineering.*
During the period under review forty tunnels were started. Two were successful and four P's/W escaped, but only one of these succeeded in reaching the U.K. The following is a brief description of these two tunnels:

20

(i) In June, 1941, work was begun on the construction of a tunnel running West from the West Barrack. The project was organised by 70419 S/Ldr. M.L. McColm R.A.F. A trapdoor was made in the wooden floor of one of the rooms in the West Barrack and the vertical shaft of the tunnel was made a short distance from it. This opening was concealed by boards covered with sand, when work was not in progress.

The lateral shaft was constructed about five feet below the surface. Very little shoring was used. After a time the air became foul and an air pump was constructed. This was a bellows which was operated under the floor of the barrack close to the tunnel entrance. The airline, which ran to the working face, was made of wallpaper. It was suspended from the roof of the tunnel by means of pieces of wire stuck into the sand.

The sand which was excavated was dispersed under the floor of the barrack.

Construction started on 26th June and the tunnel was completed on 19th August. About a dozen P's/W were engaged in the work. When ready for use the tunnel was about 100 feet in length. The details of the escape made by means of this tunnel are given later in this Chapter.

(ii) In late September, 1941, a tunnel was started from an incinerator situated close to the South fence, which separated the Compound from the Officers' Sports Field. Work was begun by 42232 F/Lt. B.A. James R.A.F., and the lateral shaft of the tunnel ran South. It was intended that the exit would be in the Sports Field.

After a few days, James was approached by 30177 F/Lt. J.T.L. Shore R.A.F., who offered to help in the project. James agreed and they worked together from then onwards.

At 10.30 hours daily there was a football match in the Sports Field and some of the P's/W stood on top of the incinerator to watch the game. This provided cover for James and Shore while they go into the incinerator. They left the trapdoor open a little for ventilation and worked until about 17.00 hours. At the end of the day's work arrangements were made for a number of spectators of the football match, then in progress, to stand on top of the incinerator to cover James and Shore whilst they emerged.

The construction of the tunnel took four days but work was interrupted by a series of searches which lasted for about three weeks. When completed the tunnel was about twenty-five feet long and was just large enough to enable a man to crawl along. A table-knife was used for excavation and the sand was carried from the face to the incinerator on a board, dumped in the incinerator and mixed with rubbish. No shoring was used. The project was completed and ready for use on 15th October.

The most active personnel in connection with tunnel construction were:

10056	F/Lt. W. Barrett	R.A.F.
104420	F/Lt. R.F. Beauclair	R.A.F.
89772	F/Lt. J.W. Best	R.A.F.
37931	F/Lt. J.B.J. Boardman	R.A.F.
33303	F/Lt. J.C. Breese	R.A.F.
74666	F/Lt. J.C.W. Bushell	R.A.F.
	Lt. (A) P.W.S. Butterworth	R.N.
41255	F/Lt. R.S.A. Churchill	R.A.F.
	Lt. (A) A. Conn	R.N.
43282	F/Lt. G.J. Cornish	R.A.F.
43954	F/Lt. J.R. Denny	R.A.F.
37467	S/Ldr. K.C. Doran	R.A.F.
70196	F/Lt. P.F. Eames	R.A.F.
72397	F/Lt. B. Everton-Jones	R.A.F.
41004	F/Lt. H.E.L. Falkus	R.A.F.
	Lt.Cdr. (A) P. Fanshawe	R.N.
332451	F/Lt. D. Ffrench-Mullen	R.A.F.
	Lt. (A) C.H. Filmer	R.N.
J.5481	F/Lt. C.W. Floody	R.C.A.F.
90252	F/Lt. N. Forbes	R.A.F.
60286	F/Lt. L.J.E. Goldfinch	R.A.F.
79573	F/Lt. H.A. Goodwin	R.A.F.
101024	F/Lt. W.J.A. Greenaway	R.A.F.
42985	F/Lt. T.F. Guest	R.A.F.
P.0554	F/Lt. Z. Gotowski	R.A.F.
88039	F/Lt. P.I. Hall	R.A.F.
70899	S/Ldr. R. Herrick	R.A.F.
84934	F/Lt. C.R. Hubbard	R.A.F.
39318	F/Lt. A.V. Hunter	R.A.F.
28157	W/Cdr. M.C. Hyde	R.A.F.
42232	F/Lt. B.A. James	R.A.F.
40714	F/Lt. K. Jones	R.A.F.
38321	F/Lt. R.G. Kerr-Ramsay	R.A.F.
90250	F/Lt. P.G. Leeson	R.A.F.
39098	F/Lt. A.J. Madge	R.A.F.

82958	F/Lt. R.C. Mordaunt	R.A.F.
42255	F/Lt. I.M. Muir	R.A.F.
40058	F/Lt. A.R. Mulligan	R.A.F.
79377	F/Lt. D.A. McFarlane	R.A.F.
40631	F/Lt. I.A. McIntosh	R.A.F.
	Lt. (A) A.D. Neely	R.N.
33331	F/Lt. A.D. Panton	R.A.F.
42356	F/Lt. V. Parker	R.A.F.
70902	F/Lt. D.E. Pinchbeck	R.A.F.
76017	F/Lt. L. Reavell-Carter	R.A.F.
42152	F/Lt. P.G. Royle	R.A.F.
39193	W/Cdr. E.N. Ryder	R.A.F.
64926	F/Lt. E.H.L. Shore	R.A.F.
79220	F/Lt. J.V. Silverston	R.A.F.
84678	F/Lt. W.G. Snow	R.A.F.
40028	F/Lt. J.W. Stephens	R.A.F.
79173	F/Lt. H.R. Stockings	R.A.F.
78536	F/Lt. J.E. Thompson	R.A.F.
05225	S/Ldr. N.H.J. Tindal	R.A.F.
60141	F/Lt. R.A. Walker	R.A.F.
40775	F/Lt. J.C. Wilson	R.A.F.
67076	F/Lt. W.A. Wise	R.A.F.

(c) *Dispersal.*
Usually the sand excavated from tunnels was dispersed under the barracks where the tunnel entrances were situated. The chief exception to this was in the case of the tunnel described in (ii) where dispersal was effected in the incinerator where the tunnel entrance was located. In all cases this work was performed by the personnel engaged on the construction of each tunnel.

(d) *Supplies.*
All supplies required for tunnel construction were collected by the members of each tunnelling team. These items included:- Boards for shoring, materials for air-pumps and airlines, digging implements, materials for providing lighting, etc. In a few instances a levy of bed boards from the other P's/W was arranged by the Escape Representatives.

(e) *Security.*
In addition to the security measures described in this Chapter, the following precautions were taken:

(i) The concealment of tunnel entrances. As a rule this was done by covering the hole with boards over which sand was spread, care being taken to ensure that the area would appear to be undisturbed. (ii) The dispersal of sand was carried out under the barracks. As far as possible this was carried out in such a manner that the suspicions of the Germans were not aroused. The chief method employed to achieve this was to remove some of the surface sand, dump the fresh sand from the tunnel and cover it with the surface sand which was darker in colour. It was necessary to spread the sand over the whole of the under barrack area in order not to make it apparent that the level of the surface was being raised. (iii) In some cases the clothing which was worn by tunnellers was left in the tunnels when the workers returned to the surface. This was done so that the Germans would not become suspicious through finding clothing in which sand was embedded. Where the tunnels were very damp the workers did not wear clothing. (iv) After the Germans had installed the microphone anti-tunnelling system, the P's/W endeavoured to overcome its effectiveness by constructing two tunnels side by side simultaneously. It was hoped that the Germans would locate one, but not the other when they approached the perimeter fence. This hope was not realised.

(f) *Comments.*
The main reasons for failure to construct a greater number of successful tunnels were:

(i) Operations were hampered seriously by the fact that the water level was at about six feet below the surface.
(ii) The concealment of entrances to tunnels was inadequate.
(iii) Lack of experience on the part of those engaged in their construction.
(iv) The efficiency of the German security measures after mid-1941 and in particular the effectiveness of the system of ground microphones: the high water level made it impossible to tunnel below their effective range.
(v) The Germans learned about tunnelling projects, and other escape activities, by means of a system of secret microphones installed in the barracks. The P's/W although warned of their presence, persisted in talking about their activities and plans.
(vi) The inefficiency of the Camp security system described in this Chapter. The employment of P's/W who were detailed for watching

duties was most unsatisfactory. If a watcher relaxed his attention for a few moments it was sufficient time for a German to enter the Compound unobserved, thus endangering any operation which was taking place at that time.

19. GATE WALK-OUT SCHEMES

(a) *First attempt.*
Shortly after the Camp was opened parties of P's/W were taken out of the Camp for walks, on parole, accompanied by guards. Two officers observed that the procedure adopted by the Germans when taking such parties out of the Compound provided a possibility of escape. The system was that all personnel forming one of these parties had to sign the Parole Book, then fall into line where they were counted. Immediately afterwards the party was marched out of the Compound under the escort of several guards. The two officers were:

37795	F/Lt. C.A. Crews	R.A.F.
39125	F/Lt. A.J. Hudson	R.A.F.

On the day they had chosen in August, 1940, they ran from their barracks to the gate and joined a party of officers just as they were about to pass through the gate on a parole walk. The guards did not trouble to ascertain whether Crews and Hudson belonged to the party and had signed the Parole Book. The whole party walked out of the Camp and through an adjacent wood.

At a bend in the path, where they were screened from the guards, Crews and Hudson ran down a gully and hid in bushes until nightfall. They walked to the coast and stole a small fishing boat in which they set sail. Owing to a high wind they were unable to make the open sea and after daybreak they were forced to land on the Island of Rugen. As they stepped ashore they were accosted by an armed civilian who questioned them, then took them to a farm and telephoned for the police. Later they were returned to the Camp.

(b) *Second Attempt.*
In February, 1941, two officers walked through the Camp gates disguised as German workmen. They were carrying a forged pass, copied from an original which had been stolen from a workman's coat while the coat was hanging on a peg in the Compound. The two officers were:

39553	F/Lt. J.C. Milner	R.A.F.
28097	S/Ldr. B. Paddon	R.A.F.

As they were walking through the town of Barth they were recognised by one of the guards from the Camp and arrested.

(c) *Third attempt.*
Parties of P's/W were taken out of the Camp for sea-bathing under similar conditions to those described in (a) above. In June, 1941, 88213 F/Lt. A.B. Trench R.A.F. joined one of these parties without signing the Parole Book. As the party passed through the wood outside the Camp he concealed himself intending to remain there until nightfall.

When the party of P's/W returned to the Camp the Germans discovered that one man was missing: Trench had been counted although he was unaware of the fact. A search of the area was instituted and he was recaptured and taken back to the Camp.

(d) *Fourth attempt.*
The third attempt to escape by walking through the Camp gates was effected by 39457 F/Lt. H.N. Fowler R.A.F.

For some time prior to his attempt to escape he was in charge of the distribution of parcels arriving in the Camp. In this capacity he worked in the Parcels Store situated in the Vorlager and was escorted from the Compound to the store by a German guard. After a time these guards became careless and he was permitted to enter the parcels room alone while the guards remained in an adjoining room.

Fowler planned to take advantage of this laxity and made a bogus German uniform and a civilian type suit with scraps of material. When these were finished he smuggled them, together with a quantity of food which he had saved, into the parcels room.

About 10.30 hours on 5th November, 1941, he entered the parcels room as usual, leaving the guard outside. He observed that there were few Germans in the Vorlager, so donned the civilian suit and bogus German uniform, placed his food in an old mail bag, sung the bag over his shoulder and walked out of the store. He walked past the Kommandantur and through the Compound in which the German quarters were situated, eventually reaching a part of the fence which was not guarded. He climbed over the fence and hid in a wood just beyond, where he discarded the German uniform. He walked for about two miles and hid in another wood until nightfall.

After dark he walked along the main road towards Stralsund and at one stage boarded a goods train which conveyed him to Velgast. He resumed walking and arrived at Stralsund about 06.00 hours on 6th November. He saw no sentries on the bridge between Stralsund and the island of Rugen, so began to walk across. A German civilian crossing

26

the bridge in the same direction spoke to him, asking him whom he knew in the district. Fowler, who understood a certain amount of German, stated that he was an Italian workman on leave visiting the island for pleasure, and tries to convey the impression that he was half-witted. This puzzled the German who began to shout, so Fowler turned back and re-entered Stralsund. He tried to steal a bicycle, but without success. Then, observing a number of workmen about to cross the bridge he mingled with them and crossed without incident.

He walked along the main road towards Sassnitz and after covering about three miles hid in a wood, where he rested for a few hours. He resumed walking until dusk, then hid in a wood. After dark he entered the railway yard at Bergen and waited for a train going to Sassnitz. He fell asleep and awoke as a train was leaving. It was travelling too fast for him to jump on it. About midnight he walked into Bergen in search of a bicycle but could not find one. He walked to Sassnitz, arriving about 11.30 hours on 7th November. He went to a position from which he could observe the docks. By this time his clothes were torn and muddy, although he had managed to shave.

A number of soldiers were paraded close to the Swedish ferry and there were numerous civilian standing about. There was a barricade at the docks and many police with dogs. Fowler threw away his haversack and walked towards the docks. As he approached some railway trucks he was confronted by a policeman with a dog. After asking several questions, he asked Fowler for his identity card. Fowler stated that he had left it at home, whereupon he was arrested and taken to the police station. There he was stripped and searched and his P/W identity disc was discovered.

He was returned to the Camp and after serving a term in cells was transferred to Oflag IV C (Colditz).

(e) *Fifth attempt.*
On 10th December, 1941, a party of officers was taken under escort to the Camp Theatre, situated in the N.C.O's Compound, to see a cinema show. A member of the party hid in the roof of the theatre, where he remained for three days. He was 70775 F/Lt. J.C. Wilson R.A.F.

He made preparations for his attempt to escape. These included the manufacture of a suit of the type worn by French workmen, which was done by altering and dyeing an R.A.F. uniform; making a cloth civilian-type cap; acquiring maps, a compass and food.

During the time he was hidden in the roof he attempted to cut through the Compound fence at night, but failed to do so and returned to his hiding place.

27

At 17.00 hours on 13th December, he joined a party of French workmen and walked out of the Camp with them. When clear of the Camp he hid in a wood until 19.00 hours, then began walking West.

On arrival at Damgarten he boarded a passenger train going to Rostock. He travelled in a lavatory, which he left after the train had stopped at Rostock. Instead of leaving the train on the platform side, he climbed down on to the tracks on the other side and left the station. He walked through Rostock to a small railway station on the line to Warnemunde, but as it was getting light was forced to hide in a disused railway carriage on a siding from 08.00 hours on 14th December, till dusk.

At 20.00 hours he boarded a train and sat on the buffers of a passenger coach until he arrived at Warnemunde about thirty-five minutes later. He left the station by climbing a fence, then walked to the docks.

He saw two train ferries, which he watched from a distance in case they were patrolled by guards. Seeing none he walked up the gangway of one of the ships and looked for a suitable hiding place. Eventually he locked himself in a first-class lavatory.

The ferry sailed at 10.00 hours on 15th December and on arrival at Gedser, Wilson left the boat and hid in the guard's van of a train, where he remained for the rest of that day and night.

At about 10.00 hours on 16th December, he left the guard's van and attempted to force his way into a wagon labelled 'Copenhagen'. He was seen by a Danish railway official who shouted at him. Wilson ran off pursued by the Dane.

The chase was joined by three other Danes who intercepted Wilson. He was taken to the Stationmaster's Office and questioned. He attempted to bluff, but was not successful and was searched by German police soon afterwards. When his watch was examined an inscription with his name and 'R.A.F.' was discovered. This led to his arrest and he was returned to the Camp a few days later.

(f) *Sixth attempt.*
About 1st January, 1942, an attempt was made by:

    90285 S/Ldr. G.D. Craig   R.A.F.
    26216 S/Ldr. W.H.N. Turner   R.A.F.

as well to walk through the gate disguised as German guards. They made their bogus German greatcoats from blankets and their leggings from sacking. They wore balaclava helmets similar to those worn by the

Germans. They carried dummy rifles which were made for them by fellow P's/W.

About dusk they joined the party of German guards who were going round the Compound closing the shutters on barrack windows. They assisted in this work and eventually marched through the Compound gate.

At this point the guards began talking amongst themselves. One turned to Craig and remarked in German on the poor quality of the greatcoats issued by the Germans, and suggested he got his changed. Further conversation followed, during which the guards became suspicious of Craig's poor German.

At the second gate the Guard Commander was called and Craig's identity was discovered amid much laughter, in which Turner joined. A German officer arrived and there was some discussion between the officer and the Guard Commander over the discovery. While this was going on the guards jokingly began to examine one another and Turner was discovered.

(g) *Seventh attempt.*
A Polish chimney sweep worked in the Camp during the Summer of 1941 and an officer became friendly with him and succeeded in borrowing his gate pass which was copied by another P/W. The officer was 90250 F/Lt. P.G. Leeson R.A.F. It was his intention to impersonate the sweep without his knowledge and after leaving the Camp to walk to Rugen and travel by the ferry to Sweden.

The sweep did not reappear in the Camp till March, 1942. Whilst waiting for his return Leeson made a sweep's outfit. This consisted of a top hat made out of cardboard and painted black, a coat and trousers covered with soot, a brush made of cardboard attached to a line with a weight on the end. He made a civilian suit which he intended to wear underneath the sweeps clothing.

On about 16th March, 1942, the sweep came into the Compound and Leeson donned his disguise. At about 11.00 hours he walked out of the Camp while the real sweep was engaged in conversation with some other P's/W. When the genuine sweep left the Camp the guards did not report his 'double' exit owing to fear of punishment.

After Leeson had walked a short distance from the Camp he discarded the bogus sweeps' outfit and tried to wash his face and hands in the snow. Owing to the fact that it was snowing heavily with strong winds, he changed his original plans and decided to make for Warnemunde.

After walking about thirty kilometres, Leeson took shelter in a barn about nightfall. He was discovered by an old farmer, but managed to convince him that he was a foreign worker on his way to Rostock. However, he was turned out of the barns so walked towards Damgarten. Owing to the snow he was unable to skirt the town and was picked up by a patrol. He was returned to the Camp a few days later.

(h) *Eight attempt.*

In March, 1942, a partly successful attempt was made to escape by walking through the gates disguised as a 'ferret'. The attempt was made by 42356 F/Lt. V. Parker R.A.F. He wore soiled overalls similar to those worn by the 'ferrets', a bogus Luftwaffe field-service cap and duty belt, and carried a dummy torch and iron spike resembling those carried by the 'ferrets'.

Parker intended to pose as an Italian workman when clear of the Camp precincts and wore suitable clothing under his overalls. He was in the possession of a forged pass for an Italian worker and carried a map and a compass.

When dressed in his disguise Parker bore a resemblance to a 'ferret' named Piltz. Choosing a time when Piltz was not in the Compound or Vorlager, he walked through the two camp gates without difficulty. In the woods adjacent to the Camp he met Piltz who arrested him and took him back to the Camp.

(i) *Ninth attempt.*

A scheme for an escape by walking through the compound gates was devised by:

> 73727 F/Lt. P.F. Cazenove   R.A.F.
> 90250 F/Lt. P.G. Leeson   R.A.F.
> 40258 F/Lt. J. Plant   R.A.F.

The plan was that Leeson, who spoke German, was to wear a bogus German uniform complete with dummy revolver and march the others, in normal P/W dress, through the Compound gate into the Vorlager with the aid of suitable forged documents. One of the documents was a gate pass authorising a guard to escort two prisoners from the Compound. All three were to wear civilian type clothing underneath their uniforms. The attempt was timed to take place when it was known that the Abwehr Officer would not be in his office.

At 13.00 hours on 5th April, 1942, the plan was put into effect and the party approached the gate leading from the Compound into the Vorlager. The guard examined the pass carefully but allowed them through. After they had gone a few yards the guard recalled them and demanded to see the pass again. He pointed to a Roman 111 printed in the top left corner. This number had puzzled the P's/W and Leeson feared that discovery was imminent. However, the explanation was simple enough, for as the guard pointed out, it was now the fourth month not the third. Leeson shrugged his shoulders and stated that the Abwehr Officer had given him the pass with instructions to escort the two prisoners to his office. He added that he was a new arrival in the Camp and not familiar with procedure. The guard accepted this explanation and let the party go. They passed the guard on the second gate, leading from the Vorlager into the German Compound, without incident.

They went towards the Abwehr Officer's office, passing the German doctor and one of the 'ferrets' on the way. Instead of entering the office they made a long detour between the buildings of the German Headquarters and climbed the single wire fence at a point where they were not visible from the windows.

When they had climbed the fence the three escapers separated, having arranged a rendezvous that evening. They discarded their uniforms, but Cazenove and Plant were discovered soon afterwards by a road patrol. That evening Leeson was discovered in a wood after having been spotted by two members of the Hitler Youth who had become suspicious because of his dyed trousers. All three officers were returned to the Camp.

20. WIRE SCHEMES
(a) *First attempt.*
In September, 1940, a new Compound was under construction to enlarge the existing Compound. This was adjacent to the West fence and contained one barrack. The new Compound was patrolled by two sentries. On the South side there was a gap in the fence. This led to the Sports Field which was surrounded by a single fence.

A scheme to take advantage of these conditions was devised and put into effect by 37467 S/Ldr. K.C. Doran R.A.F. On 15th September, he cut through the fence between the old and new Compounds. This was done in daylight and he hid in the partly built barracks until about 22.00 hours. It was dark then and he began to crawl towards the gap leading into the sports field. He was noticed by a guard as he run through the gap and cut through the single fence. Several shots were fired and the area was illuminated by the searchlights in the sentry tower, but he run towards the river close by. Although a search party with dogs was turned out, his hiding place amongst the reeds was not discovered.

About 04.00 hours on 16th September he started walking West.

31

Although he was wearing non-uniform trousers, which he had acquired in Norway after capture, and a civilian shirt, he hid in a wood from dawn until dusk. When he resumed walking he continued until he reached Saaler Bay, then hid until the evening of 17th September, when he started walking towards the nearby flying-boat base. Whilst walking across a field he was seen by some farmers and arrested.

He was taken to a nearby farmhouse, but seeing a chance to make a getaway jumped onto a bicycle in the yard. Before he had travelled more than a few yards he was apprehended by another farmer. In due course he was returned to the Camp.

(b) *Second attempt.*

In October, 1940, an escape over the fence of the Sports Field was made in daylight by 70824 F/Lt P.D. Tunstall R.A.F. He was a member of a party of P's/W which had been taken to the Sports Field for recreation. He was wearing a suit of overalls, similar to those worn by 'ferrets', under his greatcoat; also a pair of German jackboots which he had acquired. Under the overalls he wore civilian-type clothes made by converting his uniform.

When the party was being marched back to the Compound the two guards were at the rear. Tunstall, who was at the head of the column, waited until they reached a right-angled corner, took off his greatcoat and walked back past the column and the guards, disguised as a 'ferret'. The guards displayed no interest in him and he was able to climb over the fence of the Sports Field. As the P's/W had been taken back to the Compound this was unguarded.

Tunstall hid in the wood until evening, then started walking towards Stralsund. About daylight he hid in a wood, but saw a milk lorry which he assumed to be going to Stralsund so jumped onto the tailboard. He discovered that it was going towards Barth, but it was travelling too fast for him to jump off until he was close to the outskirts of the town.

At a wayside halt he boarded a local train going to Stralsund. When asked for his ticket, some time later, he told the conductor that he was a Swedish sailor who had missed his ship. This story was accepted and Tunstall travelled to Stralsund. On arrival there the conductor called a policeman and Tunstall was arrested. He was taken to the police station in Stralsund and returned to the Camp later that day.

(c) *Third attempt.*

In May, 1941, a tunnel was under construction in the Compound and a number of P's/W were apprehended by the Germans. They were sentenced to short periods of confinement in cells and one of them conceived the idea of attempting to escape from his cell. The cells were situated in the Vorlager. This officer was 39965 F/Lt. H. Burton R.A.F. He anticipated that he would have some time to wait before being taken to the cells to serve his five-day sentence, but a guard arrived at his barrack and escorted him to the cells without prior warning. He was unable to take the bulk of food, etc. which he had in readiness, but he was able to conceal a map and two bars of chocolate.

He spent the next five nights at work on loosening the bars across his cell window with the aid of a table knife. These were screwed into the wooden walls from the outside. On the fifth night about 23.00 hours, he unscrewed the bars completely, removed them and climbed through the window. He undid some of the screws fastening the grille covering the window of the cell occupied by another officer, then crawled to the double gate leading from the Vorlanger to the German Compound. He excavated a hollow under the gates with a piece of metal which he had picked up.

While the guard was being changed he ceased work and crawled back and lay under his cell window at the side of the building, as at such times an Alsatian dog was allowed to run along outside the perimeter fence. Whilst he was lying by the cell window one of his jailors came out for a smoke and a chat with the sentry.

After he had burrowed under the gates, he ran across to the German Headquarters buildings and from there crawled to the perimeter fence. He climbed this about 02.30 hours on 27th May whilst the patrolling sentry was elsewhere on his beat.

(d) *Fourth attempt.*
In June, 1941 an escape attempt was made by two officers who were serving sentences in cells for previous escapes. They were:

> Lt.Cdr. (A) J. Buckley   R.N.
> 05225 S/Ldr N.H.J. Tindall   R.A.F.

Buckley cut a hole in the wooden partition between his cell and the one occupied by Tindall and climbed through. They unscrewed one of the bars across Tindall's cell window and climber through under cover of darkness. They crawled to the fence and Tindall began to cut his way through with a pair of wirecutters which he had managed to conceal from the Germans. Whilst engaged in this they were apprehended and placed in other cells under close surveillance.

(e) *Fifth attempt.*

The next attempt to escape by negotiating the wire was made by 78536 F/Lt. J.E. Thompson R.A.F. The following account is an extract from his statement – I.S.9/REP/4/G/4/264:

"About June, 1941, I began to plan an escape which was to be effected from the N.C.O's Compound.

"For the next six months I studied the movements of guards at nights and noted the times taken by the sentries in patrolling their beats. I observed the shadows cast by small hillocks, etc. when the N.C.O's Compound and the Officers' football field were swept by the searchlights located in the four sentry towers overlooking this area. In this way I acquired a mental picture of the whole terrain and knew the exact location of every height and hollow.

"I made a pair of wirecutters using two iron bars from stoves, but these were not very efficient and I planned to use them to cut through the last fence only. I obtained a Naval Officers' uniform from Midshipman Wright, R.N., and converted it to look like a civilian suit. I obtained maps and a compass and saved a quantity of food.

"When all my plans had been completed I made an attempt to get into the N.C.O's Compound by exchanging identities with an N.C.O. at the Compound gate, but this was detected. Neither of us was apprehended.

"I was a member of the Officers' Compound football team. A match was arranged between the Officers' team and the N.C.O's team to take place in the N.C.O's Compound. The Germans consented to this arrangement and the match was fixed for 1st January, 1942.

"When the Officers' party arrived at the gate leading into the N.C.O's Compound I bribed the guard with cigarettes and was able to get into the Compound without being counted. I was wearing my 'civilian' suit under my greatcoat and carried my escape aids, food, etc.

"After the football match was over I hid in one of the N.C.O's barracks until after the evening roll call. The party of officers had returned to the Officers; Compound. I hid under a bed during the roll call.

"At about 18.00 hours I left the barrack, which had been locked up for the night, by getting through a concealed trap-door in the floor. This was the entrance to a tunnel which was under construction from underneath the barrack.

"Two N.C.O's who lived in the barrack, requested that I should allow them to accompany me. I refused, but advise them to follow my tracks the following night if my attempt should be successful. Subsequently I learned that they had attempted to do so, but had been detected. They were fired upon and one was killed.

"I crawled diagonally across the N.C.O's Compound towards the sentry tower located on the Southern perimeter fence at the point where the fence was joined to the double fence separating the N.C.O's Compound from the Officers' football field. After traversing about two thirds of this distance, I crawled away from the sentry tower and parallel to the fence dividing the N.C.O's Compound and the Officers' football field.

"In due course I reached the double gate in this fence, which had a structure of barbed wire entanglements placed between the gates. This gate was located about five yards from the gate leading from the German Administrative Compound into the N.C.O's Compound and a sentry was on duty there. An arc light was suspended above this gate and the area was well illuminated. I burrowed under the double gate leading into the Officers' football field, but this took a long time because the ground was frozen and I could not make any noise on account of the close proximity of the sentry on the other gate. The fence and the gate between the N.C.O's Compound and the Officers' football field were illuminated by the normal camp boundary lights, but there was not a sentry on patrol.

"In order to get through the hole which I had made under the gate I had to remove my greatcoat which contained my food, maps, wirecutters, etc. When I crawled through to the other side, at about midnight, I was caught in the beam of a searchlight and had to roll away from the gate to rougher ground which afforded me some degree of concealment. I decided not to take the risk of attempting to recover my greatcoat.

"In due course I learned that when the greatcoat had been discovered by the Germans on 3rd January, they assumed that it belonged to one of the two N.C.O's who had attempted to follow me.

"I crawled parallel to the fence towards the sentry tower on the Southern perimeter fence which I have mentioned previously. I climbed over this boundary fence at about 03.00 hours on 2nd January at a point about five yards from the sentry tower and when the patrolling sentry was at the other end of his beat. The sentry in the tower was sweeping the N.C.O's Compound with his searchlight at the time.

"My reasons for choosing to climb the fence so close to the sentry tower were:

(i) I believed that if in were seen by the sentry at close quarters he would be less likely to shoot than if I were at a distance.

(ii) I had observed that the sentries in the towers did not shine their searchlights directly downwards so that an area of about twenty yards from the tower was comparatively 'safe'.

"The two Compounds, over which I crawled to get to the point where I climbed the fence, were swept by four searchlights. As far as possible I crawled directly towards, or away from, the nearest searchlight during the nine hours which it took me to carry out the operation. By doing this I had to traverse a much greater distance, but my object was to ensure that the shadow cast by my body when illuminated by the nearest searchlight could be confused with the shadow cast by a small hillock. The two N.C.O's who attempted to follow me the following night did not heed my advice in this respect, but crawled diagonally across the beams of the searchlights. In my opinion, this was the cause of their failure.

"When I had climbed over the fence I crawled to a point about twenty yards outside the fence, then ran across the field to the wall surrounding the nearby Flak School. When I reached this I fainted, probably due to nervous strain and cold. When I regain consciousness I discovered that my clothing was saturated. At first I thought that this was due to having crawled over the snow, but closer examination showed that it had been caused by perspiration.

"I walked along the side of the wall to the main road on the outskirts of Barth, then through the town and along the main road to Stralsund, where I arrived about 09.00 hours. From daylight onwards I affected a crooked arm and an idiotic expression. I walked through Stralsund and across the heavily guarded bridge leading to the Island of Rugen. When I saw that I was unobserved I hid in a field.

"I remained there until dark, when I returned to the road and walked North passing through Bergen. Just before dawn on 3rd January I hid in a field, where I remained until dusk. Then I resumed walking and arrived on the outskirts of Sassnitz just before dawn on 4th January: I hid in a field.

"I remained there until the afternoon, when I decided I should have to leave my hiding place and reach the ferry to Sweden that day. This decision was forced upon me by my condition. I felt that I could not last more than another day without food and shelter and I knew that I should have to remain in hiding on the ferry until it would arrive at Trelleborg, Sweden. I believed that the ferry sailed from Sassnitz in the late afternoon, so I left my hiding place in daylight. While crossing the field I was seen by two farmers who accosted me. I swore at them in German and then ran. They chased me and were able to catch me because of my exhausted condition. Later I was returned to the Camp."

(f) *Sixth attempt.*

In January, 1942, an attempt was made by an officer to escape by climbing over the fence during a snowstorm. He was seen by a guard and a few shots were fired, but he was not hit. He was recaptured within a few minutes. He was Lt. (A) J. Kiddell R.N.

(g) *Seventh attempt.*
An escape was made from the Sports Field in January, 1942, by 42356 F/Lt. V. Parker R.A.F. In preparation for the attempt he acquired a shortened airman's greatcoat with black buttons made from poker chips, and dyed trousers. He carried false identity papers indicating that he was an Italian worker.

On the day of the attempt he went with a party of officers, under escort, to the Sports Field. The ground was covered with deep snow at the time. Parker, who was wearing his escape clothing, participated in the game of rugby which was being played. During a scrum he was buried in the snow.

He remained there until he heard a bugle played in the Compound about five hours later. This was a pre-arranged signal that it was dark. Parker climbed over the fence of the Sports Field, which was unguarded. He started walking towards Sassnitz, but was unable to walk properly as his leg was frostbitten. He was picked up in Barth by Luftwaffe personnel and taken back to the Camp.

(h) *Eighth attempt.*
During a snowstorm on about 16th March, 1942, an escape was made by climbing the fence by 61046 F/Lt. G. Hill R.A.F.

Snow had been drifting for several days and the concertina wire between the two sections of the double fence was covered with snow packed hard. During the snow-storm Hill noticed that the guard in one of the sentry towers had retired into the back of his box for shelter, also that visibility was reduced to about fifty yards. Hurriedly he acquired a pair of Naval trousers, an airman's greatcoat which had been shortened and altered to look like a civilian coat, and provided himself with food, maps and a compass.

At about 09.00 hours he was ready and choosing a moment when visibility was at its lowest, he climbed over the fence at a point about ten yards from the sentry tower. The snow was falling so thickly that none of the guards in the other sentry towers could see him and in a few minutes his tracks in the snow were obliterated.

He walked some distance to a barn where he took shelter for a time, then walked through the town of Barth towards Stralsund. That night he sheltered in another barn. Next day he resumed walking and arrived on the outskirts of Stralsund. As he was rather exhausted he sat down beside a house and began talking to the occupier. He thought that this man was satisfied with his story, but a German soldier arrived about five minutes later and arrested him. He was taken to the Submarine School in Stralsund and returned to the Camp a few days later.

(i) *Ninth attempt.*
The attempt made by Hill was witnessed by 66002 F/Lt. R. Edge R.A.F., who decided to emulate his example. His preparations were very simple and consisted of covering the buttons of his uniform and acquiring some food and a map.

He walked round the Compound close to the perimeter fence and noticed that the guard in the box, near which Hill had climbed the fence, had been changed. The new guard was more conscientious than the man he had relieved and stood in the front of his box in such a position that Edge could not approach the fence without being seen. Edge continued to walk round the Compound for about an hour, then observed that this guard also had retired to the back of the box where the windows were covered almost entirely with snow.

Edge walked up to the tower in such a way that these windows were between himself and the guard, then climbed over the fence directly under the sentry box. The weather cleared for a few moments later and he was seen about two hundred yards from the Camp. The guard fired several shots without effect and Edge took cover in a trench used for training purposes by the nearby Flak School. As he was emerging from the trench a few minutes later he was apprehended by a German from the Flak School and taken back to the Camp.

21. WALL SCHEMES
Not applicable.

22. TRANSPORT SCHEMES
(a) *First attempt.*
In September, 1940, parties of French P's/W who were engaged on construction work were brought into the Compound and taken out of it by lorry. The undermentioned officers devised a scheme to take advantage of this:

78530 F/Lt. J.B.S. Brockway   R.A.F.
90252 F/Lt. N. Forbes   R.A.F.

They converted their flying overalls into civilian clothes, made cloth caps, and acquired maps and food.

After a few days their preparations were completed and they awaited an opportune moment. About mid-day on the selected day the lorry arrived in the Compound to take the Frenchmen out. The Frenchmen climbed into the lorry and when the German officers who were supervising this operation had gone, Brockway and Forbes climbed in and lay flat on the floor at the back. The lorry moved on a few yards and six German guards climbed in, but the two escapers were not discovered.

The lorry passed through the Camp gates and as it approached the railway station at Barth the two escapers dropped off between the side of the lorry and the canvas hood. By the time they had accomplished this the lorry had entered the station yard and they were recaptured almost immediately.

(b) *Second attempt.*
During the late Spring of 1941 the Germans insisted upon issuing the food contained in Red Cross parcels from the dining room in the Compound. All tins were opened in the presence of two Germans and the contents tipped into containers which each P/W had to take with him when collecting his 'parcel'. The empty tins were thrown into a large wooden box which was taken out of the Compound on a hand-waggon by British orderlies, escorted by a guard. The tins were dumped beyond the outer fence of the Camp close to a small wooden hut. The reason for the issue of the contents of parcels in this way and the removal of the tins from the Compound was to prevent the tins being used as airlines for tunnels.

A scheme for taking advantage of the removal of the tins in this way was developed by Lt. (A) Filmer R.N. as a result of a chance remark by a fellow P/W. He asked the orderlies to make a point of dumping the tins closer to the small hut from then onwards. The box used for removing the tins was modified and fitted with a false bottom; the work being done at night in the barrack after 'lock-up'. Entrance to the space to the false bottom and the original bottom was gained through a cunningly concealed door, hinged along one of the ends of the box. The concealed space had to be very small and Filmer, a man of small stature, could just get into it by lying on his side with his head and neck bent in one corner and his knees drawn up under his chin.

Completing the alterations took several days and in the last week of April Filmer carried out a dummy run in order to ascertain whether he could endure being cooped up for the period of two hours required; also to see if things would work satisfactorily at the tin dump. He found that he suffered from cramp and that the oils and juices from the tins seeped

39

through the cracks. He was taken out of the camp and discovered that the arrangements made by the orderlies at the tin dump were satisfactory. He was taken back into the Compound without incident.

Filmer completed his preparations which included blackening the buttons of his Naval greatcoat, removing the badge of a Naval cap, making maps and a rucksack, acquired food and a little money, learning the details of his route and as much relevant information as possible. Arrangements were made for concealing his absence from the Germans and the orderlies were asked to divert the attention of their escorting guard at the tin dump.

On 2nd May, 1941, the bottom of the box was covered with absorbent paper to prevent the oils and juices from seeping through and Filmer, dressed in his 'civilian' clothes, got into the concealed space. The box was taken to the dining room and after the completion of the issue of the contents of the parcels it was lifted onto the hand-wagon and taken to the tin dump. The orderlies distracted the attention of the guard, and upon hearing a pre-arranged signal from one of the orderlies, Filmer opened the hinged flap and crawled into the small hut. He hid there under some timber until dark, then walked into the woods nearby. Here he encountered a barbed wire fence, the existence of which he had not known as it was not visible from the Camp. He climbed this fence and started walking.

He walked for three nights, hiding in the daytime, until he reached Rienitz, where he boarded an empty passenger train which was standing in the station. He travelled in this to Rostock where it stopped in the goods yard. He saw a goods train moving off so climbed out and boarded it. This took him to Bad Kleinen, where he alighted in the goods yard as it was nearly daylight. He hid during the day and boarded another goods train at the same place that night. This took him to Neumunster, where he left the train in the goods yard and started looking, though unsuccessfully, for a hiding place. Finally he decided to continue his journey and stole a bicycle from outside a factory.

He cycled North towards Denmark and reached the frontier after three days, hiding at night. During the night of 8th May he crossed the frontier by crawling between two sentry boxes. He walked for about half an hour, then hid under some bushes and fell asleep.

Sometime later he was awakened by a Danish frontier guard, who took him to a frontier post on a main road. He was interviewed by a Danish officer, but although he tried to make this officer understand that he was an escaped British P/W he was sent back into Germany. At the German frontier post he was allowed to pass although he had no papers. Apparently the guards assumed that he was a Danish workman.

Filmer walked into Flensburg, where he spent the day looking for a neutral ship, but without success. That night he made another attempt to cross the Danish frontier by climbing along the side of a small bridge over a river. He was heard by a German sentry who apprehended him and took him to a local headquarters. He attempted to bluff, but his story was not believed and he was taken to a prison in Flensburg. A few hours later he was escorted back to the Camp.

(c) *Third attempt.*

A number of large packing cases were supplied by the Germans in early April, 1942, for the purpose of packing books, theatrical equipment, canteen stores, etc. for removal to Stalag Luft III (Sagan), as all the P's/W were to be moved there a few days later. The officer who was in charge of the Canteen at that time modified and enlarged one of the packing cases so that he could fit into it. He was 70775 F/Lt. J.C. Wilson R.A.F.

His other preparations included obtaining a shortened and dyed airman's greatcoat with civilian buttons, blue civilian trousers, a camp-made peaked cloth cap dyes black, maps, a compass, food and an iron bar for forcing his way out of the packing case. The Air Force N.C.O's who were to be responsible for removing the packing case from the Compound and loading them on to the train at Barth Railway Station were advised of the markings on the case in which Wilson would be, and asked to ensure that no other luggage was placed on top of it in the railway wagon.

On the afternoon of 10th April, Wilson was nailed into the packing case and soon afterwards it, together with other luggage and similar packing cases, was loaded on to a lorry and conveyed to the railway station. These items were placed in a railway wagon and sometime later, about 17.00 hours, Wilson broke open the packing case. He discovered that the door of the wagon was padlocked and resisted all his efforts to open it.

At about 11.00 hours on 11th April the train began to move and from then until the following day Wilson made repeated attempts to open the door whenever the train was passing through the open country. The method he adopted was to swing his iron bar attached to a length of rope through the ventilator slit in such a way that it would catch under the padlock and hasp. Eventually he was able to break the hasp and slide the door open.

By this time the train had arrived at Bernau and Wilson jumped off. He walked East until he reached the river Oder North of Kustrin and spent that night in a barn. On 13th April he resumed walking and arrived at Angermunde two days later, having spent the previous two nights sleeping in the open. At about 22.00 hours on 15th April he entered the railway yard at Angermunde and eventually hid in the guard's van of a goods train which was labelled 'Stettin'.

Presently the train began to move and about 05.00 hours on 16th April arrived at Stettin. Wilson left the train and slept in a wood on the outskirts of the town until about 11.00 hours. He went to the docks and spent the remainder of that day seeking Swedish ships. He discovered only one, which was anchored mid-stream, so he returned to the wood for the night. On 17th April he returned to the docks and spent the whole of that day trying to locate a Swedish ship, but without success.

By this time his food supplies were very low and he decided to board a goods train and attempt to get to Rostock, where he hoped to be able to cross by ferry to Gedser in Denmark. At about 22.00 hours he hid in the guard's van of a goods train and fell asleep. When he awoke he discovered that he had boarded the wrong train and had arrived at Kustrin. Here he gave himself up as he was suffering from hunger and fatigue. A few days later he was taken to Stalag Luft III (Sagan).

23. MISCELLANEOUS SCHEMES

(a) *First attempt.*

For a period of several months after the opening of the Camp, Air Force N.C.O's and airmen were taken out of the Camp under escort on working parties in the district. Usually these parties returned to the camp at night. Three officers were able to effect an exchange of identities with three N.C.O's and joined one of these working parties in August, 1940 The three officers were:

41710	F/Lt. H.O. Jones	R.A.F.
37973	F/Lt. D.F. Laslett	R.A.F.
37659	F/Lt. N.M. Thomas	R.A.F.

During the day Laslett and Thomas got away from the guard on the excuse of wishing to retire, but Jones was unable to join them. They were dressed in uniform modified to look like the dress of Polish workers and had maps, food and compass.

They walked South-East and reached the outskirts of Demmin, about forty-five kilometres South of Stralsund, two days later. Whilst resting in a wood they were picked up by some Germans and returned to the Camp.

(b) *Second attempt.*

On 1st October, 1940, two officers managed to exchange identities with two N.C.O's and so join a working party engaged in digging a drain in the main street of the town of Barth. The two officers were:

> 42113 F/Lt. R.H. Edwards   R.A.F.
> 42646 F/Lt. J.P. Quirke   R.A.F.

Whilst having a mid-morning rest, they slipped off down a side street and walked to the outskirts where they were apprehended by Dock Police. Later they were returned to the Camp.

(c) *Third attempt.*
On about 5th January, 1942, 05225 S/Ldr. N.H.J. Tindal R.A.F. changed places with a British orderly and accompanied a number of other orderlies on a trip to the town of Barth under escort, to empty Camp rubbish at the refuse dump. As the party was returning to the Camp on foot it was overtaken by one of the Camp lorries which stopped to pick them up. It was dusk, and Tindal decided to run for it while the working party was in some disorder before getting into the lorry. He ran off the road into a wood, but was seen by one of the occupants of the lorry who gave chase. The German was unarmed, but gained steadily on the fugitive and jumped on his back and brought him down. It transpired that this German was one of the Camp doctors and had been a professional runner. Tindal was taken back to Camp.

24. NUMBER OF ESCAPES
There were two successful escapes from this Compound during the period under review. The individuals were:

> 39965 F/Lt. H. Burton   R.A.F.
> 39177 F/Lt. J.T.L. Shore   R.A.F.

The account of Burton's escape is later in this Chapter.

25. NUMBER OF ATTEMPTED ESCAPES
In addition to thirty-eight unsuccessful tunnelling projects involving a large number of men, thirty-eight personnel who were resident in this Compound attempted to escape in twenty-five separate attempts.

26. MASS ATTEMPTS
On 19th August, 1941, an attempt was made to carry out a mass escape by means of the tunnel described in this Chapter. About a dozen officers were to make the attempt, but the second man to leave the exit, at about

midnight, was seen by a guard and some shots were fired. Only three officers succeeded in getting clear. They were:

32108	S/Ldr. C.E.S. Lockett	R.A.F.
70419	S/Ldr. M.L. McColm	R.A.F.
36271	F/t. H.D. Newman	R.A.F.

Lockett and McColm travelled together and Newman went alone. Their statements, which have been compiled from their M.I.9/S/P.G. reports, are given below:

(i) *McColm.*
"I was dressed in a camp-made cap, navy-blue roll-necked sweater, Air Force trousers and thick rope-soled sandals. It was intended that Lockett, Newman and myself should travel together to Lubeck.

"I went through the tunnel first followed by the others. We had arranged to meet in a nearby field. After I had waited for about three-quarters of an hour, Lockett arrived. We waited for Newman, but as he did not arrive Lockett and I travelled together from then on.

"We walked South-West by night and hid in woods during the day until 26th August, when we boarded a goods train travelling towards Lubeck. On arrival at Schwann we got off the train when it was stationary and hid in a swamp until evening.

"We spent the evening and night of 27th August trying to find a goods train travelling to Lubeck. Our method was to examine the destination labels of the trucks as they arrived in the marshalling yard at Schwann. Our efforts were not successful.

"We resumed walking and boarded a goods train eventually. On arrival at Bad Kleinen a German got into the truck in which we were hiding, and heard our voices. He shone his torch on us, but we jumped out of the truck and went to a wood, where we remined until evening.

"At 0645 hours on 28th August Lockett, who could speak a little German, bought two third-class railway tickets to Lubeck. We boarded a train and arrived at Lubeck about 0900 hours. We spent the remainder of that day walking around the town. We hid our suitcases, etc., near the river and in the evening went to the docks in order to try to find a Swedish ship.

"We boarded one Swedish ship and spoke to the cook and first mate, and asked them if they would hide us. They went away and Lockett and I hid in a coal bunker. After we had been there about ten minutes, our presence was discovered by a stoker, who reported us to the chief engineer. When he arrived he told us to go ashore, or he would report us to the police. We left the ship and boarded several others without being able to obtain help.

"Eventually we found a Swedish seaman who agreed to help us to stow away on his ship. We discovered that we were being watched through binoculars by a policeman on the docks, so left the dock area.

"We returned to the place where we had hidden our suitcase and decided that we should separate and attempt to get on board different ships. We parted and I returned to the docks where I boarded a ship and stowed away amongst some auxiliary steering gear in the stern.

"On 31st August the ship sailed and when we were about eighty miles at sea I was discovered by a deck hand and taken to the Captain, who stated that he would have to hand me over to the Germans. He turned his ship about immediately and anchored near a watch-ship. On 1st September a pilot came on board and I was taken off and put on board the watch-ship.

"Some time later I attempted to steal a motor-boat moored to the watch-ship, but was captured in the act. Soon afterwards a supply boat came alongside and I was taken to Warnemunde and handed over to the Luftwaffe. On 3rd September I was returned to the Camp."

(ii) *Lockett.*
"We were all dressed to pass as Swedish sailors, in uniform trousers, polo-necked sweaters, and hats which we had made ourselves. We had camp-made compasses, a silk map, which I think McColm had managed to keep when he was captured, and a local map copied from one obtained from the Germans; also some food and five Reichsmarks.

"I was seen as I got out and fired at, but I ran away and reached the rendezvous we had selected. This was a rail/road crossing in the vicinity. There I met McColm, but Newman did not turn up, although we waited for about an hour.

"We walked South-West along the railway line, hoping to evade recapture more successfully by taking a circuitous route to Lubeck, than by going the most direct way. For the first four days we hid in potato fields and copses, and walked along the railway by night.

"In a small goods yard South of Rostock we climbed on to a stationary goods train and hid in a coal wagon. The train moved off

45

and was stopped by a signal at dawn. We got off and hid in a wood.

"The following night we climbed on to another train, which was in a small station, and travelled to Bad Kleinen, where we were seen by a man in a brake-van, so jumped out of the truck and hid in a wood.

"The next morning I bought railway tickets to Lubeck and we travelled by a workman's train at about 0530 hours, which arrived at Lubeck at about 0900 hours. We walked out of the station down to the river and sat on a piece of waste land at the edge of the river to watch shipping.

"Later we made a reconnaissance of the docks, walked on to several Swedish ships and asked to see the captains. Then we explained who we were and asked them to let us stow away, but all were too frightened. We left the docks and returned to the waste land.

"That evening we decided to split up and stow away on separate ships. As people were leaving the cinemas, we walked back to the docks and each boarded a ship. After I had looked round my ship, I decided to hide in a ventilator. I climbed into one at about 0500 hours and found a bar in which I stood for about eleven hours.

"At the end of this time I was discovered by a pantryman, who opened a door and saw my feet. The bar turned out to be part of a winch for hauling food up and my feet being on it had caused the handle to rattle. None of the crew were armed and while the police were being fetched I walked off the ship and back to the waste land by the river.

"That night I slept in a carpenter's shed and next morning went to the docks again to see if McColm's ship had left: it was still there. On my way back a policeman stopped me to ask some questions but I managed to talk my way out and went back to the waste land. I decided that the local small boys were becoming too friendly, so left and walked to the other side of the river.

"That night I spent in a shelter and the next morning I was picked up by some works police. They handed me over to the water police. I told them I was a Swedish sailor and the name of my ship, which I said was in the docks. They rowed me round the docks, but no such ship was there. I could think of no more lies so told them who I was.

"I was put into Lubeck gaol, where I spent one night, and as taken to Oflag X/C (Lubeck).

(iii) Newman.

"I was last out and hearing some shots fired I ran off alone as fast as I could. I was dressed as a workman and wore a pyjamas coat dyed blue, Air Force trousers, and a cap made out of a check scarf, the peak of which I had painted black with boot polish. I was without money or forged documents and had only a small amount of food which I had saved up.

"My aim was to reach Rostock, but soon after I got out of the Camp I lost my way in the marshy area surrounding Barth. Eventually I found I was on the wrong side of a small river and had to retrace my steps, which entailed walking through the village of Barth.

"Then I set off in a South-Westerly direction and when I reached Dunngarten I hid myself under some stooks in a field and went to sleep. Soon afterwards I was found by a farmer, who took me to the police in the village. I was taken back to the Camp.

27. SUMMARY OF METHODS

(a) *Tunnels.*

The two successful tunnels which were constructed in this Compound are described in this Chapter.

(b) *Gate walk-out schemes.*

No successful escapes were made by walking through the gate. Nine attempts of this type are described in this Chapter. These can be divided into four classes:

(i) Joining parties of P's/W being taken out of the Camp on parole, under escort, without giving parole.
(ii) Disguised as German Service personnel.
(iii) Disguised as German or foreign workmen.
(iv) Disguised as a German guard escorting a number of P's/W to the German Compound for interview at headquarters.

Accurate timing was necessary for the type of escape described in (i). A knowledge of the German language, and in some cases forged documents, was necessary to ensure success in escapes of type (ii). Type (iii) needed an effective disguise and forged documents. Type (iv) was dependent upon the 'guard', who required forged documents, an effective disguise and a sound knowledge of the German language.

47

(c) *Wire Schemes.*
There were ten attempts by negotiating the wire. Nine of these are described in this Chapter. One was successful and is also described. As a general rule this type of escape was attempted by individuals without a knowledge of German. They selected parts of the fence which were weakly guarded, or took advantage of conditions, e.g. snow, etc.

(d) *Wall schemes.*
N/A

(e) *Transport Schemes.*
Three attempts were made to escape by means of vehicles leaving the Compound. None was successful. Attempts of this kind generally were made by individuals of small stature who could not speak German.

(f) *Miscellaneous Schemes.*
Three attempts are described under this heading in this Chapter. All these were changes of identity with N.C.O's from the adjacent Compound, or with orderlies, which enabled the escapers to get outside the Camp on local working parties under guard. None were successful.

(g) *Mass attempt.*
Details of the mass escape which was to be attempted through the tunnel described in this Chapter. Only three men got clear of the tunnel because the second man to leave the exit was seen by a guard.

(h) *Comment.*
Although there was a considerable amount of escape activity during the period under review, this was not organised and individuals had to do most of their own preparatory work. It is evident that there was plenty of scope for attempts, particularly during the first year, as German security was not highly organised, but these conditions were not exploited fully. The chief reasons were:

(i) Lack of escape material of all kinds.
(ii) Failure to organise escape activities on a broad basis.
(iii) Failure to control private trading with Germans with the result that a most valuable source of supply of escape material was not developed.
(iv) Lack of information which would be useful to an escaper once clear of the Camp precincts.

During the second half of the period a larger number of attempts were made. This coincided with the arrival of clothes and food in adequate quantities; also with the nucleus of an Escape Organisation set up under the directions of the Senior British Officer at that time 05175 W/Cdr. H.M.A. Day R.A.F.

Chapter 3

Escape Material

28. REQUIREMENTS

The requirements for this type of Camp are given in the History of Stalag Luft III (Sagan) [also published by Frontline Books].

29. AIDS RECEIVED FROM I.S.9

The first parcel from I.S.9. was received in May, 1941. From that date onwards occasional parcels were received, numbering about six in all. These were games parcels which contained maps, money and compasses only. They were addressed to individual code users.

No advice was received by code message, or other means, to give warning that a parcel containing escape aids had been despatched until several months after the first parcel had arrived in the Camp.

When the recipient of the first games parcel examined its contents he showed the pipe, which was included, to one of his colleagues, who remarked that he would not care to smoke it as it was made of common wood, stained and polished. Closer examination showed that it contained a compass. From then onwards the contents of all similar parcels were examined very carefully.

30. REMARKS ON PACKING

All the gadgets in games parcels passed through the German censorship without incident. It is suggested that the best method of introducing escape aids into this type of Camp would be to despatch undisguised parcels, within the authorised weight limits, to specified individuals, but before this is done contact with the Camp must be established in order to ensure that conditions are such that these parcels could be stolen by the P's/W before censorship.

In all cases it is essential that the Camp is advised of the despatch of escape material, name and addressee, etc., by means of code messages in duplicate sent off in ample time to arrive before the parcel. If escape aids are contained in gadgets, the items in which the aids have been concealed should be specified for each parcel in order to prevent the destruction of useful items which do not contain escape aids.

31. CONCEALMENT OF ESCAPE AIDS – GADGETS, etc.
No method of concealment of escape aids in games parcels, gadgets, etc., were discovered by the Germans during this period. However, the heels of shoes were subject to special scrutiny.

32. ACQUIREMENT OF SPECIAL PARCELS
Immediately following the incident related in the final paragraph of Section 2 above, the Senior Escape Representative informed the officer who was responsible for the distribution of parcels at that time that certain games parcels contained escape aids, and asked him to advise one of the Escape Representatives of the name of any officer receiving one of these parcels from then onwards.

This was done and recipients of such parcels were approached by one of the Escape Representatives who removed the parcel and examined its contents. In some cases recipients protested that since the parcel was addressed to them its contents were their personal property.

33. DANGERS OF STEALING PARCELS
No parcels were stolen prior to censorship during the period under review. As the opportunity occurred, tins of food were smuggled away without being punctured and items of clothing removed from next-of-kin parcels during censorship sometimes were stolen.

34. MATERIAL AVAILABLE / ACQUIRABLE ON THE SPOT
Details of the materials which were available, or acquirable, in the Compound, are given [elsewhere in this book].

Chapter 4

Censorship by the Germans

35. METHOD

(a) *Parcels.*

Red Cross food parcels, next-of-kin clothing, games, book, cigarettes and tobacco parcels arrived at Barth Railway Station and Barth Post Office. These were collected by the Germans and conveyed to the Vorlager where they were unloaded by Air Force N.C.O's., under German supervision, and placed in the Parcel Store.

From the opening of the Camp until about March, 1941, Red Cross food parcels were opened and the tins punctured in the Parcel Store under German supervision, then issued to the P's/W under the directions of the Parcels Officer. From March, 1941 until September, 1941, all tins were emptied into containers which each P/W had to take with him when he collected the contents of his parcel. The reason for this was that the Germans wished to prevent the P's/W from obtaining the tins for use as air pipe-lines in tunnels. In September, 1941 the system of issuing food parcels was changed. From then onwards the requisite number of parcels were conveyed on a hand wagon from the Parcels Store to the dining room in the Compound by British orderlies working under German supervision. Then the parcels were opened and the tins punctured before being issued. In December, 1941, the Germans insisted that the contents of all tins must be emptied into containers and this system was continued until the Camp was evacuated in April, 1942. Red Cross food parcels were not examined to see whether they contained escape aids.

Next-of-kin parcels were examined by the Germans in the Parcels Store in the Vorlager until September, 1941, then issued to the addressees by the Parcels Officer. Certain listed items, especially civilian shirts, ties, etc., were confiscated. The heels of shoes were examined very closely. From September, 1941 until April, 1942, the censorship of these parcels was carried out in the dining-room in the Compound. At all times these parcels were opened and examined in the presence of the addressee.

Games parcels were dealt with similarly to next-of-kin clothing parcels.

Cigarette and tobacco parcels were slit open at one end, but as a rule the contents were not examined.

All book parcels were taken to the German Book Censoring Store, situated in the Vorlager, there they were censored. Lists of forbidden and permissible books were used. Those which were forbidden were confiscated. As a rule these were books containing anti-German propaganda, or those written by authors of Jewish origin. Books which did not appear on any list were read by the censors and issued, or confiscated, in accordance with their decision. The bindings of books were examined by the censors for concealed messages, maps, money, etc., before being issued to the P's/W.

(b) *Mail.*
All in-coming and out-going mail was censored at Dulag Luft (Oberusel) during the period under review.

36. RESULTS
(a) *Parcels.*
As far as can be ascertained no escape aids were discovered by the Germans whilst censoring parcels. All games parcels, containing gadgets in which escape aids were concealed, passed the censorship successfully.

37. OBJECT OF CENSORSHIP
(a) *Parcels.*
The object of censoring parcels was to prevent the entry into the Compound of escape aids, or concealed messages.

The purpose of puncturing food tins was to ensure that the contents would be consumed within a short time and not saved for use in an attempt to escape.

38. PARCEL MARKINGS
No parcels bearing special labels, e.g. Licensed Victuallers, etc., were received in this Compound during the period under review.

39. COMMENTS
(a) *Parcels.*
The German system of censorship was inefficient and it would have been possible to by-pass it without difficulty and gain possession of undisguised parcels known to contain escape aids, if these had been sent to the Camp.

Chapter 5

Code-Letter Mail, Radio and News Letters

40. CODE-LETTER MAIL: INTRODUCTION
With the exception of a small number of messages written by individuals who had been taught the code prior to capture and who worked independently for a time without informing anyone of what they were doing, all messages were submitted to the Senior British Officer and approved by him before they were encoded and embodied in letters despatched to the United Kingdom.

The code was introduced to this Compound by four officers who had been taught prior to capture. They were:

33245	F/Lt. D.A. Ffrench-Mullen	R.A.F.
42231	F/Lt. W.H.C. Hunkin	R.A.F.
40120	F/Lt. F.T. Knight	R.A.F.
26216	S/Ldr. W.H.M. Turner	R.A.F.

41. CODE-LETTER MAIL: ORGANISATION
The above named officers arrived in the Compound in July, 1940, and for a short time they encoded all messages. From about September, 1940, until June, 1941, a number of officers arrived in the Compound who had been taught the code at R.A.F. Stations, or at Dulag Luft (Oberursel). Some of these wrote messages independently at first, but eventually all were incorporated in the Coding Section which had been formed on the instructions of the Senior British Officer, 28097 S/Ldr. B. Paddon R.A.F., about September, 1940. Knight was appointed to be in charge.

During the next few months a number of selected officers were taught the code and registered by the original code users.

The Coding Section was re-organised by 05175 W/Cdr. H.M.A. Day R.A.F. about October, 1941, soon after his arrival in the Camp. He ruled that the coding and decoding of messages should be centralised and appointed two officers known as Coding Officers, to do this work. They were:

90900	F/Lt. J.A. Gillies	R.A.F.
40120	F/Lt. F.T. Knight	R.A.F.

A number of selected officers were taught how to incorporate the groups of figures, which were the encoded messages, into their letters, but they were not instructed how to encode or decode. They were known as 'writers'. They were instructed to pass all the letters they received from the U.K. to the Coding Officers so that any messages which had been incorporated in them could be decoded. For a short time, officers who had been taught how to code and decode were given messages in plain language by the Coding Officers and permitted to encode them: also to decode the replies, but eventually this practice was discontinued and they became 'writers'. The 'writers' did not know the contents of any messages. This system continued until April, 1942.

(a) *Sources of information.*
During the first few months after the opening of the Camp the majority of the messages despatched from this Compound were requests for escape aids and escape information, but military information was despatched also. Towards the end of the period under review this increased in volume. Military information was obtained from the following sources.

(i) New arrivals: The majority of new arrivals in the Compound were new P's/W. From July, 1940, until June, 1941, a number of such personnel were interviewed by the Senior British Officer and it was usual for any P/W who thought he had useful information to seek an interview with him. From mid-1941 onwards all new arrivals were interrogated by the Senior British Officer.
These interrogations covered the following points:
(1) Details of loss of aircraft, etc.
(2) Any military information seen or heard from time of casualty until arrival at Dulag Luft.
(3) Description of the interrogation carried out by the Germans at Dulag Luft or elsewhere.
(4) Report on the behaviour of British and American officers at Dulag Luft.

(5) Military information seen or heard on journey from Dulag Luft to this Camp.

(6) Any messages from British agents and others in civilian gaols, e.g. Fresnes Prison, Paris: also reports of conditions there etc.

(ii) P's/W on journeys outside the Camp: From the opening of the Camp until about October, 1941, the code users usually briefed P's/W who were going on journeys outside the Barth area, e.g. to hospitals, etc. about the type of information which was required and interrogated them upon their return to the Compound. From October, 1941 onwards the briefing and interrogation was done by Knight.

Throughout the period under review, information was passed to the Senior British Officer by the Air Force N.C.O's in the adjacent Compound, as a number of these were outside the Camp on local working parties. The most important source was 580224 Sgt. E.B. Lascelles R.A.F.

(iii) Recaptured escapers: All recaptured escapers were interrogated by one of the Escape Representatives upon their return to the Compound. Any information of military value was passed to the Senior British Officer.

(iv) Contacts: Because trading with Germans was not controlled during the period under review, the acquirement of information from this source was not organised. However, individual P's/W who obtained information from this source, particularly those holding official positions, e.g. Parcels Officer, Messing Officer, etc., passed it on to the Senior British Officer.

(b) *Collation.*
From July, 1940 until October, 1941, all information was collated by:

33245 F/Lt. D.A. Ffrench-Mullen R.A.F.
40120 F/Lt. F.T. Knight   R.A.F.

in collaboration with the Senior British Officer. From October, 1941, onwards this work was done by the Coding Officers:

90900 F/Lt. J.A. Gillies   R.A.F.
40120 F/Lt. F.T. Knight   R.A.F.

in collaboration with the Senior British Officer, who decided what the contents of all messages should be.

(c) *Coding staff.*
During the period July, 1940 – October, 1941, the undermentioned personnel encoded messages and decoded the replies:

37078	F/Lt. D. Barrett	R.A.F.
33303	F/Lt. J.C. Breese	R.A.F.
78530	F/Lt. J.B.S. Brockway	R.A.F.
90120	S/Ldr. R.G. Bushell	R.A.F.
	Lt. (A) P.W.S. Butterworth	R.N.
43954	F/Lt. J.R. Denny	R.A.F.
37467	S/Ldr. K.C. Doran	R.A.F.
33245	F/Lt. D.A. Ffrench-Mullen	R.A.F.
42231	F/Lt. W.H.C. Hunkin	R.A.F.
40714	F/Lt. K. Jones	R.A.F.
40120	F/Lt. F.T. Knight	R.A.F.
33120	S/Ldr. A.R.D. Macdonnell	R.A.F.
39107	F/Lt. B.A. Mitchell	R.A.F.
79220	F/Lt. J.V. Silverston	R.A.F.
79173	F/Lt. H.R. Stockings	R.A.F.
78536	F/Lt. J.E. Thompson	R.A.F.
26216	S/Ldr. W.H.N. Turner	R.A.F.
33294	F/Lt. P.E. Warcup	R.A.F.

From about October, 1941, onwards the Coding Staff consisted of two officers only. Within a very short time the above named became 'writers'. The Coding Officers were:

90900	F/Lt. J.A. Gillies	R.A.F.
40120	F/Lt. F.T. Knight	R.A.F.

(d) *Code-letter 'writers'.*
During the period under review messages were received by I.S.9. from the undermentioned personnel, although it is evident that many more were despatched from the Camp than were received:

37078	F/Lt. D. Barrett	R.A.F.
33303	F/Lt. J.C. Breese	R.A.F.
78530	F/Lt. J.B.S. Brockway	R.A.F.
43932	F/Lt. L.G. Bull	R.A.F.
90120	S/Ldr. R.G. Bushell	R.A.F.
	Lt. (A) P.W.S. Butterworth	R.N.
37595	F/Lt. V.G. Byrne	R.A.F.

90285	S/Ldr. D.G. Craig	R.A.F.
37795	F/Lt. C.A. Crews	R.A.F.
95175	W/Cdr. H.M.A. Day	R.A.F.
43954	F/Lt. J.R. Denny	R.A.F.
37467	S/Ldr. K.C. Doran	R.A.F.
33245	F/Lt. D.A. Ffrench-Mullen	R.A.F.
90900	F/Lt. J.A. Gillies	R.A.F.
42231	F/Lt. W.H.C. Hunkin	R.A.F.
40714	F/Lt. K. Jones	R.A.F.
40120	F/Lt. F.T. Knight	R.A.F.
33120	S/Ldr. A.R.D. Macdonnell	R.A.F.
39107	F/Lt. B.A. Mitchell	R.A.F.
79220	F/Lt. J.V. Silverston	R.A.F.
79173	F/Lt. H.R. Stockings	R.A.F.
78536	F/Lt. J.E. Thompson	R.A.F.
26216	S/Ldr. W.H.N. Turner	R.A.F.
70699	F/Lt. F.H. Vivian	R.A.F.
33294	F/Lt. P.E. Warcup	R.A.F.

From October, 1941, onwards all the above named, except Gillies and Knight, were 'writers' only.

(e) *Despatch of messages.*
As far as can be ascertained no checking was done of letters containing code messages during the period July, 1940 – October, 1941. From the latter date onwards all such letters were examined by the Coding Officers – Gillies and Knight. The object of this was to ensure that the groups of figures had been incorporated correctly and that the letters did not contain phrases likely to be deleted by the German censorship.

42. CODE-LETTER MAIL: SECURITY
Until October, 1941, the code users were dependent upon their fellow P's/W for giving warning of the approach of Germans whilst they were at work. Each code user was responsible for destroying the original message given to him for encoding, also his 'workings'.

About October, 1941, the Senior British Officer decided, as a result of the carelessness of individuals, to make it the duty of a Coding Staff to prepare all the messages and to be entirely responsible for all coding, destruction of 'workings', etc. Another advantage of this system was the fact that only two dictionaries were in use. This was important, as only the English sections of a dictionary were used and after a time these became soiled. In the case of persons studying a foreign language it was always the other section of the dictionary which became soiled first. At this time a system of watchers was organised to give warning of the approach of Germans and this was in operation whenever encoding, decoding, or 'writing' was in progress.

The existence of a secret method of communication between the Camp and the United Kingdom was known to very few P's/W who were not members of the Coding Organisation.

43. RADIO: SUMMARY

There was no radio receiver, or transmitter, in this Compound during the period under review. B.B.C. news broadcasts were heard over the Compound loudspeaker system at irregular intervals by the courtesy of the Abwehr Officer.

From February, 1942, onwards copies of the news bulletins, produced by the Air Force N.C.O's in the adjacent Compound by listening to B.B.C. news broadcasts on a secret radio receiver, were passed to the Senior British Officer. These were read to the P's/W in this compound after an interval of twenty-four hours.

44. NEWS LETTERS: INTRODUCTION

From late 1941 onwards letters from correspondents, who were unknown to them, were received by a number of P's/W. These contained news of the progress of the war and obviously were intended to raise morale.

A small number of handkerchiefs on which messages were written in invisible ink were received also. Instructions about how to make the writing visible were received in code-letter messages.

About ten news letters and handkerchiefs were received.

45. NEWS LETTERS: OPINIONS

The value of the news letters was diminished by the fact that B.B.C. news broadcasts could be listened to from time to time; also that news of the progress of the war, etc., was acquired from new P's/W arriving in the Camp.

The message from His Majesty, which was received by the handkerchief method about Christmas, 1941, was much appreciated.

Chapter 6

Intelligence and Anti-German Propaganda

46. INTELLIGENCE: MILITARY INFORMATION
(a) Methods of collection, etc.
Details of the methods of collection and direct despatch of military information to the United Kingdom by means of code-letter messages are given [elsewhere in this book].

(b) Best targets for the type of Camp.
This subject is dealt with fully in History of Stalag Luft III (Sagan).

(c) Value of direction from I.S.9.
Very little direction was received from I.S.9. about the type of information which was required. Detailed instructions should have been sent in duplicate by means of code-letter messages.

(d) Adherence to direction from I.S.9.
All messages which were received from I.S.9. were passed to the Senior British Officer, who took action to comply with requests for information. In most cases these were extremely vague, but every effort was made to supply the information asked for.

47. INTELLIGENCE: INTERNAL SECURITY
There was no organisation for promoting internal security until about the Autumn of 1941. None was necessary during this period as there were comparatively few P's/W accommodated in this Compound, and the majority of those were acquainted one another prior to capture. It was comparatively easy to check the authenticity of each new arrival. About October, 1941, the Senior British Officer made arrangements for the interrogation of all new arrivals. Those who were not known were

required to supply sufficient details of their service career to enable a check to be made with other P's/W.

(a) Peculiarities of Camp.
The chief peculiarities of this Compound from the security aspect were:

(i) All barracks were divided into small rooms making it virtually impossible to check conversations between P's/W and Germans with whom they are engaged in 'trading'.
(ii) The Germans used a system of concealed microphones located in the barracks and recorded the conversations of P's/W on a celluloid sound track. The P's/W were aware of this, as the Abwehr Officer informed the Senior British Officer of their existence shortly after the Camp was opened. In the Autumn of 1940 a P/W attached the electric mains to the microphone wiring and destroyed the apparatus in the control room. As far as can be ascertained the system was not repaired.

48. ANTI-GERMAN PROPAGANDA: INTRODUCTION
There was no organisation for the dissemination of anti-German propaganda amongst the Germans. However, a certain number of P's/W who were brought into contact with Germans, either by virtue of their Camp duties or in private dealings, made an endeavour to lower their morale.

49. ANTI-GERMAN PROPAGANDA: RESULTS
It is not possible to assess the results of this propaganda, but it is worthy of note that certain Germans were eager at all times to listen to it; also that garbled versions of these stories were related by other Germans.

Chapter 7

Successful Escapes

50. FIRST ESCAPE

The first successful escape from this Compound was made by 39965 F/Lt. H. Burton R.A.F. His account of his subsequent activities, complied from M.I.9/S/PG/433 is as follows:

"When I climbed over the fence at about 02.30 hours on 27th May, 1941, I was dressed in my Service trousers, which I had dyed black, and a battle-dress tunic. I took a blanket with me in which I wrapped my two bars of chocolate, shaving tackle and towels, and a pack of cards.

"I walked to the railway on the West side of the town of Barth, then followed the tracks through the town towards Stralsund until I reached some woods close to the railway, about five kilometres East of Barth, where I hid for the day. The following night I set off again, following a track, which was on my map, towards Stralsund. During the night it thundered and rained and I got very wet. About 02.00 hours on 28th May, I reached a lake about three miles West of Stralsund, where I got some water and filled a beer bottle which I had found.

"About 04.00 hours I followed the railway line right through the town of Stralsund, walking down the main platform of the station. I carried on down the railway to the bridge between Stralsund and the Island of Rugen, which I reached about 04.30 hours, when it was beginning to get light. I decided to carry on across the bridge, rather than turn back and hide close to the town. After I had walked about twenty yards on to the bridge, I noticed a sentry on the left-hand side. He had seen me, and as there was no chance of turning back, I carried on and crossed the remaining quarter mile of bridge, passing five sentries on the way, whom I greeted with: "Good morning". That day I hid in a small wood close to the railway line.

"That night I followed the railway line and passed through the town of Bergen, after which I hid in a wood. The next night I resumed walking and in one village an Alsatian dog ran out, followed by its master, who was in semi-uniform. I was walking with my shoes in my hand, as I always did through cobble-stoned villages: the old man spoke to me but did not seem to require any answer. Eventually I discovered   that he wanted to know where I was going so I said: "Sassnitz", after which he walked away.

"I reached Sassnitz at 03.00 hours on 30th May, climbed over a fence and walked towards the sea, only to find myself surrounded by coastal defence guns and anti-aircraft guns. Realising what they were I went away quickly and stayed on a cliff above the harbour, but before daylight, returned inland to a wood, where I spent part of the morning.

"After washing, I discarded my jacket and walked down into the town wearing an open-necked shirt and my dyed Service trousers. During my walk through the town I passed many German soldiers. I studied the harbour very closely, went further along the beach,   had a bathe and a sunbath for the remainder of the afternoon and watched the ships which left the harbour in order to discover at what time the Swedish ferry sailed. That night I returned to the wood in which I had spent the previous night, having discovered that the Swedish ferry left at 16.30 hours.

"Next day at 15.30 hours I went to the docks and walked past the sentry, who took no notice of me. There were quite a few sentries walking about when I passed, and there were several Naval vessels in the docks. Going down to the Swedish ship I found that it was surrounded completely by barbed wire. The alternative methods of getting on board were, either going through the entrance reserved for passengers, or through the entrance where the railway trucks were taken on board, which was well guarded also. The only possible way seemed to be by going on the trucks.

"Having studied the trucks for some time I discovered which were being loaded preparatory to be taken on the ferry. I went round to the other side and got beneath an express mail van and hung on to the axle. At about 16.15 hours the trucks were pulled on board the ferry and I sat on the deck under the truck. I remained there till the ship had been at sea for an hour, then climbed into the mail van, where I remained for several hours.

"When the ship reached Trelleborg, I hung on to the underside of the truck whilst it was pulled off on to the quay side; this was at about 20.30 hours on 31st May. I gave myself up to the Swedish police who took me to the police station, and in due course I was sent to the British Legation at Stockholm. Some time later I was repatriated to the United Kingdom.

51. SECOND ESCAPE

The second successful escape from this Compound was made by 39177 F/Lt. J.T.L, Shore R.A.F. His account of his escape, complied from M.I.9/S/PG/593 is as follows:

"When the tunnel was completed it was decided to wait for an air raid to take place between 20.00 hours and 02.00 hours. Four other P's/W wanted to use the tunnel immediately after James and myself, but I insisted on their allowing us a quarter of an hour's start after the air raid had begun. James and I each made a trapdoor from the rooms in which we were sleeping.

"Normally there was one sentry on the fence between the Compound and the football field, but during air raids the guard was trebled. However, it took half an hour to do this. We calculated that it would take five minutes to get from our respective huts through the tunnel into the football field.

"I made a haversack out of the bottom of a suitcase and in this stored a supply of chocolate, cheese, raisins, concentrated food tablets, chewing gum, etc.

"On 15th October, all preparations had been completed and we started nightly watches in order to take advantage of the first air raid warning which was heard between the times decided upon. At 22.30 hours on 19th October, I heard aircraft and the camp lights went out. I went and warned one of the party of four which was to follow James and I, then started crawling through my trapdoor in the hut. Unfortunately, I was wearing my greatcoat which got caught when I was half through the trapdoor and a German guard came along and almost stepped on me. He did not notice me, but walked on for about twenty feet and the stood still, watching something in one of the barrack rooms. Then the guard at the gate flashed his torch and the guard who was standing near us walked over to him. I walked after this guard, making my footsteps coincide with his, to the barrack in which James lived and called him.

"He came out just behind me and I went across to the incinerator, thinking he would follow me. I got into the incinerator and banged the door at regular intervals to attract James' attention, but he did not appear. Then I went through the tunnel, which was partly waterlogged, and pushed up the trap door at the other end. On looking out I saw a German guard talking to someone through the window of my hut. I got out of the tunnel and went across the football field to a ditch which had been dug by the Germans and crawled under the bottom strand of wire which was just below ground surface. I made my way across the field and remembered that I had told James that I would wait half an hour for him in the wood to the West of the Flak School.

"While waiting and watching the camp, I saw two lights and fearing recapture, went on. I set off down the main Barth-Planitz road, after squeezing lemon over my boots and clothing to destroy the scent, as I knew that the Germans employed dogs for tracking escapers. I started walking towards Barth passing one or two personnel from the Flak School.

"As I was getting near Barth I heard a car approaching from behind so left the road and lay down in a field. After the car had passed I resumed walking and on the outskirts saw what appeared to be a lighted cigarette in the archway over the road at this point. I turned off to the right about thirty yards before reaching the archway following a small road Southwards.

"I arrived just outside Stralsund at about 06.30 hours and having decided that it would be best to hide during the hours of daylight, retracted my steps to a wood which I had noticed about a quarter of a mile back. I went to sleep and about 10.00 hours was awakened by the singing of a contingent of Flak personnel marching into the wood for battery practice. There was irregular heavy gun-fire from then until about 17.00 hours, except for an interval at mid-day.

"At about 18.00 hours I left the wood and walked through Stralsund, keeping a sharp look-out for an unattended bicycle. When I got to the bridge at Stralsund I discovered that it was thirty-five miles to Sassnitz, instead of six as I had thought. I walked across the bridge and on the other side made an attempt to steal a bicycle, but a man came out of a hut opposite to where the bicycle was standing and called out to me. When I ran off and hid behind a tree the man went back into the hut and came out with a companion who had a lantern, but I was not discovered.

"I resumed walking along the road and at about 06.30 hours next morning hid in a small wood and went to sleep. I managed to find some water in the wood before leaving it that night. I knew I was about five miles from Bergen and decided to walk through that town instead of following the railway, but after passing through the town concluded I was on the wrong road. I realised that my best course would be to follow the railway line and walk through the station at night when, presumably, it would be empty. This I did and found that I was travelling East but continued as I thought that I would hit the coast and could then follow it round.

"Eventually I arrived at Binz and walking through it took a right turn and then saw a signpost marked Sassnitz. After a time this route developed into an Autobahn, and presently the Autobahn stopped and I continued on a grass track past some fishermen's houses, noticing some fishing boats which I thought I might be able to use if I could not board the Swedish ferry at Sassnitz. By this time my feet had become very painful and as it was beginning to get light I felt I ought to hide for the day. First of all I dug myself into a haystack, but considered this was not safe, so went out onto the main road again. It was then about 07.30 hours and a German sailor passed me and stared hard at me. Eventually I got into a plantation of firs where I hid until about 09.00 hours.

"When I left my hiding place I walked along the road into Sassnitz and made my way into the Swedish ferry goods yard, where I got into a tarpaulin-covered wagon, marked with a Dutch name, and spent the night and next day until about 13.30 hours. At that time the wagon was shunted and looking out I saw that I was being taken towards Sassnitz railway station. I jumped out hurriedly leaving most of my food behind.

"I returned to the harbour at about 15.30 hours as I knew that the ferry left Sassnitz at 16.30 hours. By this time I looked just like a German workman, very dirty and wearing a cap which I had made myself in the camp. I waited for a little while just above the harbour trying to pick out the right wagon. The boat came in and a number of passenger coaches were landed. I noticed a line of coaches waiting on the siding. There were one or two German Air Force guards and a number of German soldiers on duty in the harbour, but it was possible to walk about.

"I managed to get underneath a Pullman coach hoping to be able to hang on there until the train was shunted onto the ferry. Unfortunately, the train started to move off towards the station, as had happened at my first attempt, and I had to jump off. I ran up onto the bank just behind the track and hid amongst blackberry bushes and watched the ferry boat leave at 16.30 hours.

"I saw a Swedish three-masted ship standing at the main quay and decided to try to get on board, but did not think that it would be safe to do so until about 19.00 hours. Meanwhile I found some elderberries which quenched my thirst. I noticed that there were some houses at the top of the bank and climbed up hoping to find some water. I could not find any and started walking down a narrow track which led to a rubbish heap.

"On the way down I passed a woman and she looked at me very suspiciously, probably because the track led to a cul-de-sac. When I arrived at the rubbish heap I shrugged my shoulder, turned round and retraced my steps. When I passed the woman again she said something to me about the way to the station but I did not reply. I went back to my hiding place on the bank and was very sick.

"At about 19.00 hours I walked onto the Swedish three-masted ship and, as I saw a German soldier looking at me, asked a dock hand where the Captain was. As the dock hand said the Captain was not on board I left the ship. There was another Swedish boat and some Danish fishing boats further along the quay. I was walking towards them when another German soldier came up and asked me what I wanted. I said: "Hans Kultur" and "Ich bin Schweder" hoping that "Hans Kultur" was the name of my ship.

"I walked off towards the other Swedish boat followed by the German. Naturally it was not the "Hans Kultur" so I said "Nicht hier", shrugged my shoulders and slouched off again still followed by the German. When we got opposite the Danish boats he asked me for my papers and I said "Nicht verstehen". The German then went and brought two Danes from the ship so that he could show me what he meant by papers.

"At that moment a drunken Dane appeared and put his arms around me and the German. The German then turned to the other two Danes and asked them to produce their papers so that I could see what he wanted. As he turned to speak to them I walked off.

"I decided to wait for the Danish sailors to come back. As they passed me I said "Danish" to them but the replied: "Nein, gute Deutsche". I went back past the railway lines and found a water hydrant just outside Sassnitz station, where I had a drink. On the way back towards the harbour I saw two Pullman coaches and got into one of them and had another drink and a wash in the lavatory. I was feeling rather despondent and got into a second-class carriage and went to sleep, not much caring if I was discovered.

"I woke up about 03.00 hours and left the carriage as it occurred to me that there might be a ferry at about 04.30 hours as well as the 16.30 hours. I scrambled into a tarpaulin covered truck filled with piping and from there saw the funnel of the ferry. A line of trucks was being taken on to the ferry and I jumped out of my truck, ran across the intervening fifty yards, and managed to scramble on to a low truck which was passing me at right angles. This truck contained a German lorry.

"The ferry sailed at about 03.30 hours and during the voyage the trucks were not searched. I sat in the driving cab of the lorry. When we arrived at Trelleborg a man on a bicycle noticed me sitting in the lorry, but I managed to slip out and tried to get out of the goods yard. However, I walked off in the wrong direction and was soon going through a gate by a Swedish guard who came over to me. I was arrested and taken to a small office, where I said I was an escaped prisoner of war and must speak to the British Consul. On being told that this was impossible I said I must see the police.

"Two policemen arrived in a car and took me to the police station. No particulars were taken and I just said: "Harry Burton" and they recognised the name. A little later another man came in who spoke English and I was told that I would have to give an account of how I had escaped and that this report would be sent to the Swedish Foreign Office.

"I wrote an exceedingly brief statement, but was told that this would not do. I said that I could not write more until I saw the British Consul. I was informed that I must write a full report before the Consul could be sent for, so I wrote a short account. They brought me food, very small meals at frequent intervals, and afterwards I learned that when Harry Burton had arrived he had been given a large meal and had been violently sick immediately.

"Later that day I was taken to the railway station and sent to Stockholm, where I arrived at 08.00 hours next day and reported to the British Legation. A few days later I was returned to the United Kingdom.

The following is an extract from the M.I.9/S/PG report in respect of 42232 F/Lt. B.A. James R.A.F:

"On 21st October, during an air raid when the boundary lights were extinguished, we left the barrack in which I was living. Shore got to the incinerator, but I was unable to follow him owing to the presence of German guards. Shore was able to make a successful escape. I attempted to evade the guards and reach the incinerator, but I was caught.

Part 11

NCOs' COMPOUND
July 1940 to April 1942

Chapter 8

Introduction

1. LOCATION AND DESCRIPTION OF CAMP

Full details of the location of the Camp are given in Part I of this Volume. An aerial photograph of the whole camp, taken in April 1944, is at [Plate 1], and the Compound dealt with in this Part is marked by the figures '32'.

2. CAMP CONDITIONS

(a) *Number of P's/W and accommodation.*

About July 1940 the first parties of N.C.O's were transferred to this Camp from Stalag XIIA (Limburg) and Stalag VIIIB (Lamsdorf). From then until about June, 1941, parties arrived from Dulag Luft (Ober Ursel). At that time all the available accommodation was filled, the total being about 550 personnel.

The accommodation comprised three wooden barracks each divided into a number of rooms of different sizes. Each room housed from six to twenty P's/W according to size. Each barrack was fitted with a kitchen where P's/W could cook the food from their Red Cross parcels. Each barrack had a small Common Room for reading etc.

The sanitary facilities were in a building which ran at right angles to the three barracks. Cold showers were available in this building at all times. Once weekly hot showers were available for each P/W in the Vorlager.

The P's/W were locked in their barracks at dusk each day and at first all shutters on barrack windows were closed and barred on the outside during the hours of darkness. The barrack doors were opened about 06.00 hours in Summer and 09.00 hours in Winter. After some time the Germans agreed to allow one shutter of each room to be opened after "lights out" in Summer.

(b) *German Administration.*

The German Administration of the Camp was carried out by Luftwaffe personnel. All orders to the P's/W were conveyed through the Man of Confidence.

Apart from inspections of barracks for cleanliness and the supervision of parades, the Germans left the administration of the Compound to the P's/W.

(c) *P/W Administration.*
During the first few weeks after the opening of the Compound the P's/W elected a Red Cross Representative to deal with the I.R.C.S. in Geneva. He was 580309 Sgt. May, T.K., R.A.F.

The Senior N.C.O. in the Compound assumed the position of Compound Leader by virtue of his seniority. He was 564838 F/Sgt. Hall, E.L.G., R.A.F. After a short time he handed over his duties to 590230 F/Sgt. Ross, T.G., R.A.F., who was a strict disciplinarian and soon became unpopular. These two N.C.O's took charge of all parades and were responsible for the Administration of the Compound during their periods in office.

About August Ross resigned and Hall resumed the position of Compound Leader. Shortly afterwards two other F/Sgts arrived and it was decided that they would be Barrack Leaders. The three Barrack Leaders were:

564838	F/Sgt. Hall, E.L.G.	R.A.F.
561898	F/Sgt. Steele, F.J.W.	R.A.F.
590406	F/Sgt. Taylor-Gill, J.D.T.	R.A.F.

These three took charge of parades in turn and May handled all correspondence with the Germans as well as the I.R.C.S. He performed the duties of Man of Confidence.

These conditions continued until September, 1941, when the three Barrack Leadrers were transferred, together with other N.C.O's to Stalag VIIIB because of suspected connection with escape activities. A number of the senior Sgts. then approached 580114 Sgt. Deans, J.A.G., R.A.F., and it was agreed that May should continue in office; also that Deans should become a Barrack Leader, two other Barrack Leaders were appointed by popular vote:

580179	Sgt. Potter, J.	R.A.F.
564378	Sgt. Ruse, H.	R.A.F.

This administration functioned until March 1942 when a meeting was held by the N.C.O's in charge of the rooms in each barrack to discuss the

Administration of the Compound. As a result of this Deans was appointed Camp Leader by majority vote, but few changes were made because the Germans informed Deans that the Camp was to be transferred to Stalag Luft III within a few weeks. The transfer took place in April, 1942.

(d) *Roll Calls.*
Parades were held twice daily, morning and evening, by the Germans to count the number of P's/W. In fine weather the parades were held out of doors and in inclement weather the checking was done in the barrack rooms.

During the roll calls a German guard was posted at each end of each barrack to ensure, as far as possible, that no P/W could get himself counted twice.

(e) *Food.*
At first Red Cross food parcels which were addressed to individuals who had been captured some time previously arrived in the Camp. This continued until about the end of 1940, but individuals captured after May 1940, did not receive such parcels.

In early 1941 occasional consignments of parcels, which were not individually addressed, began to arrive in the Camp and these were allocated to the oldest P's/W as there were insufficient to distribute one to each person. After a time this scheme was abandoned and all parcels were divided equally according to the number available. It was not until about June, 1941, that sufficient parcels arrived to enable a distribution of one to each man weekly. From then until the evacuation of the Camp in April, 1942, each P/W received a food parcel weekly.

Throughout the period under review the German issue of rations was reasonably adequate and varied. Most of this was cooked by the P's/W under German supervision in a cookhouse which supplied both officers and N.C.O's Compounds.

(f) *Clothing.*
As P/W required clothing the Germans issued French, Belgian and Polish uniforms which had been cleaned. This practice was discontinued when British uniform began to arrive in the Camp about May, 1941. The issue of this clothing was controlled by P/W representatives working under German supervision. From then onwards supplies were adequate but not excessive, with the exception of boots which were in short supply for a considerable period.

(g) *Searches.*

Searches of the barracks and P's/W possessions were carried out at irregular intervals by members of the German Abwehr (Security) Department. These personnel worked under the direction of the Abwehr Officer and they were specially trained. In all cases warning of forthcoming searches was passed on to the Barrack Leaders by May who was on friendly terms with the Abwehr Officer.

In addition to searches the Abwehr personnel spent a lot of time in the Compound by day and by night observing the activities of the P's/W. They were disposed to be friendly in their relations with the P's/W. They were unarmed and wore dark blue overalls over their uniforms. They were nicknamed 'Ferrets' because of their habit of crawling underneath barracks in their search for tunnelling activities.

(h) *German anti-escape measures.*

The Compound was surrounded by a double barbed-wire fence about 8 feet in height. The two fences were about six feet six inches apart with concertina wire between them to a height of about three feet from the ground. Sentry towers were situated in the positions marked 7, 8, 9 and 10, on [Plate 1]. These were fitted with machine-guns and searchlights which worked independently of the main supply when the boundary lights were switched off during air-raid alarms. The boundary lights were situated at intervals of about fifteen yards along the perimeter fences and were sufficiently powerful not to leave any dark patches. Guards patrolled outside the fences, between the sentry towers.

A warning fence, which consisted of a single strand of wire, was situated inside the Compound perimeter fence at a distance of about fifteen feet from it. The area between this warning wire and the main fence was a forbidden zone, but this was not strictly enforced and personnel were allowed to retrieve footballs, etc.

Each P/W was photographed by the Germans shortly after his arrival in the Camp. The photograph was mounted on an identity card which bore the description of the individual. These identity cards were filed in the German Headquarters.

All German personnel were in possession of a Gate Pass, but this was not often used as the Germans knew one another intimately.

When parties of N.C.O's and airmen were taken out of the Camp on local working parties they were accompanied by armed guards. Such parties could not be taken out of the Compound without a special pass signed by the Abwehr Officer.

The majority of vehicles leaving the Compound were subjected to a cursory search at the gate.

Civilian workers who entered the Compound were in possession of a Gate Pass, but they were not accompanied by guards.

The system of microphones for recording the location of vibrations caused by tunnelling, which is referred to in Part I of this Volume, was installed around the perimeter of this Compound about June, 1941. As far as can be ascertained, the P's/W were unaware of this until just before the evacuation of the Camp in April, 1942. At that time a German showed the control room to May, the Man of Confidence. By means of this installation the Germans were able to locate all tunnels in this Compound before they reached the main fence.

During the summer of 1941 trenches were dug lengthwise under the Barracks. The object of this was to enable frequent inspection to be made of the area under the barrack floors. This was the place most generally used by the P's/W for starting tunnelling operations.

At about the same time a trench was dug to below water level between the wash-barrack and the main fence. Prior to this several tunnels had been started from the wash-barrack and lavatory.

It is believed that a system of microphones was installed in all barracks in this Compound during the construction of the Camp. Although this has not been proved, a sound track of conversations between P's/W was played over by the Abwehr Officer about April, 1942 to 902601 Sgt. Bristow, J.F.H., R.A.F.

Bristow formed the opinion that these recordings had been obtained by using the radio loudspeakers in each barrack Common Room as microphones.

(i) *Punishment for escape activities, etc.*
The usual punishment given to N.C.O's apprehended whilst engaged on escape activities, or after an attempt to escape was a few days in cells on normal rations. Airmen were allowed bread and water only with a hot meal every third day.

(j) *Education.*
Classes of instruction were organised by various P's/W who had special knowledge of various subjects, these included: Radio, Mathematics, Shorthand, German, etc. Progress was hampered by the lack of books.

(k) *Library.*
A small library was formed of books received from the I.R.R.C. and by P's/W in personally addressed parcels from the U.K.

(l) *Sports.*
Soccer and rugby games were organised by a committee and these games were played on a sports field within the Compound. On occasion matches were arranged between teams representing the N.C.O's and the officers.

In winter ice-skating rinks were made and ice-hockey games were played.

All the sports equipment was supplied by the Young Men's Christian Association.

Because of the enthusiasm of the P's/W for sports the standard of physical fitness was high.

(m) *Amateur theatricals.*
Some months after the Camp was opened the Germans granted permission for the use of a part of the cookhouse building as a Camp Theatre. Various Plays, Concerts, etc. were produced, but costumes, etc. were not supplied by the Germans.

(n) *Religion.*
From the opening of the Camp until about Mid 1941 religious services were conducted in the Camp Theatre each Sunday by a German clergyman. A church was built during the summer of 1941 and from then onwards the services were conducted by a Padre from the Officers Compound.

(o) *Shooting incidents, etc.*
The only serious shooting incident which occurred during this period resulted in the death of 742749 Sgt. Shaw, J.C., R.A.F. On 2nd January 1942 Shaw and 745630 Sgt. Evans, W.L., R.A.F., attempted to escape from the Camp by following the route taken by 78536 F/Lt. J.E. Thompson R.A.F., who had succeeded in getting out of the Camp the previous night. A full description of this attempt is given in Part I. Whilst Shaw and Evans were crawling across the football field they were seen by a guard who opened fire. Shaw was killed, but Evans escaped injury.

(p) *P/W Morale.*
At first the morale of the P's/W was rather low. In all probability this was due to the lack of Red Cross food, shortage of clothing, books, etc., and the depressing effect of the German news. A contributory factor was the suspected presence of an informer.
Morale improved considerably after the arrival of the Red Cross food parcels, supplies of clothing and books, etc.

When the secret radio receiver was put into operation this helped morale to some extent.

(q) *Medical.*
The Camp Sick Quarters was situated in the Vorlager. It was staffed by a Luftwaffe Medical Officer and a number of French Medical orderlies. The treatment given was adequate. The sick quarters was used for passing messages between Officers' and N.C.O's Compounds.

(r) *Reprisals.*
The Germans did not carry out any reprisals against the P's/W.

(s) *Finance.*
During the period under review an arrangement was made whereby N.C.O's and airmen were able to borrow German Camp Money from Officers. The arrangement was that repayment would be made after release. This scheme was operated by 964794 Sgt. Olliver, R.B, R.A.F.

Chapter 9

Escape Organisation

3. CONTROL BY CAMP AUTHORITIES
Attempts to escape were not controlled by the Camp Authorities and there was no Official Escape Committee.

4. PLANNING
At first an attempt was made to organise escape activities by 564838 F/Sgt. Hall, E.L.G, R.A.F. He established contact with those P's/W who were interested in escape matters and work begun on a tunnel. At a later date other groups began tunnelling activities, but these groups worked independently of one another and obtained their own supplies, etc. Information gained from any source was circulated amongst the personnel interested in escape.

Individuals wishing to make attempts to escape by means other than tunnels made their own preparations and sought the assistance of trusted companions.

There was no central organisation of escape activities, but it was generally known that maps for copying were obtainable from 536997 Sgt. Parsons, J.W.H., R.A.F.

5. SECURITY
No organised attempt was made to ensure that escape activities were not discovered by the Germans. Most of these activities took the form of tunnelling and the workers made whatever provisions they considered necessary. Usually this amounted to one of their number watching the gate to give warning when a German entered the Compound. The entrance into tunnels were usually concealed by boards covered with soil.

In at least one instance tunnellers were discovered at work because of ineffective security.

78

6. CLOTHING

Individuals used their own uniforms as escape clothing. As a rule slight alterations were effected and in some cases these were dyed. This work was carried out by the individual or his companion.

There was no organisation for the supply of clothing to intending escapers.

7. FORGERY

No attempt was made to forge documents of any kind.

8. FOOD

Intending escapers saved food in preparation for their attempts.

9. MAPS

Some months after the Camp was opened a road map of Germany was discovered in a locker which had just been brought into the Compound. This was passed round amongst all those interested in escape and each made a copy or tracing of it.

About twenty rough copies were made by 536997 Sgt. Parsons, J.W.H., R.A.F., and given to intending escapers at various times. Apart from this there was no organised map making.

10. COMPASSES

Several of the P's/W were in possession of compasses which they had concealed during the searches following capture. Personnel interested in escape and unable to obtain one of these made their own compasses by magnetising sewing needles with the magnet from a pair of earphones which the Germans had omitted to remove from a flying helmet. The magnet in a safety razor was also used for this purpose.

A number of compasses were made for intending escapers by N.Z. 401231 Sgt. Protheroe, D.E.B., R.N.Z.A.F.

11. ESCAPE INTELLIGENCE

(a) *Contacts.*

There was no scheme for obtaining escape information from German sources.

(b) *Journeys outside the Camp.*

Airmen and N.C.O's who went out of the Camp on local working parties obtained information about the area. P's/W who were sent to hospitals for treatment were able to give some information about travel conditions etc.

Further details about the vicinity of the Camp were gained by personnel who were interested when the Germans allowed parties to go for walks and sea-bathing accompanied by armed guards.

Much of the information gained from the above mentioned sources was collected by 563997 Sgt. Parsons, J.W.H., R.A.F., and circulated to intending escapers.

(c) *Recaptured escapers.*
Personnel interested in escape questioned recaptured escapers when they returned to the Compound.

(d) *New P's/W.*
New P's/W were not interrogated regarding any information they might have which could be useful to an escaper.

(e) *From I.S.9.*
As far as can be ascertained no information was received in this Compound from I.S.9. which was useful to an escaper.

12. SUPPLIES
(a) *Contacts.*
There was no 'trading' organisation for obtaining escape material from German sources, but a few individuals acquired maps, compasses, etc. by barter. Private trading by individuals to increase their own standard of living was rampant and uncontrolled.

(b) *Camp resources.*
Materials for tunnelling, e.g. bed-board for shoring etc., were gathered by the individuals engaged on the work. Intending escapers acquired items of clothing etc., from their colleagues.

(c) *New P's/W.*
In some instances maps and compasses, hacksaw blades, etc. were brought into the Compound by new P's/W who had succeeded in secreting them during the various personal searches following capture. These were not pooled but were retained by the individuals. However, in some instances intending escapers were able to acquire these items.

(d) *Parcels from I.S.9.*
As far as can be ascertained no parcels were received from I.S.9. during the period under review.

13. CARPENTRY

The only carpentry work which was done in connection with escape was the shoring of tunnels. This was carried out by the personnel engaged on tunnel construction. There was no central organisation of woodwork.

14. METAL WORK

The construction of digging implements was the only metal work which was attempted. This was done by the tunnellers.

15. LEATHER WORK

The only article of leather which was made for escape purposes was a pistol holster. This was manufactured out of an old football by 906183 Sgt. Adlam, A.F., R.A.F. The work was initiated by the P/W who intended to use the holster.

16. TOOLS

Small quantities of tools of various kinds were stolen by members of working parties who were employed for a time in the Barth area. A few were acquired by individuals from Germans by barter. In all cases these were obtained by individual initiative.

17. GADGETS

No gadgets were made for use in connection with escape.

18. TUNNEL CONSTRUCTION

(a) *General.*

Personnel interested in tunnel construction formed themselves into groups and commenced work on the site which they chose, usually beneath the barrack in which the majority lived. As few people as possible were made aware of such projects and neither Barrack Leaders nor the Camp Leader were informed.

(b) *Engineering.*

The most active personnel in connection with tunnel construction were:

755839	Sgt. Bristow, D.E.	R.A.F.
790053	Sgt. Everson, J.E.	R.A.F.
524851	Sgt. Fancy, J.	R.A.F.
520659	Sgt. Flynn, D.	R.A.F.
742039	Sgt. Garrioch, W.G.	R.A.F.
564838	F/Sgt. Hall, E.L.G.	R.A.F.

561779	Sgt. Lang, S.	R.A.F.
580224	Sgt. Lascelles, E.B.	R.A.F.
518168	Sgt. Liggett, H.	R.A.F.
	L/S Moore	R.N.
563997	Sgt. Parsons, J.W.H.	R.A.F.
620735	Sgt. Prendergast, J.N.	R.A.F.
590230	F/Sgt. Ross, T.G.	R.A.F.
550365	Sgt. Smith, W.G.	R.A.F.
580932	Sgt. Stanford, J.R.	R.A.F.
539339	Sgt. Street, W.W.	R.A.F.
625503	Sgt. Townsend-Coles, R.	R.A.F.

As far as can be ascertained ten tunnels were constructed in this Compound during the period under review. All were discovered before reaching beyond the fences and none had any special feature which justify a description of its construction, but one tunnel was shored with briquettes of fuel.

The main difficulty which was encountered was the high water level. In most parts of the Compound this was about 6 feet below the surface.

A noteworthy feature of construction was that the lateral shafts of a high proportion of the tunnels was excavated at from 1 foot to 2 feet below the surface. These were elliptical in shape and very little shoring was used. This was possible because of the adhesive properties of the sandy soil.

(c) *Dispersal.*
In all cases the dispersal of the excavated sand was effected close to the site of the entrance shaft. Where these were situated underneath barracks this was comparatively safe at first as the Germans had difficulty gaining access to the areas under barracks in order to carry out inspections. Tunnels which were begun in the lavatory building presented no difficulties of sand disposal as this was deposited in the cess-pool.

All sand dispersal was affected by the personnel engaged on the construction of each tunnel.

(d) *Supplies.*
The materials required for tunnel construction, principally bed boards for shoring and digging implements, were collected by the groups of personnel engaged on building the tunnel.

(e) *Security.*
The precautions which were taken to prevent premature discovery of tunnels are described elsewhere in this Chapter.

(f) *Comments.*
It is evident that the personnel interested in tunnel construction approached the problem with an individualistic outlook. They worked in small groups instead of amalgamating and working as a team. They distrusted one another and it was believed generally that the discovery of one tunnel after another, as the fence was approached, was due to the activities of one or more informers in their midst.

19. GATE WALK-OUT SCHEME
Only one attempt was made to escape from this Compound by walking through the gate. The personnel involved were:

625389	Sgt. Boyle, J.I.	R.A.F.
743038	Sgt. Brock, J.W.	R.A.F.
580404	Sgt. Eden, W.H.	R.A.F.
563983	Sgt. Parsons, J.W.H.	R.A.F.

About 07.00 hours one day in March, 1942, Boyle who was disguised as a German Unteroffizier in fatigue dress, marched Brock, Eden and Parsons, who wore their Service dress, through the Compound gate into the Vorlager.

Boyle was in possession of a gate pass authorising a German to take three P's/W out of the Compound. This had been stolen from the German Headquarters by a P/W about two days previously. Brock, Eden and Parsons were carrying milk cans. This was to support the story which the members of the party had prepared to enable them to leave the Camp area. The story was that the Unteroffizier was taking the three P's/W to fetch milk for the Compound.

As the party walked across the Vorlager towards the gate leading into the German Compound they met a German Interpreter who knew all four P's/W and they were marched off to the cells.

20.WIRE SCHEME
The only attempt which was made to escape from this Compound by negotiating the wire was made by:

745630	Sgt. Evans, W.L.	R.A.F.
742749	Sgt. Shaw, J.C.	R.A.F.

83

On the night of 2/3 January, 1942, they attempted to follow the route taken by F/Lt. Thompson as described in Part I. Whilst they were crawling across the football field they were seen by a guard and fired upon. Shaw was killed but Evans escaped injury.

21. WALL SCHEMES
Not applicable

22. TRANSPORT SCHEMES
(a) The first attempt which was made to escape from this Compound by hiding in a vehicle was carried out by:

938691	Sgt. Booth, H.	R.A.F.
515799	Sgt. Sands, J.C.	R.A.F.

The following account is compiled from extracts from their M.I.G./ S/PG/LIB reports:

"Owing to the bad weather conditions the Germans had become exceedingly careless in searching vehicles leaving the Camp. On the day we had selected in March, 1942, a German vehicle entered the Compound, driven by a German, and stopped at the cookhouse to unload foodstuffs and reload with empty cartons.

"We waited until the guards were looking the other way, jumped into the lorry, lay flat on the floor and were covered up with tarpaulins by the other N.C.O's who were unloading and reloading the lorry. Then we were surrounded by empty cartons in such a way as to avoid crushing us.

"We were wearing R.A.F. uniform covered by German overalls which we had stolen. We had altered our caps to look like German caps and were in possession of compasses and maps which we had made ourselves. We had food which we had saved from Red Cross parcels. We carried some tools and had about 22 Reichsmarks between us.

"The lorry was driven off from the kitchen and passed through the gate leading from the Compound into the Vorlager. It was about to drive off from there when the guard in the sentry tower about the gate shouted to the sentry on the gate asking whether he had searched the lorry. A conversation ensued which we did not understand, but the result was that the lorry was searched and we were discovered."

(b) The second attempt to escape from the Compound by means of a German vehicle was carried out by:

742402	Sgt. Baird, W.J.	R.A.F.
518168	Sgt. Liggett, H.	R.A.F.

On the eve of the evacuation of the Camp to Stalag Luft III large quantities of crates of books, theatre equipment, etc. were being taken from the Compound to the railway station at Barth. The above named personnel used this to enable them to escape. The following account of the escape has been compiled from their M.I.G. reports:

"On 20th April, 1942, we were concealed in wooden packing cases with the lids nailed down. We each had a supply of food and water. The packing cases, with others, were marked "Library Books" and despatched to the railway station at Barth, where they were loaded into a closed goods wagon.

"After an interval we broke out of the packing cases and left the railway wagon before the train started. We left the wagon separately and did not meet again until after our recapture.

Liggett: "After leaving the railway wagon I started walking and arrived at Sassnitz about 21.30 hours on 21st April. I got on board the German-Swedish ferry *Deutschland* and was discovered when the ferry was at sea at 93.00 hours on 22nd April.

"My discovery was due to the fact that I realised that the boat was going South instead of North and I left my hiding place in order to investigate. I was unaware that the ferry called at Stettin before going to Sweden."

Baird: "After I got out of the railway truck I made for Stralsund by walking across country until it was light. As I was on the outskirts of the town I hid under fir branches beside a wood pile. I fell asleep until someone stood on me. I discovered that this was one of three labourers who had come to collect wood for the farm. I was taken to the farmhouse and arrested later".

23. MISCELLANEOUS SCHEMES

From the opening of the Camp until early 1942 airmen were compelled to work on various projects in the Barth area. N.C.O's were permitted to volunteer for such work provided that they had not made previous attempts to escape. These working parties were employed on farms, a fish packing factory, the local gasworks, a radio repair shop, the railway, etc. In most cases the P's/W were returned to the Compound each night.

A number of Airmen and N.C.O's took advantage of these working parties and made attempts to escape from them. Some were partly successful but all personnel were recaptured within a few days and returned to the Camp. The following are known to have used this method:

740781	Sgt. Annan, R.S.	R.A.F.
518279	Sgt. Avery, G.	R.A.F.
580078	L.A.C. Jones, A.E.	R.A.F.
562560	Sgt. Le Voi, E.E.B.	R.A.F.
581031	Sgt. Roche, F.A.S.	R.A.F.

The above named escaped together from a barn where they were being accommodated on a farm. This took place at night on 10th August, 1940. They were recaptured near Stralsund on 14th August and returned to the Camp.

552647	Sgt. Alkison, G.A.	R.A.F.
551972	Sgt. Atkinson, J.P.	R.A.F.
549667	Sgt. Coote, C.E.	R.A.F.
619756	Sgt. Miller, A.G.W.	R.A.F.

On about 25th August, 1940, the above named escaped from the room in which they were accommodated on a farm; this took place at night. They were recaptured on the coast, about ten kilometres West of Barth, on 26th August, and returned to the Camp.

590718	Sgt. Mirfin, J.R.	R.A.F.

Slipped into the woods from a working party engaged on road repairs in August, 1940. Recaptured three days later and returned to Camp.

525214	Sgt. Fisk, R.J.	R.A.F.
625503	L.A.C. Townsend-Coles, R.	R.A.F.

Escaped from a working party in September, 1940, whilst the guards attention was distracted. They were recaptured in a railway yard near Stettin two days later and returned to Camp.

580770	Sgt. Donaldson, P.R.	R.A.F.
580932	Sgt. Stanford, J.R.	R.A.F.

Escaped from a working party in June, 1941, through a lavatory window. Recaptured about twelve hours later near Stralsund and returned to camp.

| 741250 | Sgt. Phillips, F. | R.A.F. |
| 640070 | Sgt. Tebbutt, P.R. | R.A.F. |

Escaped from a working party in June, 1941, whilst another P/W engaged the guard in conversation. They walked along the main road toward Stralsund. When about ten kilometres from Barth a German from the Camp, who was driving a tractor along the road, recognised Phillips and took the two of them back to the Camp.

| A.400051 | Sgt. Damman, R.G. | R.A.A.F. |
| 619759 | Sgt. Graham, R.R.McK. | R.A.F. |

Escaped from a working party employed near the railway line between Barth and Zingst, whilst the guards attention was distracted, on 10th August, 1941. They climbed on the buffers of the rear coach of a train as it began to move off, but were seen by a guard who fired two revolver shots. After the train had travelled about fifty yards they jumped off and parted company. Both were recaptured a few days later and returned to the Camp.

| 745910 | Sgt. Young, D. | R.A.F. |

Escaped from a working party at a flour mill near Barth Railway Station in September, 1941. Was recaptured about two and a half hours later by a guard from the Camp and taken back to the Camp.

| 966856 | Sgt. Bernard, D.H. | R.A.F. |

Escaped from a working party at a fish cannery in Barth during a lunch interval in September, 1941. When about five kilometres from the town, on a road to Stettin, he was accosted by some members of the Hitler Youth Movement. As he was unable to produce identity papers they sent for a policeman and he was arrested and returned to the Camp.

| 74208 | Sgt. Blair, D. | R.A.F. |
| 580896 | Sgt. Hill, C.A. | R.A.F. |

Attempted to escape from a working party employed on unloading barges at Barth, whilst the guards attention was distracted by two other P's/W in

October, 1941. As they were leaving the lavatory the door slammed and attracted the guards attention. He ran after them and opened fire. They were not wounded, but Hill fell on the cobble stones and they allowed themselves to be recaptured. They were returned to the Camp.

    521960   Sgt. Bowes, A.E.   R.A.F.
    581031   Sgt. Roche, F.A.S.   R.A.F.

Were members of a working party at Barth in December, 1941. Roche ran across the yard under cover of a cloud of steam and stole a bicycle which was leaning against a wall. He rode through the town and along the Stralsund road. Bowes was to have followed, but he was apprehended whilst crossing the yard.

Roche turned off the main road, after riding about three kilometres, but discovered that the lane led to a farm. He returned to the main road and after riding about four kilometres was overtaken by a motor-cycle and sidecar. He was arrested by a German interpreter from the Camp, who was in the sidecar, and taken back.

22. NUMBER OF ESCAPES
No successful escapes were made during the period under review.

23. NUMBER OF ATTEMPTED ESCAPES
In addition to the construction of approximately ten unsuccessful tunnels involving about twenty or thirty men, thirty-four personnel who were accommodated in this Compound attempted to escape in fifteen separate attempts. All were unsuccessful.

24. MASS ATTEMPTS
No mass attempts were made from this Compound.

25. SUMMARY OF METHODS
(a) *Tunnels.*
The construction of tunnels was the main escape activity. It is probable that the reason for non-success were:

(i) The lack of co-ordination of effort with the result that a number of small groups of enthusiasts worked independently, seriously hampering the scale of operations.
(ii) The premature discovery of tunnels by the Germans led the P's/W to assume that there was an informer amongst the number. If adequate provision had been made to ensure that security was

good it would have been apparent that this was not the case and another reason for discovery would have been sought. Because the theory of an informer was accepted, the same mode of construction was repeated time after time and an attempt was made to ensure success by limiting the number of personnel who knew of each project. No attempt was made to devise improved methods of concealing entrances, dispersal of sand etc.

(iii) The apparent lack of co-operation from the Air Force Officers in the adjacent Compound. The officers knew of the existence of the microphone system for locating the sites of tunnelling activity, but it would seem this information was not passed on to the N.C.O's.

(b) *Gate Walkout Schemes.*
The only attempt of this kind which was made is described in Section 17 of this Chapter. It was well planned and the individuals were unfortunate in meeting a German who recognised them. It is probable that other attempts to escape by this method were not made for the following reasons:

(i) Few of the N.C.O's who were interested in escape could speak German.

(ii) Passes etc. for copying were not required, except for the attempt referred to above, because there was no organisation for obtaining these, and other escape aids, from Germans by bribery.

(iii) Clothing was in short supply and there was no organisation for providing clothing for escapers.

(iv) Personnel who desired to make attempts to escape could get out of the Camp as members of working parties, provided that they had not made previous attempts.

(c) *Wire Schemes.*
The only escape which was attempted via the wire is referred to elsewhere. The escapers were seen and one was shot. It is not possible to ascertain why other attempts were not made by this method, but in all probability escapes from working parties appeared safer and easier to effect.

(d) *Wall Schemes.*
Not applicable.

(e) *Transport Schemes.*
Two methods of getting out of the Camp on German vehicles are

described in this chapter. The first attempt failed because the lorry was searched at the Compound gate. The second attempt was well planned. Observation had shown that the Germans were lax about checking the contents of boxes before they left the Camp.

(f) *Miscellaneous Schemes.*
Eleven separate attempts were made. All were effected from working parties employed outside the Camp, where the guards were comparatively lax.

(g) *Comments.*
Only a small percentage of P's/W in this Compound were interested in making attempts to escape. One of the reasons for this may have been the fact that living conditions in the Compound were better than those experienced by some P's/W in other camps; also that two batches of personnel who made attempts to escape from this Camp were sent to Stalag VIII B (Lamsdorf) where conditions were known to be bad.

26. AIDS RECEIVED FROM I.S.9.
As far as can be ascertained, the only escape aids which were received in this Compound were not despatched by I.S.9., but by the Military Attaché in Stockholm. In June, 1941 a parcel was received by 740910 Sgt. Hollidge, R.L., R.A.F. This contained food, etc. and as he had not received any warning to expect escape aids he distributed the contents of the parcel amongst the occupants of his room. When examined these items were found to contain money, maps and compass needles.

27. MATERIAL AVAILABLE/ACQUIRED ON THE SPOT
Because of the lack of organisation of escape activities the acquirement of escape material from camp resources was not fully exploited.

Chapter 10

Censorship and Communication

28. CENSORSHIP BY THE GERMANS

(a) *Parcels.*
This subject is dealt with in Part I of this Volume.

(b) *Mail.*
All in-coming and out-going mail was censored at Dulag Luft (Ober Ursel) and is dealt with in Chapter IV of the History of that Camp.

29. CODE-LETTER MAIL

(a) *Introduction.*
The incorporation of code messages in letters was introduced to this Compound in October, 1940 by 620735 Sgt. Prendergrast, J.N., R.A.F., who had been taught the "dictionary" code prior to capture.

(b) *General Organisation.*
Whilst at Dulag Luft (Oberursel) Prendergrast had informed the Senior British Officer, 05175 W/Cdr. H.M.A. Day, R.A.F., that he knew the code and was instructed to report this fact to the Camp Leader upon arrival at Stalag Luft I. Prendergrast did so and it was decided that he should teach the code to the three Barrack Leaders:

564838	F/Sgt. Hall E.L.G.	R.A.F.
590230	F/Sgt. Ross T.G.	R.A.F.
590406	F/Sgt. Taylor-Gill J.D.T.	R.A.F.

Until January, 1941, Prendergrast and Hall worked together and despatched messages, but as far as can be ascertained Ross and Taylor-Gill did not despatch any messages at any time.

In December, 1940 an N.C.O., who had been taught the "box" code, arrived in the Compound. He was 740910 F/Sgt. Hollidge, R.L., R.A.F.

For some months he worked independently as he did not know that there were other code users in the Compound. Eventually Hall received a message from I.S.9. stating that Hollidge was a code user and instructing him to get into touch with him.

In January, 1941, Prendergrast left the Camp and was in various hospitals and other Camps until July, 1941, when he was returned to this Compound.

Hall and Hollidge worked together from the time of receipt of the instructions from I.S.9. until Hall was transferred to Stalag VIII B(Lamsdorf) about September, 1941.

About July, 1941, they received instructions from I.S.9. that in future all messages were to be coded in the "box" code only.

About September, Prendergrast taught the code to 629281 Sgt. Walker, L.A., R.A.F. It is understood that Walker wrote a certain number of messages, but there is no record of any having been received by I.S.9.

(c) *Sources of information.*
Until early 1941 the information which was acquired from the under mentioned sources was obtained by the code users during the course of informal conversations. After that time the information was collected by the Barrack Leaders by interrogation and passed to the code users. The sources from which military information was obtained were:

(i) New arrivals. A percentage of new arrivals were able to give details of the locations of military installations, etc. which they had noticed.

(ii) P's/W on journey outside the Camp. Those P's/W who left the Camp on working parties, visits to hospitals, etc. often were able to supply details of the locations of airfields, Flak batteries, etc. Certain personnel were given an indication of what to look for.

(iii) Recaptured escapers. On occasion recaptured escapers were able to supply information similar to that indicated in (ii) above.

(iv) Contacts. A limited amount of information was obtained from Germans, the two N.C.O's who were most active in this connection were:

580370 Sgt. Hart, C.S.   R.A.F.
580309 Sgt. May, T.K.   R.A.F.

(d) *Collation.*
The collation of all information was done by the code users working in

collaboration with the Camp Leader, Barrack Leaders and the Man of Confidence.

(e) *Coding Staff.*
The following were the registered code users in this Compound during the period under review from whom messages were received by I.S.9.:

564838	F/Sgt. Hall, E.L.G.	R.A.F.
740910	Sgt. Hollidge, R.L.	R.A.F.
620735	Sgt. Prendergrast, J.N.	R.A.F.

(f) *Despatch of letters.*

The code users generally checked the encoding of each others messages and censored the letters in which they were incorporated. The object of this censorship was to ensure that no stilted phrases were used and that no statement likely to be deleted by the Germans censorship had been made. The letters, or postcards were posted in the normal way.

30. SECURITY
The encoding and decoding of messages was carried out by the code users in the rooms in which they lived. No special security precautions were taken and they relied upon the other occupants of their rooms to give warning of the approach of a German. The other P's/W were not aware of the nature of the work on which the code users were engaged, but they knew it was something which was forbidden and dangerous.

31. COMMENT
The reason for the non-development of the despatch of information to the U.K. from the Compound by means of code messages were:

(i) When the code users were taught the code at R.A.F. Stations they were instructed that they were not to inform anyone of their activities if they should become P's/W.
(ii) When they were being taught how to use the code no indication was given of the type of information which would be most useful, or how to obtain it most efficiently having regard to security.

32. CRITICISM
During 1941 Hollidge received two letters from Sweden which he considered to be very suspicious in appearance. He attempted to decode them using his own code-word, but was able to decipher only one of

them. The other code users attempted to decode the remaining letter without success. It was passed to the Officers' Compound and it is believed that after some months they succeeded in decoding it, but the information contained was not passed back to this Compound.

33. RADIO
(a) *Introduction and Construction.*
About November, 1941 work was begun on the construction of a wireless receiver this was undertaken by 902601 Sgt. Bristow, J.F.H., R.A.F., who began this task on his own initiative. He designed the set and was assisted in the manufacture of all components, other than valves by:

905095	Sgt. Hurrell, H.L.	R.A.F.
580468	Sgt. Stubbs, P.	R.A.F.
903307	Sgt. Young, D.G.	R.A.F.

these parts were made from tin, old scraps of metal, tinfoil, wire, paper, etc.

The valves were obtained from a wireless repair shop in Barth by an arrangement made between Bristow and the Abwehr Officer, Hauptmann Buckwick, (?) Luftwaffe. The Abwehr officer arranged for four N.C.O's to work in the shop repairing radio sets and the valves were acquired by one of their number, 515799 Sgt. Sands, J.C., R.A.F. The set was used for the first time on 11th February, 1942.

(b) *Operation.*
The receiver was operated daily, usually to obtain the 1800 hours or 2100 hours, B.B.C. news broadcasts, by Bristow assisted by Stubbs and Young.

(c) *Maintenance.*
All maintenance was effected by Bristow assisted by Stubbs and Young. Parts which needed replacement were made by them.

(d). *Security.*
The receiver was split up into four units to simplify concealment. The units were hidden in a piano accordion, a model ship, a model aeroplane and a portable gramophone which could still be played. The earphones were wrapped in paper and kept in the bottom of a dried milk tin with powdered milk covering them. Despite numerous searches by the Germans the receiver was never discovered.

Whilst the receiver was being operated a watch was kept to ensure that no German could enter the barrack without previous warning being given. This arrangement was most satisfactory and Bristow and his colleagues were never caught at work.

The longhand notes of the B.B.C. News broadcasts were not distributed to the news readers until the day following the broadcast. This was a security measure designed to mislead the Germans, in the event of one of the news sheets being discovered, into assuming that it had been compiled from information brought into the Camp by a German.

A watch was kept to ensure that no German could approach the barrack whilst the news bulletin was being read.

Before the P's/W were transferred from this Compound to Stalag Luft III (Sagan) in April, 1942, the radio receiver was dismantled and the components packed into tins containing food. These passed through a search on leaving the Camp and another on arrival at Stalag Luft III, but nothing was discovered.

(e). *Dissemination of News.*
The B.B.C. news broadcasts were taken down in shorthand by 744979 Sgt. Mogg, R.P.L., R.A.F. He transcribed these notes into longhand and on the following day a copy was passed round the various Barrack Leaders who read the bulletin to the occupants of their barracks. As a rule this was done at a meal time.

A copy of the bulletin was passed, by various means, to the Senior British Officer, W/Cdr. H.M.A. Day, R.A.F., so that the news could be distributed in the Officers Compound.

(f). *Value and Remarks.*
The reception of the B.B.C. news broadcasts by means of the secret radio receiver and the dissemination of the news amongst the P's/W was a most important feature in the maintenance of high morale. This was important because of German propaganda.

(g) *W/T Communications.*
No w/t broadcasts containing code messages were received in this Compound during the period under review.

34. TRANSMITTER
There was no radio transmitter in this Compound.

35. NEWS LETTERS
(a) *Introduction.*
A few letters were received by certain P's/W from correspondents who

95

were unknown to them. These contained news of the progress of the war, etc., and obviously were designed to raise morale.

(b) *Opinions.*
In some cases the recipients thought that the contents of the news letters were intended for German consumption.

Chapter 11

Intelligence and Internal Security

36. MILITARY INFORMATION
(a) *Methods of collection.*
Details of the methods of collection and direct despatch of information to the United Kingdom by means of code messages are given elsewhere. In addition, from about September, 1940, onwards a certain amount of information was obtained by the undermentioned N.C.O's at the request of the Senior British Officer, 28097 S/Ldr. B. Paddon R.A.F., and passed to him in the Officers Compound.

The N.C.O's were:

564838 F/Sgt. Hall, E.L.G.   R.A.F.
580224 Sgt. Lascelles, E.B.   R.A.F.
620735 Sgt. Prendergrast, J.N. R.A.F.

The information which was collected by Hall and Prendergrast consisted of statistics of the causes of the loss of aircraft. This was obtained by questioning new arrivals in the Compound. The resultant data was passed to the Senior British Officer.

Lascelles, who worked independently, volunteered to go out of the Camp on local working parties. This was about September, 1940, after Squadron Leader Paddon had informed him that he was in communication with the United Kingdom by means of code. From then until April, 1941, he passed information to the Officers Compound. After Paddon's departure from the Camp in early February, it was received by Lt. Cdr. (A) P. Fanshawe R.N.

The messages which were written in an elementary code and embodied in notes, which were exchanged between Lascelles in the N.C.O's Compound and Paddon or Fanshawe in the Officers Compound, were usually passed through the agency of 550365 Sgt. Smith, W.G., R.A.F.

This N.C.O. was engaged on boot repairing and was enabled to go from the N.C.O's Compound to the Officers Compound from time to time accompanied by a German guard. Some of these messages were passed through the Administrative Staffs of the two Compounds, e.g. Parcel Representatives, Sick Quarters personnel etc.

The following is an extract from the M.I.9/S/P.G. report in respect of Fanshawe:

"When Lascelles went out of the Camp on working parties he obtained information which was passed on to Paddon. This system was still in operation when Paddon was posted from the Camp following his attempted escape on 31st January, 1941. Before this attempt Paddon informed Lascelles that I would carry on in his stead, and gave me a sheaf of messages which he had received from Lascelles. These contained local information and the names and addresses of several Poles who would be prepared to assist escapers.

"Lascelles signed messages "Leatherneck" Paddon informed him that I would sign messages "Hornblower". This was my nickname in the Camp at that time.

"After Paddon left the Camp on 31st January, 1941, I carried on the exchange of messages with Lascelles using a different code word. About May, 1941, I changed the signature on my message to "Murgatroyd". I retained the messages from Lascelles which Paddon had handed to me, and subsequent messages between Lascelles and myself. They were hidden in a concealed panel in the wall of the Canteen.

"One of the messages sent to me by Lascelles contained information about German troop movements. Another message referred to a tunnel on which Lascelles was working and suggested arrangements for two officers to use it when it would be completed. These messages were concealed in the wall of the Canteen also.

"I am of the opinion that I destroyed those messages which contained names and addresses of Poles, in the early summer of 1941. I cannot be definite about this.

"About April, 1941, the Germans carried out a very thorough search of the Officers Compound & the concealed panel in the Canteen, in which the messages were hidden, was discovered.

"I sent a message to Lascelles informing him of what had occurred. At that time he was a patient in Sick Quarters. A few days later he was encoding a message in reply to this, when he was apprehended by a German. I learned, subsequently, that Lascelles kit was searched and other messages discovered. They were decoded in Berlin. His tunnel was discovered also.

"Lascelles was arrested and placed in cells pending investigation. He remained there for a few weeks before being taken to Gestapo Prison at Stettin.

"On 9th September, 1941, I was arrested by the Camp Abwehr and placed in cells. On 10th September, I was interrogated by two Gestapo officials in connection with the messages which had been found. I admitted that my nickname was "Hornblower", but denied everything else. After this interrogation I remained in the Camp cells until 2nd October.

"On that day one Gestapo official, in uniform, arrived and interrogated me along the same lines as on the previous occasion. I maintained my denials. Then he informed me that I would be kept in cells indefinitely. I told him that I was the recipient of the messages. Then he interrogated me on the messages. I stated that the messages were for escape purposes only. He pointed out that one of the messages contained military information. I replied that I had not asked for this information and did not know why it had been sent, and in any case no use could be made of it.

"Then he interrogated me about a message which I had sent to Lascelles, the gist of which was: 'I must inform A.M. that the Polish addresses have been compromised.'

"I stated that I had to report to the Senior British Officer that certain Polish addresses had been found. The "A.M." was passed of successfully as a coding error. No further reference was made to Poles.

"Then I was asked about the information which had been passed to me. I stated that it was for the purpose of making a personal attempt to escape and that I had not passed the information to anyone else. I denied that any Camp Escape Organisation existed.

"My reasons for admitting my connection with the receipt of messages was to clear up the case as Lascelles had been held in the Gestapo Prison at Stettin for three months, and that the Germans had proof of the part he had played.

"On 3rd October, I was taken to the Gestapo Prison at Stettin, where I was placed in solitary confinement. I remained there until 10th October. During this period I was interrogated by a senior Gestapo official, who was wearing civilian clothes. He wanted me to expand upon the statement which I had made on 2nd October. I replied that I could not add to it, as I had given all details. The interrogation was not pressed.

"On 10th October, I was escorted to Stalag Luft I (Barth) and released in the Officers Compound.

"On 19th November, 1941, I was arrested by the Camp Abwehr and placed in cells. The charges, which were read to me, related to the collection of military information. I was informed that I was to be sent to a Military Prison in Berlin by order of the Kreigsgericht.

"On 20th November, I was taken to the Military Investigation Prison at Tegel, Berlin: this was an O.R's prison. I remained there until 20th March, 1942. During this period, about 12th December, 1941, I was interrogated at the Reich Kreigsgericht, Charlottenburg, about the message containing details of troop movements and about the other messages in general. I was interrogated about my life since childhood. I gave full details until the time of my entry into the Royal Navy, then refused to disclose further particulars and the matter was not pressed. No reference was made to the addresses of the Poles.

"On 18th March, 1942, the Commandant of the prison sent for me and informed me that the charges against me had been dismissed. On 20th March, I was returned to Stalag Luft I. Lascelles, who had been in this prison also was returned with me."

The following is an extract from the M.I.9/S/P.G. report in respect of Lascelles:

"During this time (September, 1940 – April, 1941) I had made contact with Squadron Leader Paddon, who was in the Officers Compound. He told me he was using a code to the U.K. I volunteered to go on working parties out of the Camp in order to get information. I got plans of a Flak School, an aerodrome near Barth and the gun emplacements near Zingst. Also during this time, some P's/W who were wounded or ill, and were being repatriated to England came through Barth in transit. I interrogated all the N.C.O's and was able to report to Squadron Leader Paddon that German troops were moving Eastwards in large numbers.

"When I was in hospital (Camp Sick Quarters) with impetigo, I got a note from Paddon using an elementary code which told me that this information had been found by the Germans during a search and that the tunnel scheme had been discovered also: Paddon knew of this scheme.

"I was arrested and put into solitary confinement, but not immediately charged: Paddon was not arrested. At the end of June I was formally charged with espionage. After this, I was moved

100

around to various prisons but not tried. I got no medical attention although the impetigo had spread to my chest.

"About the middle of August, 1941, I was sent to the Gestapo Headquarters at Stettin. I was interrogated over a period of four months and they tried to get evidence against me. I admitted getting the plans and information, but made out that it was for escape activities. I was sent back to Barth for one day.

"Lieutenant Commander Fanshawe, who had taken Paddon's place, had been arrested and put in the cell next but one to me, they tried to see if we would communicate, but failed. The Gestapo were trying to make out that I was not a pilot, but that I had been dropped as an agent.

"From there I was sent to a prison at Berlin. Fanshawe was sent to Berlin also. I waited there until April, 1942, awaiting courts-martial. Then the charge was dropped because the Germans could not find any link with England through me".

(b) *Value of direction from I.S.9.*
The code users considered that the direction which they received from I.S.9. was inadequate.

(c) *Adherence to direction.*
The code users followed instructions received from I.S.9. to the best of their ability.

37. INTERNAL SECURITY
(a) *Organisation.*
There was no organisation to promote internal security. A small number of N.C.O's performed the self-appointed task of endeavouring to check the bona fides of new arrivals in the Compound. The personnel who attempted to do this security work were:

580224	Sgt. Lascelles, E.B.	R.A.F.
590230	F/Sgt. Ross, T.G.	R.A.F.
590406	F/Sgt. Taylor-Gill, J.D.T.	R.A.F.

It was found to be impossible to check whether information was being given to the Germans by P's/W, but this was suspected because of the inevitable premature discovery of tunnels. Apparently, the real reasons for such discoveries were the anti-tunnel and the concealed microphones in barracks.

101

38. ANTI-GERMAN PROPAGANDA

(a) Introduction and Method.

No organised attempt was made to disseminate anti-German propaganda to Germans, but certain P's/W endeavoured to lower German morale by making statements designed to have this effect to those with whom they came into contact.

(b) *Results.*

It is not possible to assess the results of these statements, but it is noteworthy that many of them were repeated at a later date by other Germans, usually in an exaggerated form.

Part III

NCOs' CAMP
October 1942 to November 1943

Chapter 12

Introduction

1. LOCATION AND DESCRIPTION OF COMPOUND

This Compound was used for the accommodation of Air Force officers from July, 1940 until April, 1942, and is described in Part I of this volume.

2. CAMP CONDITIONS

(a) *Number of P's/W and accommodation.*

In October, 1942 a party of about 150 Air Force N.C.O.'s were transferred to this Compound from Stalag Luft III (Sagan). This party was made up of a number of volunteers from the R.A.F. and Dominion Air Forces. Until the arrival of this party the Camp had not been used for the accommodation of British P's/W since April 1942.

During the next few months batches of new P's/W arrived from Dulag Luft (Oberursel) and in January, 1943, the Compound housed about 600 men. They were accommodated in three wooden barracks, each of which was divided into rooms. Each room occupied by 6 men.

When this Compound had been used for the accommodation of Air Force officers prior to April, 1942, only 250 had been housed there. Shutters on all barrack windows were closed and bolted on the outside at night.

Although the N.C.O.'s became very cramped as their numbers increased, the accommodation was better than the older P's/W had experienced in previous Camps. Each barrack had indoor sanitation, a wash room and a kitchen.

The German dry rations were issued from, and the cooked rations cooked in, the cookhouse situated in an adjacent Compound which had been occupied by Air Force N.C.O.'s during the period July, 1940 – April, 1942. The preparation of meals was done by volunteer P's/W working under German supervision. They were taken from this Compound to the cookhouse each morning by a German guard and returned each evening.

In April, 1943 the Compound which had been occupied by N.C.O.'s during the July 1940 – April 1942 period was opened because of the influx of new P's/W and the transfer from Stalag Luft III (Sagan) of Polish and Czech nationals serving in the R.A.F. as N.C.O.'s and U.S.A.A.C. N.C.O.'s. During the hours of daylight the P's/W could move freely from one compound to the other, but the Germans forbade them to change their place of residence.

During the next few months batches of new P's/W arrived from Dulag Luft (Oberursel) and accommodation became very crowded. About September, 1943, the total strength of the Camp was approximately 1,200 N.C.O.'s of the R.A.F., R.A.A.F., R.C.A.F., R.N.Z.A.F., S.A.A.F., Naval Air Arm and U.S.A.A.C.

In November, 1943, the Germans decided to evacuate the N.C.O.'s in order to use the Camp for the accommodation of Air Force officers. During that month all the N.C.O.'s except a few who elected to remain for the purpose of assisting the officers, were transferred in batches of about 200 to Stalag Luft VI (Heydekrug), where they were accommodated in "K" Compound.

(b) *German administration.*
The Camp was administered and guarded by about 200 German Air Force personnel. Approximately 150 of these were guards, 12 were interpreters connected with the Abwehr (Security) Department, and the remainder were German administration staff.

Except for roll calls, anti-escape measures, and inspections for cleanliness, the administration of the Camp was left to the Camp Leader.

(c) *P/W administration.*
In October, 1942 prior to the departure from Stalag Luft III (Sagan) of the party of N.C.O.'s which had been transferred to this Camp, the Senior British Officer, Group Captain H.M. Massey, D.S.C., D.F.C., approved of the appointment of 580309 W/O. May, T.K., R.A.F. to the position of Camp Leader. He was to be in charge of the party and was to assume his duties as Camp Leader immediately upon arrival in this Camp.

May carried out his duties to the best of his ability, but after a short time a large number of the P's/W became discontented with his leadership.

This was due to the following factors:
(i) May was a good administrator, but no leader of men.
(ii) The overcrowded conditions and the lack of recreational facilities caused the P's/W to become interested in Camp politics.

A bitter dispute developed in the Camp concerning the treatment of Germans. This reached a crisis at Christmas 1942 when the band from the nearby German Flak School gave a concert in the Compound and the bandsman lost certain items of clothing. May felt that the Germans had been doing a kind act in giving the concert and should not suffer for it. Those who had stolen the clothing thought that sentiment should not enter into such questions.

Several days later, after much unpleasantness, May prevailed upon the robbers to return the clothing. At the same time May, who was highly respected by the Germans, told the Kommandant that he was unable to maintain discipline in the Camp and requested that two British officers should be sent to Stalag Luft III (Sagan). The Germans agreed, and the S.B.O. at that Camp was asked to submit the names of two officers. He nominated:

26183   Group Captain J.C. Macdonald   R.A.F.
26216   Squadron Leader W.H.N. Turner   R.A.F.

These two officers were acceptable to the Germans and they were transferred to this Camp, where they arrived on 21st January, 1943.

In early January, 1943, May resigned his position as Camp Leader and another N.C.O was elected in his place. He was NZ.405362 W/O. Barnes, J.G., R.N.Z.A.F., who held the position for about three weeks, until the arrival of Group Captain Macdonald and Squadron Leader Turner. The reasons for this were:

(i) Group Captain Macdonald had made a very strong written protest through the Kommandant to the Protecting Power, and a verbal one to Goering's official interpreter during his visit to the Camp, on the torture to which allied P's/W were being subjected at Dulag Luft (Oberursel).

(ii) Group Captain Macdonald had not met the wishes of the Kommandant when he was asked to disclose the name of a P/W who had escaped.

During the period from 21st January, 1943 until 12th July, 1943, Barnes worked as an assistant to Group Captain Macdonald. Before the latter was transferred from the Camp he addressed all the P's/W and informed them that Barnes would act as Camp Leader from then onwards. From then until November, 1943, when the majority of the P's/W were transferred to Stalag Luft VI (Heydekrug), Barnes carried out his duties satisfactorily.

(d) *Roll Calls.*

The German method of counting the P's/W was very similar to that at Stalag Luft III (Sagan). Despite these elaborate precautions, the Escape Organisation was able to cover up the absence of all those who succeeded in escaping from the Camp. In each case this was only necessary for a short time. The method generally employed was the use of a concealed trap door between the rooms which enabled a man to be counted twice.

(e) *Food.*

In October, 1942, consignments of Red Cross food parcels were re-directed to this Camp from Stalag Luft III (Sagan). Within a reasonably short time supplies arrived direct from Geneva, but at times the quantity available for distribution was not sufficient for the issue of one parcel per man each week. This was due to the time lag in increasing supplies when the strength of the Camp was being increased by new intakes of P's/W.

Throughout the period under review the German rations were meagre. The P's/W attempted to vary their diet by cultivating garden plots. Seeds, tomato plants, etc. were purchased from the Germans through the Camp Canteen. No milk was supplied at any time.

(f) *Clothing.*

Supplies of R.A.F. O.R.'s uniforms, boots, greatcoats, underwear, shirts, socks, etc. were forwarded through the agency of the International Red Cross Society. These items were distributed amongst the P's/W through their own administration under German supervision, but no restrictions were imposed regarding the quantities issued.

A limited quantity of this clothing was available at all times for escape purposes, but stocks were never in excess of requirements because of the gradual increase in the Camp strength.

(g) *Searches.*

At first unpredictable searches of the barracks and Compounds were carried out at irregular intervals by members of the Abwehr Department (German Anti-Escape Organisation). After January, 1943, prior warning of searches was obtained by the P's/W through the 'Evading' Organisation.

Whenever these searches took place the doors of the barrack, or barracks, were locked and armed guards were posted to ensure that no P's/W could gain entry. The possessions of the P's/W and the structure of the barrack were subjected to scrutiny of varying degrees of thoroughness, in an endeavour to discover escape aids, tools, entrances to tunnels, radio sets, diaries, etc. As a rule, hoards of food were not interfered with.

(h) *German anti-escape measures.*
The German Abwehr Department was very highly organised under the direction of Hauptmann Von Miller zu Aichholz, who had been an interrogating officer at Dulag Luft (Oberursel) from July, 1940 until July, 1942. His chief assistant was Unteroffizier Siemens who had held a similar position at this Camp during the period of the earlier occupation by Air Force P's/W. Siemens had a staff of six interpreters. The duties of the Abwehr staff were:

(i) to keep a continuous listening watch on the microphone system installed for the detection of tunnels.
(ii) to patrol the Compound at night accompanied by dogs. They were also instructed to listen at the windows of the barracks, etc.
(iii) to search all parcels issued to the P's/W and supervise the Parcel Store.
(iv) to carry out searches of the barracks, etc.

Siemens was seldom seen in the Compound during the hours of daylight, but he spent a considerable amount of his time lying under the barracks at night.

The Lagerfuhrung (Camp management) Department was responsible to the Abwehr Section for certain aspects of Camp security. This department was under the direction of Hauptmann Eilers, who had not had previous experience of P's/W. He was assisted by six interpreters. The duties of this Department were:

(i) to check all P's/W twice daily in order to ascertain whether any had escaped.
(ii) to escort P's/W from the Compound to other parts of the Camp, i.e. the Cookhouse, Sick Quarters, etc.
(iii) the superintending of various Camp Duties, i.e. removal of rubbish, supply of fuel, etc.

It will be seen from the foregoing that there were twelve interpreters, which is a very large number for such a small Camp. Two of these were always in the Compound during the hours of daylight for the purpose of observing the activities of the P's/W and listening to scraps of conversation.

The perimeter fence of the Camp was composed of two barbed wire fences about 6 feet, 6 inches apart and 8 feet in height. The area between the fences was filled with concertina wire to a height of about 2 feet 6 inches. The fence was lit from dusk to dawn, except during air-raid alarms, by arc lights spaced about 25 yards apart. Sentry towers, which were fitted with searchlights and machine guns, were situated at strategic points (see [Plate 1]).

During air-raid alarms the sentries outside the fence, between the sentry towers was doubled. At night this was done before the boundary lights were switched off. When necessary the searchlights could still be operated.

All German personnel, other than members of the Abwehr staff, had to report to the guardroom, situated outside the Vorlager, when entering and leaving the Camp. During the hours of daylight an interpreter of the Lagerfuhrung department was constantly on duty there to scrutinise all personnel.

All German personnel, irrespective of rank, had to produce their special passes when passing through each of the three gates between the Compound and the area beyond the Camp boundaries.

All vehicles were searched at the Vorlager gate before leaving.

At the end of March, 1943, the Germans became aware that a number of tunnels were under construction. They transferred all the P's/W to another Compound for one day and during that time a trench was dug along the whole of the length of the Northern side of the Compound between the barracks and the fence. The trench was about 5 feet in depth and went below water level. This was then filled with rubble, broken glass, old tin cans, etc. All the tunnels which had been under construction were discovered. Before the P's/W were allowed to return to the Compound in the evening they were addressed by the Abwehr Officer who lost his temper and dared them to get through his new defence.

At the end of May, 1943, the Germans suspected that a tunnel was being built, but they could not discover it. Three whole day searches took place. On the first day a steam roller was driven round the Camp between the barracks and the fence, but without result. On the third day the area under all barracks was flooded by means of fire hoses and the tunnel collapsed. The tunnel detector system was in operation throughout this period.

(i) *Education.*
About December, 1942, an Education Section was formed by W/O. Wood R.A.F., as soon as supplies of paper, text books, etc. began to

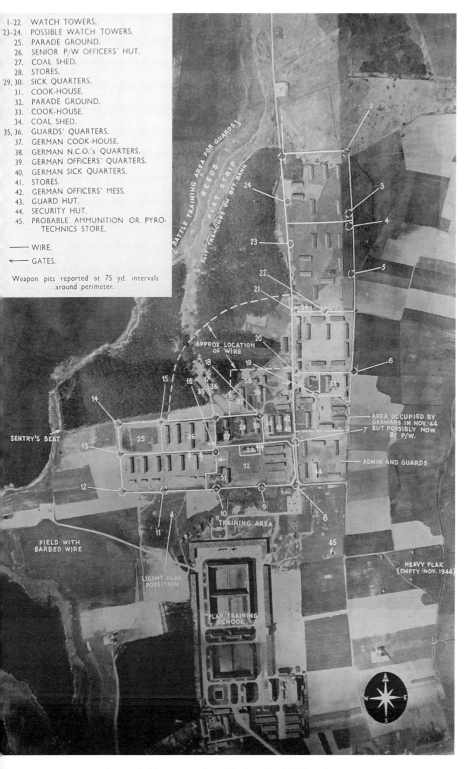

1-22. WATCH TOWERS.
23-24. POSSIBLE WATCH TOWERS.
25. PARADE GROUND.
26. SENIOR P/W OFFICERS' HUT.
27. COAL SHED.
28. STORES.
29, 30. SICK QUARTERS.
31. COOK-HOUSE.
32. PARADE GROUND.
33. COOK-HOUSE.
34. COAL SHED.
35, 36. GUARDS' QUARTERS.
37. GERMAN COOK-HOUSE.
38. GERMAN N.C.O.'s QUARTERS.
39. GERMAN OFFICERS' QUARTERS.
40. GERMAN SICK QUARTERS.
41. STORES.
42. GERMAN OFFICERS' MESS.
43. GUARD HUT.
44. SECURITY HUT.
45. PROBABLE AMMUNITION OR PYRO-
    TECHNICS STORE.

——— WIRE.
←——— GATES.

Weapon pits reported at 75 yd. intervals
around perimeter.

Plate 1: An annotated aerial photograph of Stalag Luft I, Barth.

Plate 2: The photographic equipment used by the Forgery Section. The bellows of th camera extension was made of brown paper, the film holder of wood, and the ligh reflector from a milk tin. The copy board, shown on the left of the photograph, coul be moved up or down, and to the left or right as desired. The camera could be move towards or away from the copy board and locked in position with wing nuts. A pas is shown in position on the copy board.

Plate 3: One of the methods employed by the Escape Organisation for concealin documents, small maps, money, etc. The book was opened approximately at th middle, the binding of the pages was cut and the cover boards slit open. Th documents, etc., were placed inside and the binding of the pages glued. If the wor was done neatly, it was impossible to discern that the book had been tampered wit Owing to the enormous number of books in the Camp it was impossible for th Germans to examine more than a few of the total during any one search. This metho was never discovered.

Plate 4: A forged Camp Pass which was reproduced by hand by a member of the Forgery Section.

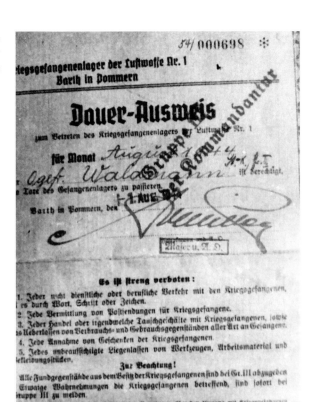

Plate 5: The back of the Camp Pass shown in Plate 4. The complicated design was reproduced by hand.

Plate 6: A battery-operated radio receiver used by the prisoners at Stalag Luft I. The hinged panel is open showing the position of the receiving unit, and the wires running to behind the adjoining panel, where fifty to sixty flash-lamp batteries were concealed These were connected together to supply the power for the set.

Plate 7: The panels behind which a radio receiver and batteries were concealed. (1) and (2): Screwdrivers in position for tuning and reaction control. These were inserted through holes in the wooden panel. When the receiver was not being used the holes were filled with wooden plugs which were disguised as towns on the map, all towns being indicated with black spots. (3): Aerial clipped to a nail which passed through the panel and was connected to the receiver. (4) and (5): Earphone leads connected to nails which passed through the panel and were connected to the receiver. (6) Bookshelf, a common feature in most rooms in the Camp. The nails mentioned in (3), (4) and (5) helped to support it. (7): Alarm clock used to waken the operators for the 'Voice of America' programme at 0200 hours daily.

Plate 8: A view of one of the guard towers/sentry posts at Stalag Luft I at Barth. (Historic Military Press)

Plate 9: A view of one part of the complex of Stalag Luft I at Barth. (Historic Military Press)

Plate 10: A second photograph of part of the complex of Stalag Luft I at Barth. (Historic Military Press)

Plate 11: Prisoners of war at Stalag Luft I, near Barth, enjoying a festive meal on Christmas Day 1940. (Historic Military Press)

Plate 12: This group photograph shows members of the NCOs' soccer team at Stalag Luft I in 1941. (Historic Military Press)

Plate 13: A view of 'Johnnie Fenders band' at Stalag Luft I at Barth in 1941. One account states: 'Two rival bands of Stan Parris and Johnny [*sic*] Fender, practiced long and hard and provided the music for the shows. Johnny Fender of Failsworth, Lancashire, an RAF regular of 148 Squadron Bomber Command was captured of the Dutch Coast on 29th August 1940 and spent the war in Stalag Lufts, 1, 3, 6 and Stalag 357 Thorne and Fallingbostal.' (Historic Military Press)

Plate 14: A view of players of an officers v. NCOs rugby match held at Stalag Luft I (Historic Military Press)

Plate 15: Some of the players pictured during an officers v. NCOs rugby match held at Stalag Luft I in 1941. (Historic Military Press)

Plate 16: An officers v. NCOs hockey match underway at Stalag Luft I in February 1942. (Historic Military Press)

Plate 17: Another photograph of the officers v. NCOs hockey match underway at Stalag Luft I in February 1942. (Historic Military Press)

Plate 18: A group of Canadian officers at Stalag Luft I in 1941. (Historic Military Press)

Plate 19: A view of prisoners dressed up to play their roles in the production 'Aubrey Goes West' at Stalag Luft I in 1941. Note the RAF issue flying boots worn by the PoWs. (Historic Military Press)

Plate 20: A PoW dressed up as a pirate standing with another prisoner at Stalag Luft I in 1941. Note the watch tower in the background. (Historic Military Press)

Plate 21: Prisoners dressed up to play their roles in the production 'Jack and the Beanstalk' at Stalag Luft I during the Christmas of 1941. The individual second from the right is Alfred George Fripp. He was shot down in 1939 and held in twelve different PoW camps. As the last of the '39ers' (those taken prisoner in the first year of the war), he was the oldest surviving and longest serving British PoW. (Historic Military Press)

Plate 22: Members of the prisoners' band called the 'Luft Orpheans' at Stalag Luft I during 1942. (Historic Military Press)

Plate 23: Another prisoners' band, this time called 'MOs Gefangeners', pose for the camera at Stalag Luft I during 1941. (Historic Military Press)

Plate 24: A view of a Christmas party or meal held at Barth in 1941. (Historic Military Press)

Plate 25: One of a series of images taken before and during the funeral of 23-year-old Sergeant Pilot 742749 John Cecil Shaw, 49 Squadron, during January 1942. Shaw was a Hampden pilot whose aircraft P4404, was shot down on the night of 6/7 December 1940. Having taken off from Scampton, Shaw and his crew was tasked with attacking German airfields in Northern France. The Hampden Mk.I, coded EA-R, was hit by anti-aircraft fire, resulting in Shaw making a crash-landing south of Paris. Shaw and his crew eventually ended up in Stalag Luft I near Barth on the Baltic. On the night of 4 January 1942, Shaw attempted to escape from the camp by using the 'invisible man' act, in which he crawled across the snow to the perimeter wire whilst covered by a white sheet. He was spotted by one of the guards, but on standing up and raising his hands, as well as turning to face the sentry, he was shot and killed. This image shows Shaw's body lying in rest prior to being taken to the cemetery. (Historic Military Press)

Plate 26: Part of the Allied contingent at the funeral of Sergeant Pilot John Cecil Shaw. The picture shows Pilot Officer B.H. Evans, Shaw's navigator (first RAF officer third from left), with Wing Commander 'Wings' Day (on his left) saluting at the graveside. Sergeant David Young and Sergeant W.K. O'Leary, also from Shaw's crew, wait to lay wreaths. It was a tragic irony that Evans was later himself to die by a German bullet, being one of the fifty men executed after 'The Great Escape'. (Historic Military Press)

Plate 27: This image shows the German Fire Party firing a volley after Shaw's coffin was lowered into the grave. Today Shaw lies in Berlin 1939-45 War Cemetery. (Historic Military Press)

Plate 28: Part of the officers' arts and craft exhibition at Stalag Luft I, March 1941. One account states: 'Model makers were also in good supply and some excellent models were produced and entered into model making competitions. One hut held a large collection of British and German airplanes in suspended flight, whilst the fire pool became a regular place for various model boats to be shown off and sailed.' (Historic Military Press)

Plate 29: A group of 'would be escapees recaptured' at Stalag Luft I in 1941 or 1942. Note that the individual on the left appears to be dressed in a fake German uniform. (Historic Military Press)

arrive in the Camp from the Young Men's Christian Association and the International Red Cross Society.

Wood, who had been a schoolteacher prior to joining the R.A.F., formed a Committee of N.C.O's who were qualified to teach various subjects and were willing to impart their knowledge to others. A number of classes were formed and candidates were prepared for Matriculation Examinations, etc. the classes were well attended and excellent results were obtained when candidates sat for their examinations in the Camp by virtue of arrangements made by the Education Section of the British Red Cross Society.

Materials for forgery, map making, etc. were supplied to the Escape Organisation by the Education Section. The classrooms were utilised for such work at times when instruction was not in progress.

(j) *Library*.

Quantities of books of all kinds began to arrive in the Camp during December, 1942. These were supplied by the International Red Cross and British Red Cross Societies. In order to render this literature available to the whole community a library was organised by 923213 W/O. Barnes, J.F., R.A.F. A record was kept of all books which were borrowed and a time limit set for their return. Offenders against this rule were debarred from obtaining other books for a time.

After January, 1943, escape aids were hidden in concealed panels in the walls of the library. This was considered to be a very safe hiding place as hundreds of books would have had to be moved before the Germans could begin to conduct a search.

(k) *Sports*.

From October, 1942, until April, 1943, the P's/W had very few opportunities for engaging in sports. This was due to the fact that there was no space in the Compound which was occupied during this period. There were Sports Fields in two adjacent unoccupied Compounds, but the Germans were unwilling to provide the additional guards needed to ensure that P's/W would not escape from them whilst games were in progress. However, the Germans were prevailed upon to allow these Sports Fields to be used on rare occasions. This reform took place after strong representations had been made to the Kommandant by 26183 Group Captain J.C. Macdonald R.A.F. soon after his arrival in the Camp.

In April, 1943, there was an influx of new P's/W and the Compound formerly occupied by N.C.O's during the July, 1940 – April, 1942 period was brought into use. This contained a Sports Field and from then onwards full use was made of it as there was free access to both

111

Compounds. Soccer, rugby, cricket and softball were very popular. As a rule each barrack had a representative team for each of these games. Inter-Compound matches were also played.

The bulk of the sports equipment was supplied by the Young Men's Christian Association.

(l) *Amateur Theatricals.*
The Camp Theatre was situated in the same building as the Cookhouse. After some months various plays, Concerts, Gramophone recitals, etc. were produced and were most popular. As a rule, the Germans were most helpful in all matters connected with the Theatre and did everything possible to meet requests for materials, costumes, etc. which were supplied on parole.

(m) *Religion.*
A room in which Religious Services were held was situated in the same building as the Cookhouse and Camp Theatre.

(n) *Shooting Incidents, etc.*
There were no shooting incidents during this period.

(o) *P/W Morale.*
At first, the morale of the P's/W in this Camp was rather low. Undoubtedly, this was due to the overcrowded living conditions, lack of sports and recreational facilities, lack of a secret radio receiver and an obsession with Camp politics.

After the arrival of Group Captain Macdonald and Squadron Leader Turner in January, 1943, morale and discipline improved considerably.

(p) *Medical.*
Sick parades were held daily in the Camp Sick Quarters which were situated in the Vorlager. The staff consisted of Captain Nicholls R.A.M.C. and a number of P's/W who had volunteered to act as orderlies. This staff lived in the Sick Quarters. A German Medical Officer, an eye specialist, visited the Sick Quarters daily. Patients suffering from serious illnesses were transferred to a hospital at Neu Brandenburg with the German Medical Officer's consent.

Chapter 13

Escape Organisation

3. CONTROL BY CAMP AUTHORITIES

Amongst the N.C.O.'s who had volunteered to transfer to this Camp from Stalag Luft III (Sagan) were a number who had done so with the object of attempting to escape. They were of the opinion that conditions would be easier in this Camp, where there were no Air Force officers, than at Sagan. The keenest of these formed themselves into an Escape Committee which assumed control of all escape activities. The members of this committee were:

515590	W/O. Axford, J.L.	R.A.F
741990	W/O. Dunphy, D.C.	R.A.F.
R.56516	W/O. Smith, A.J.	R.C.A.F.
1375121	W/O. Thompson, R.C.	R.A.F.

Axford was elected Chairman and the details of the Escape Organisation which was set up by the Committee are given in the succeeding Sections of this Chapter under the sub-heading "October, 1942 – January, 1943".

As stated, Group Captain Macdonald and Squadron Leader Turner arrived in this Camp on 21st January, 1943. After reviewing the situation, Group Captain Macdonald instructed Squadron Leader Turner to reorganise escape activities. The main reasons for this were:

(i) There was little team spirit amongst the P's/W due to jealousy of authority.

(ii) Escape equipment was not being shared and was being lost during searches.

(iii) Camp security was bad, due to the difficulty of persuading personnel to carry out watching duties, etc.

(iv) Personnel interested in making attempts to escape had to do most of the preparation themselves. This was not only due to lack of organisation, but also a distrust of the discretion of fellow P's/W.

(v) Trading with Germans was uncontrolled and no attempt had been made to acquire escape aids by this means.

It must not be assumed from the above remarks that there was little interest in escape amongst the P's/W. A number had made attempts to escape from the Camp during the previous three months, and there were many who had experience of tunnel construction.

Squadron Leader Turner informed the P's/W that he intended to organise escape on the same lines as the Escape Organisation at Stalag Luft III (Sagan) East (Officers') Compound. He instructed the occupants of each of the three barracks to elect a representative. This was done and from then until about 12th July, 1943, the Escape Committee was composed of the following:

> 1105939   W/O. Booth, G.S.   R.A.F.
> N.Z.391384 W/O. Howard, P.N.   R.N.Z.A.F.
> R.56516   W/O. Smith, A.J.   R.C.A.F.
> 26216   S/Ldr. Turner, W.H.N.R.A.F.

Squadron Leader Turner acted as Chairman of the Committee and directed policy. He caused a nominal role of all P's/W to be made and each individual was asked to state his civilian trade and any foreign languages which he could speak. From this information the various departments of the Escape Organisation were arranged.

When Group Captain Macdonald and Squadron Leader Turner were transferred from the Camp on about 12th July, 1943, the position of Chairman of the Escape Committee was taken over, on Turner's authority, by 968327 W/O. Kerr, W.E., R.A.F.

Within a short time the Committee acquired two new members. They were:

> 515590   W/O. Axford, J.L.   R.A.F.
> 964794   W/O. Olliver, R.B.   R.A.F.

This Committee, with the exception of Smith who was repatriated to the U.K. on medical grounds about September, 1943, continued to function until the evacuation of the Camp in November, 1943.

Throughout the period under review personnel interested in making attempts to escape sought the advice and assistance of the Escape

114

Committee. No attempt was made without the permission of the Committee.

4. PLANNING

Individual P's/W, or groups, who had ideas for attempts to escape, approached the Escape Committee and the scheme was discussed in full detail. If the committee considered it to be feasible, the resources of the Escape Organisation were employed to facilitate it.

In general, these conditions applied to the whole of the period under review.

5. SECURITY

(a) *October, 1942 – January, 1943.*
During this period the Escape Committee organised the nucleus of a Security Organisation. The following were appointed:

A402117	W/O. Gillespie, B.C.	R.A.A.F.
R61024	W/O. Sikal, M.F.	R.C.A.F.

Gillespie was in charge of this section, and Sikal made all arrangements in connection with recording the entry into, and exit, from the Compound of all Germans. Gillespie was responsible for the safe custody of all the escape aids held by the Escape Committee. He was assisted by A.406196 W/O. Evans, J.D., R.A.A.F.

Sikal's chief assistant was 546056 W/O. Carruthers, P.W., R.A.F.

Although a number of other N.C.O.'s were engaged on security work for a time, i.e. watching for the approach of Germans whilst tunnels were being constructed, etc., it became increasingly difficult to get volunteers for this work and towards the end of the period the above-named were doing most of the security without assistance. As a result of the inadequate security measures several men were apprehended by the Germans whilst engaged on tunnel construction.

(b) *January, 1942 – July, 1943.*
When Squadron Leader Turner re-organised the Escape Committee he appointed an N.C.O. to be in charge of all security. He was 968327 W/O. Kerr, W.E., R.A.F. Kerr selected the following to organise various aspects of the Security Organisation:

925696	W/O. Drummond,	R.R.R.A.F.
A402117	W/O. Gillespie, R.G.	R.A.A.F.
R.61024	W/O. Sikal, M.F.	R.C.A.F.

Kerr co-ordinated the work of all Sections.

Drummond made all arrangements in connection with the appointment of 'watchers' whose duty it was to give warning of the approach of any German to those areas where escape activities were in progress. His chief assistant was 546056 W/O. Carruthers, P.W., R.A.F.

Gillespie was responsible for the safe custody of all escape equipment held by the Escape Organisation. His chief assistant was A. 406196 W/O. Evans, J.B., R.A.A.F.

Sikal organised the 'duty pilot' system by which the movements of all Germans in the Compound were recorded by relays of 'watchers' throughout the 24 hours.

All N.C.O.'s who were not engaged on other Camp Duties, were expected to take their turn on all 'watching' duties.

During this period security improved to a marked extent.

(c) *July, 1943 – November, 1943.*
The organisation outlined in sub-Section (b) above was retained during this period. Kerr controlled all security, assisted by 741990 W/O. Dunphy, D.C., R.A.F.

A good standard of security was maintained.

6. CLOTHING
(a) *October, 1942 – January, 1943.*
German uniforms and civilian clothes were made from dyed blankets, R.A.F. O.R.'s uniforms and greatcoats, also bed-sheets. All the clothing used by escapers was made by this Clothing Section. The manufacture of clothing for escape purposes was under the control of 515590 W/O. Axford, J.L., R.A.F., who did a considerable amount of the work personally. He was assisted by:

366001	W/O. Ayres, C.A.	R.A.F.
546056	W/O. Carruthers, P.W.	R.A.F.
	Driver May,	R.A.S.C.

(b) *January, 1943 – July, 1943.*
When the Escape Organisation was re-arranged by Squadron Leader Turner, the Clothing Section became the responsibility of 1105939 W/O. Booth, G.S., R.A.F., who was a member of the Escape Committee. Booth appointed the following to make and alter clothing:

515590	W/O. Axford, J.L.	R.A.F.
366001	W/O. Ayres, C.A.	R.A.F.

	Cpl. Baines, W.	Army
546056	W.O. Carruthers, P.W.	R.A.F.
1181464	W/O. Humber, L.E.J.	R.A.F.
	Driver May	R.A.S.C.
787798	Sgt. Schneider, K.	(Czech) R.A.F.

The more highly skilled work was done by Ayres, Baines, May and Schneider.

(c) *July, 1943 – November, 1943.*
During this period the workers in the clothing section were:

	W/O. Ayres, C.A.	R.A.F.
366001		
	Cpl. Baines, W.	Army
546056	W.O. Carruthers, P.W.	R.A.F.
	Driver May	R.A.S.C.

7. FORGERY
(a) *Papers, October, 1942 – January, 1943.*
No attempt was made to reproduce documents during this period.

(b) *Papers, January, 1943 – July, 1943.*
A Forgery Section was organised about the end of January, 1943, by Squadron Leader Turner. The work of the department was supervised and directed by 64794 W/O. Olliver, R.B., R.A.F., who spoke and could read German fluently. The actual forgery was carried out by:

1225763	W/O. Alger, J.K.	R.A.F.
621818	W/O. Gregory, G.R.E.	R.A.F.
755530	W/O. Harrison, C.E.	R.A.F.
1181464	W/O. Humber, L.E.J.	R.A.F.
962982	W/O. Kilminster, A.R.	R.A.F.
968023	W/O. Maddocks, R.	R.A.F.
1652550	W/O. Watkins, H.D.	R.A.F.
1258657	W/O. White, D.	R.A.F.

Kilminster was the most highly skilled and he did most of the detailed work. The first documents to be reproduced were copies of German identity cards, and letters purporting to come from German firms. The original forgeries of these were brought to this Camp from Stalag Luft III by Group Captain Macdonald and Squadron Leader Turner.

117

A little later a German guard was persuaded to lend his Camp Pass for copying. A hurried tracing was made by Kilminster and later he made a detailed reproduction.

In the Spring of 1943 an Identity Card for Polish workers was obtained from a Pole and copied.

About the same time a Leave Pass for French workers was obtained from a Frenchman who was working in the district. This was copied.

When the forged Camp Pass referred to above was discovered by the Germans as an escaper attempted to walk through the gate in disguise, the design of the pass was altered. Subsequently a German was prevailed upon to lend his pass for copying and an accurate tracing was made by Kilminster. This was copied exactly and the signatures and stamps were in the same positions as on the original. This forgery was used by an escaper who was apprehended at the Camp gate. The forgery was examined by the Gestapo and compared with all the original passes which had been issued to members of the German Camp Staff. In this way the owner of the pass which had been copied was discovered and he was sentenced to three years imprisonment. Thereafter care was taken not to copy original signatures, etc. too faithfully.

The reproduction of Camp Passes and nearly all Identity Cards was done by hand, usually with a fine sable-hair artists' brush of very high quality. A supply of these had been sent to Kilminster by his parents at his request. These brushes were unobtainable in Germany.

About February, 1943, a duplicating machine of the jelly type was obtained from the Germans for the purpose of producing a Camp newspaper. This was not on parole and was used for making certain kinds of spurious documents. These included letters of introduction from German firms and all typewritten documents. The 'master' copies were made by imitating typewritten characters with a pen using duplicator ink. When some documents produced by this method were discovered by the Germans following an unsuccessful escape the duplicator was confiscated.

About May, 1943, shortly after the confiscation of the German duplicating machine, a three-colour duplicating machine arrived in the Camp from the Swedish Red Cross Society. The Germans demanded that a parole should be given that it would not be used for work in connection with escape before they would allow the machine to be taken into the Compound, but Group Captain Macdonald refused to accede to this demand. Eventually the Germans were persuaded to allow it into the compound but it was confiscated very shortly afterwards. However, some of the special duplicating ink was retained without their knowledge.

A large number of experiments were made to make a duplicating machine using table jellies from Red Cross food parcels as a duplicator base. In due course excellent results were obtained, although the soft nature of the jelly caused great trouble. Attempts to harden it with formalin were unsuccessful.

(c) *Papers, July, 1943 – November, 1943.*
Following the departure of Group Captain Macdonald and Squadron Leader Turner, who were transferred back to Stalag Luft III (Sagan) about mid-July, there was a marked decline in the number of personnel engaged in work connected with the Forgery Section. The department continued under the direction of Olliver and the work was done mainly by Kilminster assisted by Alger and Maddocks. Comparatively few documents were made.

(d) *Photographs, October, 1942 – January, 1943.*
No photographic work was undertaken during this period.

(e) *Photographs, January, 1943 – July, 1943.*
In cases where identity photographs were required for affixing to forged identity cards and the individual concerned did not possess a suitable photograph of himself, a photograph of some other person having a similar appearance was altered by hand to improve the likeness. Such work was carried out by Kilminster.

This method was not very effective as photographic tints were not available and the ink which had to be used stood out on top of the photograph making retouching rather obvious. To cover this defect forged identity cards were generally enclosed in a celluloid case which was intentionally somewhat soiled and the celluloid scratched.

(f) *Photographs, July, 1943 – November, 1943.*
The method outlined in the preceding paragraph was used during this period.

(g) *Stamps.*
All work in connection with stamps was done by the Forgery Section.

(h) *Stamps, October, 1942 – January, 1943.*
During this period no stamps were made for use on forged documents.

(i) *Stamps, January, 1943 – July, 1943.*
A few stamps were made for use on the forged documents which were

119

produced during this period. At first these were cut in rubber, usually pencil erasers or the heels of boots, but the results were rather rough. At a later date lead foil was melted down and the required design carved out of the solid. These stamps were rough but useable.

(j) *Stamps, July, 1943 – November, 1943.*
The impression of a rubber stamp was imitated by means of the jelly duplicator in use during this period for the reproduction of certain types of documents. This gave excellent results.

8. FOOD
(a) *October, 1942 – January, 1943.*
During this period the supply of food for intending escapers was the responsibility of A.406196 W/O. Evans, J.D., R.A.A.F., who worked in conjunction with the British Medical Officer, Captain Nicholls R.A.M.C.

The food was obtained from the Red Cross food parcels and usually consisted of biscuits, dried fruit, cheese, chocolate, etc. the ration supplied to each individual was calculated to last a certain number of days based on a formula prepared by Captain Nicholls.

(b) *January, 1943 – July, 1943.*
After the Escape Organisation was re-organised in January, 1943, the supply of food for intending escapers was controlled by A.402117 W/O. Gillespie, B.C., R.A.A.F. Most of the actual work was carried out by A.406196 W/O. Evans, J.D., R.A.A.F.

(c) *July, 1943 – November, 1943.*
During this period the Section continued to function as outlined above. There were no changes in personnel.

9. MAPS
(a) *October, 1942 – January, 1943.*
Some of the maps of Germany which had been received by the N.C.O's in the Centre Compound at Stalag Luft III (Sagan) from I.S.9. were brought to the Camp in October, 1942, by 515590 W/O. Axford, J.L., R.A.F. Soon afterwards he formed a Mapping Section which reproduced a number of copies of these maps by hand. His assistants were:

632266 W/O. Croft, S.R.	R.A.F.
970053 W/O. Everson, J.E.	R.A.F.

(b) *January, 1943 – July, 1943.*
When the Escape Organisation was re-organised in January, 1943, Squadron Leader Turner appointed 515590 W/O. Axford, J.L., R.A.F., to be in charge of the Mapping Section. His assistants were:

970053　W/O. Everson, J.E.　　R.A.F.
968023　W/O. Maddocks, R.　　R.A.F.

In March, 1943, Axford relinquished his position and was succeeded by 621818 W/O. Gregory, G.R.E., R.A.F., who re-organised the Section. His helpers were:

632266　W/O. Croft, S.R.　　　R.A.F.
970053　W/O. Everson, J.E.　　R.A.F.
755530　W/O. Harrison, C.E.　R.A.F.
968023　W/O. Maddocks, R.　　R.A.F.
R.56516　W/O. Smith, A.J.　　R.C.A.F.
1652550　W/O. Watkins, H.D.　R.A.F.
1258657　W/O. White, D.　　　R.A.F.

There was a large increase in the number of maps produced and about thirty books, each containing twelve maps; also fifty editions of a three-coloured folder of the whole of Germany, were made. Reproduction was by means of the "jelly" method of duplication, using the duplicating machines.

(c) *July, 1943 – November, 1943.*
During this period the production of maps was carried out along the lines outlined above, though on a much smaller scale. Those engaged on this work were:

632266　W/O. Croft, S.R.　　R.A.F.
970053　W/O. Everson, J.E.　R.A.F.
968023　W/O. Maddocks, R.　R.A.F.

About August, Croft ceased his activities in this Section.

10. COMPASSES
During the period under review – October, 1942, until November, 1943 – about a dozen compasses were made out of razor blades by 962982 W/O. Kilminster, A.R., R.A.F.

121

The method employed was to magnetise the razor blades by means of a coil connected to the mains. As the supply was AC the coil contained a very fine fuse so that this burned out at the peak of the cycle and gave maximum magnetising effect. These compasses were passed to the Escape Committee.

The supply of compasses referred to in the preceding paragraph was augmented when new P's/W arrived in the Camp with compasses which they had concealed during various searches following capture. From then onwards the Escape Committee was always able to meet the demands of intending escapers.

11. ESCAPE INTELLIGENCE

Escape information was obtained from the following sources and made available to intending escapers who were briefed by the Escape Committee:

(a) *Contacts, October, 1942 – January, 1943.*

There was no organised attempt to gain escape information from German sources during this period.

(b) *Contacts, January, 1943 – July, 1943.*

When Squadron Leader Turner re-organised the Escape Organisation in January, 1943, he assumed the role of Intelligence Officer. He had been briefed on all aspects of Escape Intelligence before leaving Stalag Luft III (Sagan) by Squadron Leader R. Bushell, R.A.F., the Chief of the Escape Organisation in the East Compound at that Camp. Squadron Leader Turner appointed 964794 W/O. Olliver, R.B., R.A.F. as his understudy and kept him fully informed in case he and Group Captain Macdonald were moved to another Camp.

From then onwards additional escape information was obtained from the 'Trading' organisation.

An Unteroffizier in the Abwehr department was bribed to give warning of all searches. Although these activities were suspected by the superiors and an attempt made to put a stop to it, the Unteroffizier was able to give five minutes' warning of all searches. This was done by means of a signalling system.

(c) *Contacts, July, 1943 – November, 1943.*

Following the departure of Squadron Leader Turner the position of Escape Intelligence Officer was taken over by Olliver as planned and the latter controlled the 'Trading' Organisation. He briefed the 'traders' about what information was required and all reports were made to him.

122

(d) *Journeys outside Camp, October, 1942 – January, 1943.*
Very few personnel were permitted to leave the Camp during this period, but those on visits to the dentist in Barth and to the hospital at Neu Brandenburg were briefed by the Barrack Leaders to obtain as much local information as possible. The Barrack Leader was briefed by 515590 W/O. Axford, J.L., R.A.F.

(e) *Journeys outside Camp, January, 1943 – July, 1943.*
Squadron Leader Turner briefed all personnel leaving the Camp on visits to the dentist and the hospital at Neu Brandenburg. They were advised about the type of information which was required and were interrogated by Squadron Leader Turner when they returned to the Camp.

(f) *Journeys outside Camp, July, 1943 – November, 1943.*
The same conditions applied a during the preceding period, except that the briefing and interrogation was carried out by 964794 W/O. Olliver, R.B., R.A.F.

(g) *Recaptured escapers, October, 1942 – January, 1943.*
All recaptured escapers were interrogated, following their return to the Compound, by 515590 W/O. Axford, J.L., R.A.F. This also applied to those who were captured before leaving the precincts of the Camp.

(h) *Recaptured escapers, January, 1942 – July, 1943.*
During this period all recaptured escapers were interrogated by a member of the Escape Committee after their return to the Compound.

(i) *Recaptured escapers, July, 1943 – November, 1943.*
The scheme which is outlined in the preceding paragraph was continued during this period.

(k) *New P's/W, October, 1942 – November 1943.*
All new P's/W were interrogated soon after arrival by an Escape Committee representative.

(l) *From I.S.9., October, 1942 – November 1943.*
No information was received from I.S.9, other than target maps of German ports.

(m) *From other sources.*
Details of the district in which the Camp was situated were supplied to intending escapers by 970053 W/O. Everson, J.H., R.A.F. He had feigned

stomach trouble during his previous stay at the Camp in 1941 in order to visit Stralsund Hospital for the purpose of gaining local topographical knowledge. The Escape Committee arranged such briefings.

12. SUPPLIES

Material for use in connection with escape activities were obtained from the following sources:

(a) *Contacts, October, 1942 – January, 1943.*
During this period trading with the Germans was not controlled by the P/W Administration, or the Escape Organisation, with the result that a large amount of trading was carried out by individuals who had no interest in escape matters. Prices were exorbitant, e.g. 1,500 cigarettes were paid for a pair of ice skates.

The Germans were able to obtain the goods they wanted in exchange for articles which should have been available in the Camp Canteen with the result that no items of value to the Escape Organisation were obtained by bribery.

In addition, this uncontrolled trading which was carried on solely to increase the personal comfort of those P's/W engaged in it was the cause of much jealousy and rivalry amongst the P's/W as a whole.

(b) *Contacts, January, 1943 – July, 1943.*
Shortly after the arrival of Group Captain Macdonald and Squadron Leader Turner in January, 1943, the former issued an order that no P/W was to hold conversation with a German or to have trading relations with the enemy unless specially authorised to do so. A few days later a small number of N.C.O.'s were selected by Squadron Leader Turner and briefed by him about the methods to be used to acquire materials from the Germans. At first non-contraband goods were to be obtained in exchange for cigarettes, chocolate, etc. A scale of prices was fixed and the goods were distributed in this Camp.

When this scheme had been in operation for some time the 'traders' were instructed to induce their 'contacts' to supply inks, pens, dyes, paper, uniform insignia, tools, etc., in return for larger quantities of cigarettes, chocolate, etc. This was successful and some of each of these materials was passed on to the Escape Organisation. Wireless parts were obtained also and some Germans lent their Gate Passes for copying. However, a certain amount of unauthorised trading was carried on throughout this period.

The personnel engaged on authorised 'trading' were:

970434 W/O. Eames, J.J.W.	R.A.F.
970053 W/O. Everson, J.E.	R.A.F.
Driver May,	R.A.S.C.
Pte. Milner, D.	
550365 W/O. Smith, W.G.	R.A.F.

During this period all personnel who were being sent to the hospital at Neu Brandenburg for treatment were briefed by Squadron Leader Turner and instructed to obtain civilian clothes, wireless parts, identity documents, etc., from the French orderlies there. This was very successful and such items were acquired in exchange for cigarettes. When the P's/W returned to the Camp these items were concealed on their persons or amongst their possessions. They were then handed over to the Escape Organisation.

(c) *Contacts, July, 1943 – November, 1943.*
The 'trading' Organisation outlined above continued to function with the same personnel during this period working under the direction of 964794 W/O. Olliver, R.B., R.A.F. Contact was maintained with the French orderlies at Neu Brandenburg Hospital.

(d) *Camp resources, October, 1942 – January, 1943.*
The main escape activity during this period was tunnelling and materials required for this purpose, i.e. bed boards for shoring, etc. were supplied by the personnel engaged in this work. Tools, pens, inks, rope, etc. were stolen from the Germans; also German uniform caps.

(e) *Camp resources, January, 1943 – July, 1943.*
Escape materials which were required during this period were collected by the barrack representatives on the Escape Committee. Items which had been confiscated by the Germans were stored in a building in the Vorlager. Some of these were recovered for the Escape Committee by Driver May R.A.S.C.

(f) *Camp resources, July, 1943 – November, 1943.*
The position outlined above continued during this period.

(g) *New P's/W, October, 1942 – January, 1943.*
No escape materials were obtained from the new P's/W during this period.

(h) *New P's/W, January, 1943 – July, 1943.*
When Group Captain Macdonald and Squadron Leader Turner arrived

125

from Stalag Luft III they brought copies of forged Identity Cards and other documents concealed in the binding of books. Escape maps and compasses were obtained from new P's/W who had managed to conceal them during searches following capture.

(i) *New P's/W, July, 1943 – November, 1943.*
New P's/W were induced to hand over maps, compasses, etc. which they had managed to conceal.

(j) *Parcels from I.S.9., October, 1942 – January, 1943.*
A small number of games parcels containing escape aids were received by individuals, but no warning had been sent of their impending arrival; also the recipients were unaware of their contents.

The Escape Committee endeavoured to keep trace of such parcels in order to examine them, but were not always successful. They found it impossible to discover why these games parcels containing escape aids were addressed to personnel who had no interest in escape, or why no advice had been sent to the camp by means of a code message. The N.C.O. in charge of the Coding Section had no information.

(k) *Parcels from I.S.9., January, 1943 – July, 1943.*
During this period a small number of games parcels containing escape aids were received. Generally these were acquired by the Escape Organisation before being issued to the addressee as a specially briefed N.C.O. worked in the Parcel Store.

(l) *Parcels from I.S.9., July, 1943 – November, 1943.*
A number of parcels containing food were received during this period by individuals who were unaware that the tin might contain escape aids. The addressees used the food and discarded the tins. It would appear that the Escape Organisation did not take any steps to check the tins.

13. CARPENTRY
(a) *October, 1942 – January, 1943.*
The only carpentry work which was undertaken during this period was in connection with tunnel construction and hiding places for escape material. The shoring of tunnels was done by the personnel engaged in tunnel construction. The making of hiding places in walls of barracks, etc. was done by the person concerned.

(b) *January, 1943 – July, 1943.*
The shoring of tunnels was done by the personnel engaged in their

126

construction. About March, 1943, a false bottom was made for a hand-wagon used for transporting materials from the Compound to the Vorlager, etc. This was to be used to conceal a man whilst he was taken to a dump, situated about half a mile from the Camp, where empty food tins were disposed of about twice weekly. The scheme was not put into effect because the German who accompanied the wagon and was agreeable to the scheme, was posted away from the Camp. The construction of the false bottom was done by:

NZ.403486 W/O. Blakeway, R.B. R.N.Z.A.F.
NZ.391384 W/O. Howard, P.N.   R.N.Z.A.F.

A concealed hinged panel was made between two rooms in order to enable a P/W to be counted twice to cover an escape.

(c) *July, 1943 – November, 1943.*
The only woodwork which was done in connection with escape during this period was the shoring of tunnels; done by the personnel engaged on their construction.

14. METAL WORK
(a) *October, 1942 – January, 1943.*
No metal work was done during this period.

(b) *January, 1943 – July, 1943.*
A number of Polish and Czechoslovakian P's/W, who were serving with the R.A.F., were skilled in moulding metal. The Germans allowed them to have plaster-of-paris for making models of aircraft, etc. These men also made uniform badges, buttons, belt-buckles, etc. for use on imitation German uniforms. A number of pairs of wire-cutters were made from ice-skates by:

905095 W/O. Hurrell, H.C.   R.A.F.
550365 W/O. Smith, W.G.   R.A.F.

(c) *July, 1943 – November, 1943.*
As above.

15. LEATHER WORK
(a) *October, 1942 – January, 1943.*
No leather work was undertaken due to lack of materials and tools.

(b) *January, 1943 – July, 1943.*
Various items of leather goods were made during this period. These included belts, pistol holders, conversion of flying boots into field boots, etc. Most of this work was done by 550365 W/O. Smith, W.G., R.A.F.

(c) *July, 1943 – November, 1943.*
As above.

16. TOOLS
(a) *October, 1942 – January, 1943.*
A few chisels, etc. were taken to this Camp from Stalag Luft III by the first batch of P's/W in October, 1942. These were concealed in loaves of bread.

(b) *January, 1943 – November, 1943.*
A small number of tools were acquired from Germans by the 'Trading' Organisation. The majority of tools used in connection with escape were stolen. These included about six pairs of wire-cutters, chisels, saw blades, hammers, gardening trowels, etc.

One of the P's/W who worked as a carpenter in the German workshop in the Vorlager was able to 'borrow' certain tools for a few hours at a time.

All tools were under the control of NZ.391384 W/O. Howard, P.N., R.N.Z.A.F.

17. GADGETS
No gadgets were made for use in connection with escape activities between October, 1942 and November, 1943.

18. TUNNEL CONSTRUCTION
(a) *General, October, 1942 – January, 1943.*
During this period the construction of tunnels was undertaken by groups of personnel working under the direction of 515590 W/O. Axford, J.L., R.A.F., the Chairman of the Escape Committee.

The policy was to have one tunnel under construction from each barrack at a time. No tunnels were started by groups of individuals working independently of the Escape Committee.

(b) *Engineering, October, 1942 – January, 1943.*
There were no special engineering features in any of the tunnels which were attempted during this period. Approximately ten tunnels were started, but all were discovered prior to completion. This was

128

due to discovery through the use of dogs and the tunnel detector system.

The most active personnel in connection with tunnel construction were:

741918	W/O. Adams, D.A.	R.A.F.
515590	W/O. Axford, J.L.	R.A.F.
N.Z.403486	W/O. Blakeway, R.B.	R.N.Z.A.F.
N.Z.405222	W/O. Bowling, R.	R.N.Z.A.F.
546056	W/O. Carruthers, P.W.	R.A.F.
947674	W/O. Chown, C.M.	R.A.F.
632266	W/O. Croft, S.R.	R.A.F.
741990	W/O. Dunphy, D.C.	R.A.F.
A.406196	W/O. Evans, J.D.	R.A.A.F.
790053	W/O. Everson, J.E.	R.A.F.
619031	W/O. George, O.F.	R.A.F.
A.402117	W/O. Gillespie, B.C.	R.A.A.F.
N.Z.391384	W/O. Howard, P.N.	R.N.Z.A.F.
	L/S James	N.A.A.
31341	A/Sgt. Korsen, L.	S.A.A.F.
778298	W/O. Laing, J.K.B.	R.A.F.
968023	W/O. Maddocks, R.	R.A.F.
R.64816	W/O. Miller, T.B.	R.C.A.F.
964794	W/O. Olliver, R.B.	R.A.F.
550365	W/O. Smith, W.G.	R.A.F.
628502	W/O. Thompson, E.	R.A.F.
904944	W/O. Thrower, D.B.	R.A.F.

(c) *Dispersal, October, 1942 – January, 1943.*
The dispersal of the sand excavated from these tunnels was effected by spreading it under barrack floors, in the incinerator, and by mixing it with the soil in the gardens around the barracks. Wash bowls were used for the conveyance of the sand from the tunnel face to the dispersal site.

(d) *Supplies, October, 1942 – January, 1943.*
Bed boards for shoring were the only materials used during this period. These were collected from other P's/W by the personnel engaged in building the tunnels, but comparatively little shoring was needed because of the nature of the soil.

(e) *Security, October, 1942 – January, 1943.*
A member of each tunnelling team was always on duty as a watcher

whilst tunnelling or dispersal was in progress to give warning of the approach of Germans. Before work commenced the Compound was searched by the tunnellers to ensure that no German was in any of the barracks. Owing to the large number of small rooms in each barrack this was difficult and on one or two occasions Germans were not located with the result that personnel were apprehended.

(f) *Comments, October, 1942 – January, 1943.*
It would appear that the main reasons for failure to construct a successful tunnel during this period were:

(i) Lack of organisation and lack of co-operation between the personnel engaged on tunnel construction and those who had no interest in escape.
(ii) The collapse of tunnels due to the large number which had been constructed in a limited area over a period of years.
(iii) The efficiency of the German security measures, in particular the anti-tunnel device, and the failure of the P's/W to overcome this.

(g) *General, January, 1943 – November, 1943.*
Groups of individuals who were interested in tunnel construction approached their Barrack Escape Representative and required permission to begin work from the site which they had selected. The Escape Committee discussed the project and the site was examined by NZ.391384 W/O. Howard, P.M., R.N.Z.A.F., who had been appointed by the Escape Committee to be in charge of tunnelling. If the proposal was sound the Escape Committee gave authority to start work and rendered assistance where needed. From then on, the tunnellers made all their own arrangements and Howard supervised operations and gave advice.

(h) *Engineering, January, 1943 – November, 1943.*
Approximately eighteen tunnels were attempted during this period. Nine if these were under construction simultaneously in an attempt to overcome the German anti-tunnel device, but none was successful. Following this the Germans dug a trench.
    The P's/W attempted to overcome this new anti-escape measure and the details of this tunnel are given in paragraph (i) below. The other unsuccessful tunnel is described in paragraph (ii) because of the ingenuity shown.
        (i) As soon as the P's/W were permitted to return to the Compound following digging of the anti-tunnel trench, work was

commenced on the construction of a tunnel designed to reach beyond the fence in the minimum time. To accomplish this very little shoring was used.

The tunnel entrance was made under one of the barracks close to the site of one of the nine which had just been discovered. Within two days the lateral shaft had reached just beyond the fence and it was intended that the tunnel should be used that night. During the afternoon of that day, whilst eight men were at work in the tunnel warning was received from a German who had been bribed that an immediate search was to take place.

The eight men left the tunnel, concealed the entrance and disposed of their working clothes before the Germans arrived outside the barrack in a van three minutes after the warning signal had been received. They knew the approximate location of the tunnel through the anti-tunnel device and dug it up at once, but were most annoyed at not being able to apprehend those responsible.

(ii) Following the events related above it was ascertained that the only part of the perimeter of the Camp which had not been fitted with an anti-tunnelling device was close to the gate leading into Vorlager. It was decided to construct the tunnel from the wash-house, the distance to traverse being seventy feet to opposite the sentry tower beside the gate, the lateral shaft to run parallel to the fence to a point opposite the sentry tower, then at right-angles to under the sentry tower, where it was proposed to make the exit. The entrance shaft was made under the wooden steps leading into the wash-house.

Although these steps were in the open they could not be observed by any of the guards, and a watch was kept to give warning of any German approaching the gate. When work was not in progress the shaft was covered with boards over which sand was spread. When the vertical shaft had been sunk to a depth of about two feet a number of bricks were removed from the foundation wall of the wash-house and a space excavated in the sand below the concrete floor.

From this stage onwards when work was not in progress the bricks were replaced and the vertical shaft under the steps filled with sand to the level of the adjacent area. The lateral shaft was constructed through the sand beneath the concrete floor of the wash-house. A considerable amount of shoring was used, chiefly because the tunnel passed beneath one of the showers. The shower was not used and the drain plugged. The reason for this was that the water from the shower was not drained off, but merely seeped away through the sand.

At the end of approximately four weeks the tunnel had reached the end of the wash-house, a distance of about forty feet. In order to facilitate the disposal of the sand from the second half of the tunnel, which was very much darker in colour, the existing tunnel was enlarged to about four feet in height and five feet in width.

About this time the Germans became suspicious about the wash-house and conducted a surprise search whilst six men were at work in the tunnel. However, the entrance had been closed and by means of pre-arranged signal those men were instructed to remain quiet. The Germans spent three hours in the area, probing the floor of the wash-house and the soil around the building with crowbars, but without making any discovery. When they had left the Compound the tunnellers were released and the entrance re-sealed. Work was suspended for a fortnight as the Germans were watching the area through field-glasses from the Flak Training School situated about 200 yards distant. At the end of that time this watch was withdrawn and work on the tunnel was resumed.

At the end of two weeks the tunnel had reached the area under the sentry tower and was ready for use. It was intended that seventy men should attempt to escape by this means and as a safety measure it was decided the attempt would be made at the end of the moon period – about five days later.

During this waiting period a new P/W who had just arrived in the Camp used the shower situated above the tunnel. He removed the plug from the drain and ran the shower at full strength for some time. By the time this was discovered by those connected with the tunnel water was seeping through the loose bricks under the steps and a large area of damp was visible. The tunnelling team endeavoured to cover this with dry sand, but the guard in the nearby sentry tower noticed this activity and advised the Abwehr by telephone. A few minutes later a number of Germans entered the Compound to investigate.

At first they were unable to locate the tunnel entrance, but after a time they broke through the concrete floor and discovered the tunnel, which was filled in forthwith. This was about July or early August, 1943.

The most active personnel in connection with tunnelling were:

741918	W/O. Adams, D.A.	R.A.F.
983733	W/O. Abbott, A.W.	R.A.F.

515590	W/O. Axford, J.L.	R.A.F.
NZ.403486	W/O. Blakeway, R.B.	R.N.Z.A.F.
NZ.405222	W/O. Bowling, R.	R.N.Z.A.F.
546056	W/O. Carruthers, P.W.	R.A.F.
632266	W/O. Croft, S.R.	R.A.F.
741990	W/O. Dunphy, D.C.	R.A.F.
A.406196	W/O. Evans, J.D.	R.A.A.F.
A.402117	W/O. Gillespie, B.C.	R.A.A.F.
R.52692	W/O. Hayward, A.H.	R.C.A.F.
NZ.391384	W/O. Howard, P.N.	R.N.Z.A.F.
905095	W/O. Hurrell, H.L.	R.A.F.
778298	W/O. Laing, J.K.B.	R.A.F.
968023	W/O. Maddocks, R.	R.A.F.
928687	W/O. Macdonald, L.A.	R.A.F.
R.64816	W/O. Miller, T.B.	R.C.A.F.
NZ.414516	W/O. Moynihan, T.C.	R.N.Z.A.F.
964794	W/O. Olliver, R.B.	R.A.F.
R.142360	W/O. Rathburn, A.L.	R.C.A.F.
NZ.41192	W/O. Rowley, D.K.R.	R.N.Z.A.F.
550365	W/O. Smith, W.G.	R.A.F.
628502	W/O. Thompson, E.	R.A.F.
904944	W/O. Thrower, D.B.	R.A.F.

(i) *Dispersal, January, 1943 – November, 1943.*
The sand excavated from all the tunnels referred to above was disposed of under the barracks, mixed with the soil of gardens, etc. Dispersal of the sand from the tunnel was carried out in a most ingenious manner. At first the sand was dumped into the cesspool in the wash-house and lavatory building, but because this was becoming apparent it was decided to adopt a new method. Two tenni-quoit courts were marked out close to the wash-house and at certain periods, whilst play was in progress, the sand which had been excavated from the tunnel was deposited on the pitches. As the surface of the courts was of loose sand spread from a pit which had been dug nearby with the permission of the Germans, no suspicions were aroused. The dispersal of the dark sand from the second half of the tunnel was accomplished by packing it along the sides of the first portion, which was enlarged for this purpose.

(j) *Supplies, January, 1943 – November, 1943.*
The only supplies which were used in connection with tunnel construction during this period were bed boards and gardening trowels. The former were collected from their barracks by the members of the

Escape Committee. The gardening trowels were obtained from the Germans for cultivating garden plots.

(k) *Security, January, 1943 – November, 1943.*
The general Camp security system was employed to ensure that personnel were not apprehended whilst engaged on tunnel construction. This was very satisfactory.

(l) *Comments, January, 1943 – November, 1943.*
Failure to construct a wholly successful tunnel during this period may be attributed to the following factors:

(i) For the first few months no attempt was made to circumvent the German anti-tunnel device although the P's/W knew how it operated. Eventually a tunnel was constructed which passed under the fence at the only point which was not protected in this way. The tunnel was discovered by the Germans when completed and ready for use because of lack of foresight on the part of the personnel responsible for the construction. It was realised that the use of a particular shower, situated above the lateral shaft, would endanger the project. The method adopted to avert this was to discontinue using that shower and to plug the drain. The inadvertent removal of the plug and use of the shower by a new P/W led to the discovery of the tunnel. If a pipe-line of tins had been made to lead water from the drain-hole of the shower to well below the level of the floor of the tunnel, the shower could have been used in the normal way thus increasing security and it is probable that the tunnel would have been successful.
(ii) The German anti-tunnelling device was successful in this Camp because the water table was about five to six feet below the surface in most parts of the Camp. This made it impossible to tunnel at a sufficient depth to be beyond the effective range of the microphones.
(iii) During the first few months the Germans knew that tunnelling was being done, quite apart from the warning given by the anti-tunnel device because no means had been found by P's/W to dispose of excavated sand in such a way that no suspicions were aroused.

19. GATE WALK-OUT SCHEMES
(a) *First attempt.*
In December, 1942, two N.C.O's walked out of the Compound disguised as German personnel. They were:

964794   W/O. Olliver, R.B.   R.A.F.
           W/O. Wood, G.   R.A.F.

Their "Luftwaffe" uniforms and forged gate passes were produced in the Camp. They passed through the Compound gate successfully, which took them into the Compound in which the Camp theatre was situated. They went into the theatre and hid in a cupboard with the intention of waiting until nightfall before attempting to leave the Camp by cutting through the perimeter fence.

Apparently, they had been seen entering the theatre, because a search of the building was carried out about half and hour later and they were discovered.

(b) *Second attempt.*
On 8th February, 1943, an attempt was made to walk out of the Camp disguised as a German by 742018 W/O. Blair, D., R.A.F. His "Luftwaffe" uniform consisted of an altered airman's greatcoat fitted with Luftwaffe buttons and insignia. He passed through the Compound gate without difficulty, but before he reached the gate leading into the Vorlager he met a German who recognised him.

(c) *Third attempt.*
About February, 1943, an attempt to walk out of the Camp disguised as a German guard was made by 580370 W/O. Hart, C.S., R.A.F. His "Luftwaffe" uniform was produced in the Camp. It was his intention to leave the Compound with the party of Germans which locked the barracks and closed the shutters at dusk. He could speak fluent German. As he approached the Compound gate one of the Germans noticed an irregularity in his dress and he was arrested.

20. WIRE SCHEMES
(a) *First attempt.*
In November, 1942, an escape was effected by 629843 W/O. Parkes, H., R.A.F. At this time he was working in the cookhouse, which was situated in an adjacent, unoccupied, Compound. This was guarded by only one sentry tower. Parkes was permitted to go to the cookhouse without an escort.

One morning it was extremely foggy and Parkes asked the guard on the Compound gate to allow him to take an assistant with him to the cookhouse. This was agreed to and the assistant reported to the cookhouse instead of Parkes.

135

Under cover of the fog Parkes climbed over the fence of the unoccupied Compound and began walking towards Stralsund. After about four hours he was stopped by German civilians and asked where he was going. He answered in rather poor German and was taken to a house whilst the police were informed. He was taken to Stralsund by car and interrogated. An hour later he was returned to Camp.

(b) *Second attempt.*

The second escape made via the fence was carried out by 628502 F/Sgt. Thomson, E., R.A.F. In December, 1942, a party of Russian P's/W arrived in the Camp and were accommodated in the Compound in which the cookhouse was situated. Thomson observed that when the Air force N.C.O's finished using the cookhouse each day, the guard locked up and went off duty. A party of N.C.O's was escorted from their own Compound to the cookhouse to collect the food which had been prepared, using a hand-wagon for transport. Thomson decided to get into the other Compound unobserved by hiding in this.

The Escape Committee approved of his scheme and supplied him with a Polish Army greatcoat and a pair of civilian trousers made from a German blanket. He had saved some food and was in possession of a compass.

On the selected day in December Thomson was hidden in the hand-wagon and taken to the cookhouse by the ration party. Whilst the attention of the guard was diverted he climbed out and hid in a coal bin. He remained there until all the Germans had left the Compound after locking up for the night, then climbed over the fence.

He walked towards Lubeck for about four and a half hours, but did not cover a great distance as he had to retrace his steps owing to having taken a road which led to an aerodrome. He got to a railway level-crossing and after watching the man in the box for some time, decided he was asleep and began to cross the line. He was grabbed by a guard who handed him over to the police. He was returned to the Camp.

(c) *Third attempt.*

In early May, 1943, a partly successful attempt to escape was made by 787232 W/O. Kopal, G., R.A.F. This N.C.O. who was a Czech serving in the R.A.F., noticed that the German guards had become very lax with the Russian P's/W and were allowing them to pass from their own Compound into the Vorlager unescorted. He decided to impersonate a Russian as part of a plan to get out of the Camp and approached the Escape Committee. He was supplied with a foreign worker's pass, Russian-type clothing, etc., and arrangements were made for his admission to the Camp Sick Quarters.

On the selected day he walked out of the Sick Quarters dressed as a Russian P/W and entered the Russian Compound with a plank on his shoulder. He hid in a barrack in this Compound until about 2200 hours, when he climbed the single strand fence into the Vorlager. He walked across to the German Officers' Mess and passed through a wicket gate which led outside the Camp.

He walked South until about 0200 hours when he missed his way in the darkness and got close to a large factory. As he was walking away from it the air raid alarm was sounded and he was challenged by a watchman. He was forced to go into an air-raid shelter where he was questioned, then arrested. He was returned to the Camp next morning.

(d) *Fourth attempt.*

In May, 1943, a plan was formulated by 968327 W/O. Kerr, W.E., R.A.F., to cut through the double fence of the Compound during the hours of darkness on a suitable night. When his plans were completed he invited R.64816 W/O. Miller, T.B., R.C.A.F., to accompany him, as he needed assistance to get through the fence. Miller agreed and they obtained civilian shirts, pullovers and Camp-made caps. They had concentrated food, German money, toilet equipment etc. but no identity papers.

It was raining and stormy on 12th May, 1943, and they got ready to make the attempt. About 1800 hours they hid underneath the stage of the Camp Theatre, which was out-of-bounds during the hours of darkness as it was situated close to the perimeter fence. At 2200 hours, after the Germans had completed their nightly search of the theatre, they burrowed underneath the wooden wall of the side of the theatre at a spot which was partially obscured from the searchlights situated in the sentry towers on the fence. One tower was about forty yards from the theatre on one side, and the second tower was about twenty yards distance on the other side.

They emerged in a patch of ground which had been roughly dug in preparation for a vegetable garden. They had blackened their faces and wore socks over their shoes and gloves. They crawled over the rough ground to a slight depression about twenty-five yards from one of the sentry towers.

At this point the grass was about eighteen inches in height. Kerr cut through the first part of the fence, which was lighted by arc lamps at intervals of about twenty yards and patrolled on the outside by one sentry who passed the selected spot at five minute intervals. He used wire cutters obtained from a German by bribery. While Kerr was cutting through the fence Miller watched the two sentry towers and the patrolling guard from a position about five yards from the fence on the rough ground. When he saw the patrolling sentry approaching on his beat he whistled softly and Kerr left the fence and joined him. After the sentry had passed Kerr returned to the gap he had made, completed pegging the entanglements and cut through the second fence. Then he threw the wire cutters to Miller, who buried them for recovery by the P/W who looked after the garden, as pre-arranged. During this time Kerr crawled through the gap in the fence, then Miller followed while Kerr watched for the patrolling sentry.

When Miller joined Kerr, after closing the gap in the outside fence, they crawled about thirty yards to a wooden fence surrounding the nearby Flak School. They lay there until they sighted the sentry patrolling the gun positions, which were about forty yards distant. When he had passed round the side of the nearest gun, they crawled along the fence until they were beyond the patrolled area: this was about midnight.

They stood up and began to walk South-East across country towards Grimmen, where they intended to board a train for Stettin, thus avoiding the military concentrations around Stralsund. At dawn on the 13th May they hid in a small copse, where they remained until dusk. They walked through wooded country throughout that night and the following day.

At 1800 hours on 14th May they arrived at Grimmen and hid in a wood near the railway station until midnight. They went into the goods yard and found an empty wagon labelled "Stettin" and due to be delivered next day. They climbed into it and about 0700 hours on 15th May a goods train drew alongside. They could see that the labels on the wagons were marked "Stettin". They left the wagon in which they had been hiding just as the train was moving off and clambered into an open wagon. The train stopped outside the station and the wagon in which they had spent the night was hitched on.

A railway worker jumped on to the side of the wagon in which they were lying. He signalled to the train driver and the train began to move. Just as he was about to jump off, he looked into the wagon and saw Kerr and Miller. He signalled to the driver to stop and asked them what they were doing there. They stated that they were Italian and he told them it was forbidden to travel in that way. He took them to the Station Master who telephoned for the police.

When two policemen arrived shortly afterwards and asked for their identity papers they admitted that they were escaped P's/W. They were taken to the Police Station and searched, then placed in a cell. Later that day they were returned to the Camp.

(e) *Fifth attempt.*
About June, 1943, an escape was attempted via the wire by:

781607   W.O. Grabowski, E.   R.A.F.
928063   W.O. Sadezsky, L.W. R.A.F.

The attempt was approved by the Escape Committee and arrangements were made for Grabowski and Sadezsky to be admitted to the Camp Sick Quarters; also for assistance from the Russian P's/W.

Under cover of darkness they left the Sick Quarters and entered the barrack occupied by the Russians through a window which had been left open for them. Sadezsky left the barrack first, but was apprehended before he reached the fence.

Grabowski left the barrack a few minutes later, climbed the single strand fence into the German Compound and walked past the German Officers mess into the woods. Shortly afterwards he was captured by German guards through having entered a forbidden zone. He was returned to the Camp.

(f) *Sixth attempt.*

In August, 1943, civilian workmen were repairing the roofs of the barracks. Whilst they were away for their midday meal two civilian jackets and a pair of overalls which they had left unattended were stolen by 628505 F/Sgt. Thomson, E., R.A.F. He had planned to make an attempt to escape with 632266 W.O Croft, S.R., R.A.F., and as soon as the clothing had been acquired, they approached the Escape Committee. Their scheme was approved and they were supplied with a pair of wire cutters.

They prepared a hiding place under the floor of the Camp Theatre in which to conceal themselves when the Germans carried out their nightly search of the buildings. It was arranged they would be followed by:

742018   W.O Blair, D.   R.A.F.
N.Z.404447 W.O. McKay, L.   R.N.Z.A.F

During the afternoon of 8th August, 1943 the four of them hid in the theatre. About midnight they burrowed under the side wall of the building and crawled to the perimeter fence. It took between two and three hours to cut through the fence as work had to be stopped each time the sentry passed on his beat outside the wire.

When the cutting had been completed the wirecutters were buried in the garden for recovery by the gardener and returned to the Escape Committee. Croft and Thomson crawled through the gap, but Blair and McKay turned back as it was getting light. They returned to the theatre where they were picked up by the Germans some hours later.

139

Croft and Thomson crawled across a field for some distance, then walked South across country. They reached the outskirts of Stralsund during the afternoon of 9th August, and hid until dark. They walked to the railway yard, where they were apprehended by a railway worker and handed over to the police. They were returned to the Camp next day.

(g) *Seventh attempt.*
On 12th August, 1943, an escape was made by climbing the fence in broad daylight by 515590 W.O. Axford, J.L., R.A.F. He had observed that on some occasions there was a period of four minutes when a stretch of the fence was unguarded during the change-over of the guards.

At noon on this day he was prepared for his attempt and saw that the fence was unguarded. As he climbed the fence he was seen by two girls who informed the Camp, but he was able to hide in some rushes at the side of a nearby creek. He remained there until about 2330 hours, but he was apprehended by a cycle patrol as he was crossing a road a few minutes after leaving his hiding place. He was returned to the Camp.

(h) *Eighth attempt.*
On 6th September, 1943, an attempt to escape by:

515590	W.O. Axford, J.L.	R.A.F.
632266	W.O. Croft, S.R.	R.A.F.

They were occupants of the same cell, serving sentences for their attempts to escape as related above. Axford had managed to conceal a hacksaw blade when he was taken to the cell, and whilst he and Croft were serving their sentence they bribed the German guards to bring them money, food, a needle and cotton, etc. They altered their tunics to resemble civilian jackets.

When their preparations were completed, they sawed through the bars of their cell and got out of the building about 2200 hours. They crawled across the Vorlager to the perimeter fence and were attempting to cut through it when they were seen by a patrolling sentry. They were put into other cells.

21. WALL SCHEMES
Not applicable.

22. TRANSPORT SCHEMES
Nil.

23. MISCELLANEOUS SCHEMES

(a) *First attempt.*

On 17th October, 1942, an attempt to escape was made by 74208 W.O. Blair, D., R.A.F. He had discovered by observation that the Compound in which the cookhouse was situated was not well guarded. On this day he persuaded a member of the party of P's/W who worked in the cookhouse to allow him to take his place.

During the morning he had eluded the German in charge of the cookhouse and got into the theatre, located in the same building. He removed the badges and R.A.F. buttons from his battle-dress blouse and affixed a Polish worker's "P" badge to it. He was wearing German ski-trousers.

He left the theatre and collected a wheelbarrow and shovel from another part of the Compound, and walked to near the perimeter fence where a Polish worker had been laying a pipeline. He began to extend the trench under the fence, but about an hour later he was arrested.

This was brought about by the fact that a fellow P/W had gone to the lavatory and locked the door, then climbed through the window and returned to the kitchen in order to provide an alibi if the German should ask for Blair. The guard had not noticed Blair's absence, but when he wished to use the lavatory he could not get in. When he got no reply after knocking on the door, he went outside and looked through the window. When he saw that it was empty he concluded that one of the P's/W had escaped and caused a search to be made of the Compound.

(b) *Second attempt.*

An unusual type of escape was effected in February, 1943, by 632266 W.O. Croft, S.R., R.A.F. He had heard that it was easy to escape from the hospital in Neubrandenburg so proposed a scheme which was approved by the Escape Committee.

He persuaded the German doctor in the Camp Sick Quarters that he ought to have his tonsils removed and was sent to the hospital at Neubrandenburg. He was under observation there for twelve days, but his tonsils were not removed. During this time, he acquired civilian clothing, money and food from Polish orderlies.

At about 1900 hours on the twelfth day he walked out of the hospital building disguised as a Serbian worker. There were sentries on patrol outside the fence surrounding the hospital at intervals of about fifty yards and the fence was illuminated by searchlights. Croft climbed over the fence without being seen.

He walked to Pasewalk, about sixty kilometres distant, arriving the next afternoon. He went to the railway station, but whilst in the goods

141

yard he was seen by railway workers who gave chase. He managed to evade them by jumping on a train which was just leaving the station at that moment.

The train arrived at Stralsund that evening and Croft hid there, in the station, until next morning.

At about 0630 hours he boarded a goods train and arrived at Stettin about 1730 hours. He went to the docks and wandered around for about four hours looking for a neutral ship. Finally he was challenged by a policeman and, as he had no identity papers, he was taken to Stettin Military Prison. He admitted that he was an escaped P/W and was returned to Stalag Luft I three days later.

(c) *Third attempt.*

In April, 1943, an attempt was made to escape by 742018 W.O. Blair, D., R.A.F. He was a member of a party of P's/W on a visit to a dentist in the town of Barth. Whilst the party was waiting outside the dentist's house the guard was engaged in conversation with some girls. Croft slipped into the dentist's house unobserved, removed his tunic and walked out of another door with the tunic over his arm. He was wearing his R.A.F. trousers and pullover. As he walked along the street a civilian, whom he had passed, raised the alarm and he was apprehended by a railway worker.

(d) *Fourth attempt.*

An abortive attempt was made in November, 1942, by:

A.402117	W.O. Gillespie, B.C.	R.A.A.F.
R.61024	W.O. Sikal, M.F.	R.C.A.F.

They were hidden in palliases and carried out of the Compound by a number of fellow P's/W on a visit to the coal-shed, situated in the Vorlager, for fuel. The palliases were left in the coal shed and Gillespie and Sikal intended to remain in hiding until nightfall before attempting to get out of the Vorlager.

Some time later a German entered the coal shed and searched amongst the palliases. They were discovered and arrested.

24. NUMBER OF ESCAPES

During the period under review no escaper was successful in leaving German-occupied territory.

25. NUMBER OF ATTEMPTED ESCAPES

During this period twenty-three personnel were involved in fifteen separate attempts to escape. In addition, eighteen tunnels were started.

26. MASS ATTEMPTS
Nil.

27. SUMMARY OF METHODS
(a) *Tunnels.*
The tunnel described [earlier in] this Chapter is worthy of special note. The method of dispersal of the darker sand from the second half of this tunnel was most ingenious.

(b) *Gate-walk out schemes.*
All attempts of this type are described in Section 17 of this Chapter. It is remarkable that not one escaper succeeded in getting out of the Camp by this method.

(c) *Wire schemes.*
There were eight separate attempts to escape by negotiating the wire. All were carefully planned to take advantage of conditions.

(d) *Wall schemes.*
Not applicable.

(e) *Transport schemes.*
Nil.

(f) Comments.
It is clear that a number of P's/W were very enthusiastic. However, it is evident that the majority were not well prepared with information or equipment. It is apparent that no escaper was supplied with adequate identity documents for use after leaving the Camp.

Chapter 14

Escape Material

28. AIDS RECEIVED FROM I.S.9

The escape aids which were received from I.S.9. during this period were mainly maps, compasses and money. It has not been possible to ascertain what quantities of these materials arrived in the Camp, but it is believed that few parcels were received.

29. REMARKS ON PACKING

(a) *Material received.*
The escape aids referred to above were packed in games parcels and in double-sided milk tins in comforts parcels. The method of packing was satisfactory for the type of material received.

(b) *Suggestions for the future.*
Paper suitable for making certain types of forged documents could be sent in the form of inner wrappings of parcels.

Large quantities of escape aids of the type required by this Camp could have been dispatched in parcels without camouflage. They could have been received safely if advice concerning their despatch and particulars of the addressee had been sent to the Camp by means of code messages. It is suggested that this method should be adopted in similar circumstances in the future.

30. CONCEALMENT OF ESCAPE AIDS – GADGETS ETC

As far as can be ascertained all the methods employed by I.S.9. for concealing the escape aids which were received during the period under review were successful.

31. AQUIREMENT OF SPECIAL PARCELS

No special parcels were received other than the games and food parcels already referred to. These passed through the German Camp censorship in the normal way.

32. MATERIAL AVAILABLE / ACQUIRABLE ON THE SPOT

Comparatively little escape material was available or acquirable in the Camp. This was due to uncontrolled or partially controlled, trading with the Germans and to the German security measures.

Chapter 15

Censorship and Communication

33. CENSORSHIP METHOD

(a) *Parcels.*

All parcels except those containing cigarettes and tobacco, which arrived in the Camp for the P's/W, whether individually addressed or for general distribution, were opened in the Parcel Store, situated in the Vorlager, by P's/W who worked under German supervision.

As a general rule all tins which contained food were punctured at one end. All parcels containing books, clothing, games, etc. were subjected to examination by a German. This censorship varied in intensity from time to time. Cigarette and tobacco parcels were not opened and were issued to the P's/W in their original wrappings.

In some cases parcels which the P's/W suspected of containing escape aids were mixed with those which had been censored and then taken into the Compound, but this was not the general practice.

(b) *Mail.*

The censorship of all mail for the P's/W in this Camp was carried out at Stalag Luft III (Sagan).

34. CENSORSHIP RESULTS

(a) *Parcels.*

The Germans did not discover any escape aids during the censorship of parcels.

(b) *Mail.*

The German censorship of mail appears to have been reasonably efficient. All obscure sentences, stilted phrases and groups of figures were blacked out. It is almost certain that the P/W code was not discovered.

146

35. OBJECT OF CENSORSHIP
(a) *Parcels.*
The object of censoring parcels appears to have been to prevent escape aids from entering the Camp and to puncture tins of food to prevent storage for escape purposes.

(b) *Mail.*
It is evident that the object of censoring mail was to delete passages, or possible keys to a code, which might convey useful information; also to discover, by tests with acid, whether messages were written in invisible ink.

36. PARCEL MARKINGS
The value of special markings on parcels containing escape aids despatched to individuals by I.S.9. e.g. Licensed Victuallers Association labels, etc. was not fully appreciated in the Camp. The Escape Organisation were unable to control such parcels and in many cases the addressees claimed their contents as their own property.

37. CENSORSHIP COMMENT
(a) *Parcels.*
The P's/W did not take full advantage of the German system of censoring parcels in order to get parcels containing escape aids into the Compound without censorship. This was due to friction and lack of co-operation between the Escape Organisation and the P/W Administration. The chief reason for the inability of the Escape Organisation to control parcels dispatched by I.S.9. was that they did not know who the addressees were. Full details should have been sent by I.S.9. by means of code messages, timed to arrive before the parcels.

(b) *Mail.*
Nil.

38. CODE-LETTER MAIL: INTRODUCTION
A number of N.C.O's who were transferred to this Camp in October, 1942, from Stalag Luft III, N.C.O's Compound, were taught the P/W code prior to leaving that Camp.

39. CODE-LETTER MAIL: ORGANISATION
Soon after the opening of the Camp a Coding Section was organised by the Camp Leader, 580309 W/O. May, T.K., R.A.F. The details of this

organisation are given in the following Sections of this Chapter under the heading: "October, 1942 – January, 1943".

When Group Captain Macdonald and Squadron Leader Turner arrived in the Camp in January, 1943, it was decided to reorganise the Coding Section. Squadron Leader Turner took control and tested all the N.C.O's who were using this code. As a result of this, six of the code users were suspended because they were not sufficiently expert in the use of the code. Ten other N.C.O's were trained, making a total of fifteen.

Before Squadron Leaded Turner left the Camp in July, 1943 he appointed 580309 W/O. May, T.K., R.A.F. to assume charge of the Coding Section and instructed him to continue along the lines then in operation.

(a) *Sources of information, October, 1942 – January, 1943.*

(i) New P's/W. All new arrivals in the Camp were interviewed by the Camp Leader who ascertained how each individuals aircraft was shot down, what military targets he had seen whilst travelling through Germany, etc. Such personnel were not informed that the information was to be sent to the United Kingdom.

(ii) P's/W on journeys outside the Camp. All personnel who went on journeys from the Camp beyond the Barth area, i.e. to hospital, etc. were interviewed on their return by the Camp Leader. They were asked to give details of anything of importance which they had seen, but they were not informed of the reasons.

(iii) Contacts. The Camp Leader obtained a certain amount of information from English speaking Germans with whom he came into contact.

(b) *Sources of information, January, 1943 – July, 1943.*

(i) New P's/W. All new arrivals in the Camp were interviewed by 25696 W/O. Drummond, R.R., R.A.F. [and] 580309 W/O. May, T.K., R.A.F., who worked under the directions of Squadron Leader Turner. The interrogations covered loss of aircraft, military targets seen in enemy occupied territory, details of German methods of interrogation at Dulag Luft, etc. The new arrivals were unaware of the purpose of the interrogation.

(ii) P's/W on journeys outside the Camp. All P's/W who went on journeys outside the Camp were instructed by Squadron Leader Turner to keep a sharp lookout for military installations, etc. He interrogated all such personnel when they returned to the Compound.

(iii) Contacts. All information collected by P's/W engaged in conversation with Germans was passed to Squadron Leader Turner. (iv) Recaptured escapers. All recaptured escapers were interrogated by Squadron Leader Turner when they returned to the Compound. A small amount of military information was obtained this way.

(c) *Sources of information, July, 1943 – November, 1943.*
During this period information was acquired from the sources described for the preceding period. All interrogations and briefings were carried out by 925696 W/O. Drummond, R.R., R.A.F. [and] 580309 W/O. May, T.K., R.A.F.

(d) *Collation, October, 1942 – January, 1943.*
The collation of information obtained from all sources was done by the Camp Leader, 580309 W/O. May, T.K., R.A.F., who compiled the messages for dispatch to the U.K.

(e) *Collation, January, 1943 – July, 1943.*
All the information was collected by 26183 G/C J.C. Macdonald R.A.F. [and] 26216 S/Ldr. W.H.N. Turner R.A.F., who originated all messages despatched to the U.K.

(f) *Collation, July, 1943 – November, 1943.*
All collation of information was done by 925696 W/O. Drummond, R.R., R.A.F. [and] 580309 W/O. May, T.K., R.A.F. They originated all messages sent to the U.K.

(g) *Coding staff, October, 1942 – January, 1943.*
The following were the registered code users, from whom messages were received by I.S.9.

    755011 W/O. Gough, E.W.E.   R.A.F.
    976383 W/O. McMullen, F.   R.A.F.

It is known that several other code users were taught and registered by 580309 W/O. May, T.K., R.A.F., but there is no record of any messages being received from him by I.S.9.

(h) *Coding staff, January, 1943 – July, 1943.*
At the beginning of this period all registered code users in the Camp were tested by Squadron Leader Turner. As a result six men were

suspended from using the code because they were not sufficiently expert in its use. Ten other P's/W were taught the code and registered, making a total of fifteen N.C.O's. The following were the registered users from whom messages were received by I.S.9:

1286392	W/O. Draper, E.C.	R.A.F.
755011	W/O. Gough, E.W.E.	R.A.F.
580078	W/O. Jones, A.E.	R.A.F.
976383	W/O. McMullen, F.	R.A.F.
564766	W/O. Robson, F.	R.A.F.
741584	W/O. Williams, J.F.	R.A.F.

All the above were using the box code.

| 26183 | G/CJ.C. Macdonald | R.A.F. |
| 26216 | S/Ldr. W.H.N. Turner | R.A.F. |

These two officers were using the "dictionary" code. It is known that a number of new code users were taught and registered by 580309 W/O. May, T.K., R.A.F., but there is no record of any messages from him being received by I.S.9.

(i) *Coding staff, July, 1943 – November, 1943.*
Messages were received by I.S.9. from the following:

1286392	W/O. Draper, E.C.	R.A.F.
755011	W/O. Gough, E.W.E.	R.A.F.
580078	W/O. Jones, A.E.	R.A.F.
976383	W/O. McMullen, F.	R.A.F.
564766	W/O. Robson, F.	R.A.F.
741584	W/O. Williams, J.F.	R.A.F.

It is known that the personnel who had been taught how to use the code by 580309 W/O. May, T.K., R.A.F., and registered by him, dispatched messages during this period. There is no record of any messages having been received from May by I.S.9.

(j) *Despatch of messages, October, 1942 – January, 1943.*
After the messages had been encoded by the code users and incorporated in their letters and postcards, they were posted in the normal way in the Camp post box.

(k) *Despatch of messages, January, 1943 – July, 1943.*
All letters and postcards which contained code messages were censored by Group Captain Macdonald or Squadron Leader Turner before being despatched from the Camp. The object of this was to ensure that no phrases which might be deleted by the German censorship were used, also that the phraseology was not stilted.

(l) *Despatch of messages, July, 1943 – November, 1943.*
As for the preceding period except that the censorship was done by 925696 W/O. Drummond, R.R., R.A.F. [and] 580309 W/O. May, T.K., R.A.F.

40. SECURITY
(a) *October, 1942 – January, 1943.*
No special arrangements were made for providing watchers whilst the code users were at work. As a rule the messages were encoded and decoded by the individuals in their own barrack room. In most cases this work was done in the evening after the barracks had been locked up. Code users destroyed their own "workings" etc.

(b) *January, 1943 – July, 1943.*
All "workings" and draft of messages were destroyed by the code users in the presence of Squadron Leader Turner, or Warrant Officer Drummond. There were no special watchers whilst encoding or decoding was in progress. This work was done in the barracks in the evening after "lock-up".

(c) *July, 1943 – November, 1943.*
As in the preceding period except that the "workings" etc. were destroyed in the presence of Drummond or May.

41. COMMENT
It is evident that a large amount of information was lost because of non-receipt of messages from Warrant Officer May.

42. RADIO: INTRODUCTION AND CONSTRUCTION
In October, 1942, work was begun by 905095 W/O. Hurrell, H.L., R.A.F., on the construction of a radio receiver. He was greatly handicapped by the fact that components were not obtainable from German sources by bribery so that he was forced to manufacture parts from scraps of material. He made a transformer with wire which was stolen from the

Germans, condensors from tinfoil obtained from cigarette packets and paper boiled in paraffin wax. The wax was acquired by bribery or from the wrappings of certain types of biscuits sent in Red Cross food parcels.

About April, 1943, Hurrell acquired an assistant who helped him considerably. He was 970434 W/O. Eames, J.J.W., R.A.F. Soon afterwards Eames was able to obtain some radio valves by bribing a German, but the receiver was not ready for use during the period under review.

43. RADIO SECURITY
The partially constructed receiver was concealed in a specially constructed cavity in a brick chimney in a barrack room. This was never discovered by the Germans.

44. NEWS LETTERS: INTRODUCTION
A small number of letters were received by certain P's/W from correspondents who were unknown to them. These contained topical news and out-of-date war news.

45. NEWS LETTERS: OPINIONS
It was thought that the news letters were intended to bolster morale, but this was not necessary as the progress of the war was known through the constant arrival of newly captured aircrew personnel.

Chapter 16

Intelligence and Anti-German Propaganda

46. MILITARY INFORMATION

(a) *Methods of collection.*
The means by which military information was obtained and despatched to the U.K. are described [elsewhere].

(b) *Value of direction from I.S.9.*
More detailed instructions from I.S.9. would have been welcome. The code users did not know exactly what information was most useful, nor how much detail was wanted.

(c) *Adherence to direction.*
As far as possible all instructions received from I.S.9. were obeyed. In a number of cases messages were received relating to personnel who were not accommodated in this Camp.

47. INTERNAL SECURITY

(a) *Organisation.*
All new arrivals were interrogated as related [earlier]. If any individual was considered to be doubtful he was required to give sufficient details of his Service career to enable a check to be made with other P's/W. There were no other internal security measures.

(b) *Peculiarities of Camp.*
The use of a large number of English-speaking Germans in an endeavour to obtain information through careless talk amongst the P's/W. They are known to have listened outside barracks after "lock-up".

The use by the Germans of an electrical system for indicating the location of vibrations caused by tunnelling as the perimeter fence was approached.

153

48. ANTI-GERMAN PROPAGANDA: INTRODUCTION
There was no organisation for the dissemination of propaganda amongst the Germans. However, a certain number of P's/W who were brought into contact with Germans did their utmost to lower the morale of these individuals. This was done during "friendly" conversations.

49. ANTI-GERMAN PROPAGANDA: RESULTS
It is not possible to assess the results of the propaganda ... but it is worthy of note that certain Germans always displayed a show of eagerness to hear what the P's/W had to say. There were many instances of propaganda stories being related by other Germans at a later date in an exaggerated form.

It is known that German personnel received frequent lectures from their officers about the evils of listening to tales told by the P's/W.

Part IV

OFFICERS' CAMP
November 1943 to May 1945

Chapter 17

Introduction

1. LOCATION AND DESCRIPTION OF CAMP

The location of the Camp is given in Part I. An aerial photograph of the whole Camp, which was taken in April, 1944, is at [Plate 1].

Towards the end of the period under review four Compounds were in use for the accommodation of the P's/W. The following is a brief survey of the expansion of the Camp:

(a) *South Compound.*

This Compound was in use for the accommodation of Air Force N.C.O's during the periods dealt with in Parts II and III of this volume. After the evacuation of the N.C.O's in November, 1943, the fifty who remained were accommodated in this Compound and the other Compound which had been in use during that period closed. After an interval of some days, parties of Air Force officers began to arrive. In December, 1943 all British and Dominion personnel were transferred to the West Compound and from that date onwards only American personnel occupied this Compound.

(b) *West Compound.*

As already stated, British and Dominion personnel were transferred to this Compound from the South Compound in December, 1943. A few weeks later the South Compound became filled with American personnel and during the next few months new arrivals of British and American personnel were placed in this Compound.

(c) *North Compound.*

This was a newly constructed Compound which was opened for the accommodation of American personnel in February, 1944. It comprised the area North of the points marked '20' and '6' on [Plate 1]. Access to it from the other Compounds could only be gained by passing through Vorlager.

(d) *South-West Compound.*
This Compound, which formed the officers' football field during the period dealt with in Part I of this volume, was opened for the accommodation of British and American personnel about March, 1944. The playing field was replaced by the enclosure marked '25' on [Plate 1].

2. CAMP CONDITIONS
(a) *Number of P's/W and accommodation.*
In November, 1943, just prior to the transfer to Stalag Luft VI of the N.C.O's who had been accommodated in this Camp, about fifty of them volunteered to remain behind in order to act as batmen to the Air Force officers who were due to arrive shortly after the transfer of the N.C.O's would be completed. The Germans agreed to this proposal and welcomed it as it was known that most of the officers would be new P's/W.

From November, 1943 until April, 1945 frequent batches of British and American Air Force officers arrived in the Camp and were accommodated in the various Compounds as indicated in Section 1. The final strength of the Camp was approximately two thousand British and Dominions and eight thousand American personnel. This total included a number of Air Force N.C.O's and Army personnel transferred from other Camps to act as orderlies.

In those Compounds that contained British and American personnel, the two services occupied separate barracks.

With the exception of the North Compound, personnel could pass freely from one Compound to the other, except during roll-calls and the hours of darkness, when the gates of all Compounds were locked.

The privilege of visiting North Compound was restricted to Compound Senior Officers and their assistants who attended weekly conferences there with Senior Allied Officers, to the orderlies engaged in dealing with the issue of parcels and other Camp duties, and to the N.C.O. who acted as liaison between the Senior British Officers and the Senior Allied Officer. He was 925696 W.O. Drummond, R.R., R.A.F. The accommodation provided by the Germans has been described in previous Parts of this volume.

(b) *German Administration.*
During the first few months of the period under review the Camp was guarded and administered by about two hundred German Air Force personnel. As the Camp expanded this number increased gradually to approximately five hundred. Except for roll-calls, anti-escape measures

and inspections for cleanliness, the administration of the Camp was left to the Senior Allied Officer.

(c) *P/W Administration.*
From the time of the evacuation of the main body of N.C.O's in November, 1943 until the arrival of the first party of officers some days later, the Camp was administered by 580309 W.O. May, T.K., R.A.F. The Senior officer of the first party to arrive in the Camp was 65517 S/Ldr. A. Abels R.A.F., and he assumed the position of Senior British Officer.

During the next few weeks the position of British Senior Officer was assumed by other, more senior, officers who arrived in this Camp. These were:

> 45667 S/Ldr. M.J. Harris   R.A.F.
> 63074 W/Cdr. J.A. Lee-Evans R.A.F.
> 32195 W/Cdr. F.W. Hilton   R.A.F.

In January, 1944 the large influx of American officers caused a change to be made in the Camp Administration. As a result of discussion between the Senior British Officer and the Senior American Officer, it was decided that the most senior officer in the Camp should be known as the Senior Allied Officer; also that the next ranking British and American Officer would be subordinate to him, each being in command of his own Service. This system operated until the evacuation of the Camp after the cessation of hostilities.

During the period January 1944 – May, 1945 the Senior Allied Officers were:

> Col. Hatcher   U.S.A.A.C.   January, 1944 – March, 1944
> Col. Barley   U.S.A.A.C.   March, 1944 – August, 1944
> Col Zemke   U.S.A.A.C.   August, 1944 – May, 1945.

During the period December, 1943 – May, 1945 the Senior British Officers were:

> 32195 W/Cdr. F.W. Hilton R.A.F.
>   December, 1943 – April, 1944
> 34006 G/C W.D. Marwood-Elton R.A.F.
>   April, 1944 – August, 1944
> 32195 W/Cdr. F.W. Hilton R.A.F.
>   August, 1944 – January, 1945
> 33075 G/C C.T. Weir R.A.F.   January, 1945 – May, 1945

In December, 1943 Wing Commander Hilton appointed the Senior Officer of each barrack to be responsible to him for the administration of that barrack. To assist him in the administration of the Camp he appointed officers to the following posts: (a) Senior Administrative Officer, (d) *Adjutant.*

This Staff, assisted by junior officers and N.C.O's administered the Camp after the fashion of a R.A.F. Unit. When the Americans took over their own administration it was done on similar lines. After Group Captain Marwood-Elton became Senior British Officer he appointed Wing Commander Hilton to be his Senior Staff Officer, but no changes were made in the mode of administration which continued until the evacuation of the Camp.

(e) *Roll Calls.*
The method adopted by the Germans for counting the P's/W was similar to that described in the History of Stalag Luft III (Sagan). Despite these elaborate precautions, first the Escape Committee and later the Security Organisation generally managed to cover up the absence of any P/W who had succeeded in escaping from the Camp. The method employed was to arrange for the attention of one or more guards to be detracted for a few seconds at a given moment in order to enable a P/W who had been counted to mingle with a group which had not been counted. At least four escapers were 'covered' in this way for short periods.

(f) *Food.*
The German rations were inadequate without the addition of Red Cross food parcels. For the first year sufficient Red Cross food parcels arrived in the Camp to permit of the issue of one to each P/W weekly. From November, 1944 until February, 1945 the quantity received was less than requirements and one parcel was divided between each two P's/W weekly. From February onwards no parcels arrived in the Camp and about this time the German issue of food was reduced in quantity also.

Throughout the period under review a vegetable plot was cultivated by 580721 W.O. Wells, J., R.A.F., but the space allotted to him in the Compound by the Germans was much too small. Other P's/W attempted to grow vegetables on the space between barracks. The reason for this was that the Germans did not supply sufficient quantities of fresh green vegetables.

The Germans did not supply milk to the P's/W at any time during this period.

In early 1944 a system was devised whereby P's/W could exchange items from their Red Cross parcels. This was organised as a private enterprise with the approval of the Senior British Officer, by 108911 F.O. A. Hassell R.A.F. The concern was known as 'Foodacco' Hassel had a number of partners.

When a P/W wished to dispose of any quantity of food, cigarettes, or tobacco he handed it to 'Foodacco' and was allotted a number of points. The scale of points varied with the supply and demand in respect of the various commodities. The P/W could obtain any other commodity in stock in exchange for the points he had gained, or he could have them placed to his credit for use at a later date.

The partners of 'Foodacco' deducted a small percentage of points from each transaction as payment for their work. The accounts were audited on behalf of the Senior British Officer.

Intending escapers were able to augment their food supply by trading such items as jam, margarine, fish, etc. for chocolate, biscuits, dried fruit, etc. through the agency of 'Foodacco'.

(g) *Clothing*.
Supplies of uniform, greatcoats, boots, underwear, shirts, socks, etc. were forwarded through the agency of the International Red Cross Society. At first the British were able to help the Americans with clothing, since the latter were badly equipped. At a later stage, the Americans received large supplies and were extremely generous in helping the British. British personnel always made a point of appearing on parades dressed in R.A.F. uniform.

All clothing of this type was distributed to the P's/W through their own administration. This was done under strict supervision by the Germans.

Items of uniform required for escape purposes had to be removed from the Clothing Store, situated in the Vorlager, without the knowledge of the Germans.

The officer in charge of clothing was 65517 S/Ldr. A. Abels R.A.F. His chief assistants were:

903431	W.O. Culley, J.M.	R.A.F.
745334	W.O. Read, L.R.	R.A.F.

(h) *Searches*.
The system of searches for forbidden articles, escape activities, etc., which was adopted by the Germans was the same as is described in Part III.

(i) *German anti-escape measures.*
During this period all the anti-escape measures described in Part III …
were continued. The number of English speaking Germans was
increased to four. A new measure which was adopted was for Germans
to listen to conversations between P's/W from outside the barracks
during the hours of darkness with the aid of amplifiers.

The members of the Abwehr department were very expert at
detecting freshly excavated sand from tunnels.

When the South-East Compound was brought into use about March
1944, the tunnel detector system, which is described in Part I, Chapter
I, Section 2, sub-Section (h) was not extended. It is believed that this
system was abandoned by the Germans about this time, in the other
Compounds, as it was proving to be unreliable.

(j) *Punishment for escape activities, etc.*
The usual punishment for attempted escapes, etc. was as is outlined in
Part I. However, the normal maximum sentence was increased to
fourteen days.

In the Autumn of 1944 the Germans posted notices in the various
Compounds to the effect that escaping was no longer a sport, that
certain areas in Germany were forbidden zones and any unauthorised
person entering them was liable to be shot.

Soon after this an American major escaped from the Camp. When he
was recaptured and returned to the Camp he was denied food or water
until he divulged the method of his escape. He was sentenced to a
longer term in cells than was usual prior to the posting of the warning
notices.

Owing to the changed attitude of the Germans, and after a talk with
a representative of the Protecting Power, the Senior British Officer
banned any further attempts to escape. This took place about
September, 1944. Soon afterwards a code message was received from
I.S.9 to the effect that escape was not considered to be a duty.

(k) *Education.*
Both the British and Americans appointed officers to be in charge of
education in the Camp. The British officer was 139379 F/O T.G. Wilson
R.A.F. An Education Representative was elected in each barrack and
these formed a committee. A syllabus of lectures was drawn up and
lecturers appointed. The classes were conducted in the Common Room,
or Library, situated in the West Compound. The Americans in the North
and South Compounds made their own arrangements.

Candidates were prepared for matriculation, banking, accountancy, and other examinations under the scheme sponsored by the British Red Cross Society Education Department.

Materials and books for education purposes were supplied by the British Red Cross Society and the Young Men's Christian Association.

When required, the Education Committee supplied paper, pens, inks, notebooks, etc., to the Forgery and Radio Sections.

(l) *Library*.
A library for the P's/W accommodated in the West and South-West Compounds was formed in the Common Room of the West Compound. Quantities of books were received from the International Red Cross Society and the Young Men's Christian Association. Contributions to the Library were made by P's/W who received parcels of books from the United Kingdom and the Dominions. The Librarian was 139484 F/O H.E. Peake R.A.F. Maps, money and documents for escape purposes were concealed in books in the Library.

(m) *Sports*.
The football field, which was situated on the South side of the West Compound, was in use until early, 1944 when barracks were erected and it became the South-West Compound. About this time a new football field was constructed on the West side of the West Compound. It is marked '25' on [Plate 1]. This was in use by the occupants of the West and South-West Compounds until the cessation of hostilities.

During the whole of the period under review the occupants of the South Compound used the space, marked '32' on [Plate 1] for their sports activities.

The occupants of the North Compound used spaces between their barracks for sporting activities.

Soccer and rugby were popular in all Compounds. Hockey, cricket and soft-ball games were played also. There were frequent matches between the British and Americans.

During the early Summer of 1944 bathing parties were taken out of the Camp to the beach a few hundred yards distant. The P's/W were on parole and accompanied by armed guards. They did not continue for long, however, because some Americans, who were members of one of these parties, stole wood.

Until mid 1944 the Sports Officer for the West and South-West Compounds was 103829 S/Ldr. D.J. Kilgallin R.A.F. Regiment. He handed over his duties to 43479 F/Lt. D.I. Pike R.A.F.

Sports equipment which was received from the Young Men's Christian Association was kept in a store in the West Compound, where it was available to the occupants of that Compound and the South-West Compound.

(n) *Amateur theatricals, etc.*
The Camp Theatre was situated in the same building as the cook-house and is marked '31' on [Plate 1]. It has been constructed after the opening of the Camp in 1940.

During the period dealt with here it was used by the occupants of the West, South-West and South Compounds. Plays, concerts, gramophone recitals, etc. were produced and were most popular.

The entertainment which was provided was of very high standard, due largely to the untiring efforts of:

132516   F/O W.C.H. Johnson R.A.F.   Producer
1252991 W/O Esheley, R.A.F.   Manager.
1165292 W.O. Vaughn, J. R.A.F.   Stage Scenery

It is understood that the Americans in the North Compound had their own theatre.

(o) *Religion.*
Roman Catholic and Church of England services were held each Sunday in the church which was situated in the same Compound as the cook-house. This was built during the earlier occupation of the Camp and is referred to in Part II.

Religious services were held each Sunday in the North Compound by the same padres, after they had conducted the services referred to in the preceding paragraph.

The padres, who resided in the West Compound, were:
Father Hall, until Mid 1944
Padre Charlton, H.L.I., mid 1944 – May, 1945
Rev. Drake-Brockman, until mid 1944
Rev. Mitchell, N.Z. Church Army, mid. 1944 – May, 1945

(p) *Shooting incidents.*
There was no serious shooting incidents until early, 1945, when two incidents occurred within a few days. Both were due to P's/W breaking a new order issued by the Germans that no one was allowed to be in the open during an air raid alarm.

The first occurrence of this kind was when an American Officer (name unknown) walked out of his barrack in the West Compound, not realising that there was an "alert". He was shot and killed.

The second incident occurred a few days later when a South African officer (name unknown) jumped out of a window of a barrack in the West Compound during an "Alert". He was shot in the abdomen, but was operated on at once by the British Medical Officer and recovered.

(q) *P/W Morale.*
During the greater part of the period under review the morale of the P's/W was very high. It was lowest in December, 1944 during the period of the Ardennes offensive. Although morale improved after that time, the general attitude was one of scepticism until the cessation of hostilities.

Great reliance was placed upon the daily news service. The fact that the B.B.C. news bulletins were being listened to on a secret radio receiver was the greatest single factor in maintaining morale throughout the period.

(r) *Medical.*
The medical services during this period were similar to those described in Part III. Most of the work was carried out by Captain Nicholls R.A.M.C. He performed several emergency operations with the minimum of equipment.

Medical supplies were inadequate at all times, but the standard of health of the P's/W was maintained at a very high level by the efforts of the Sick Quarters Staff.

The only death to occur in the Camp was when the American officer was shot as related in above.

(s) *Reprisals.*
In early 1944, when a German officer was passing through a barrack in the West Compound, a P/W passed a derogatory remark about him. The German took exception to this and endeavoured to discover the identity of the guilty party. He was unable to do so, and as the individual would not admit the offence, all the occupants of that barrack were confined to the barrack for two days.

In the summer of 1944 sea-bathing was stopped owing to the fact that some Americans had stolen wood while they were out of the Camp on a bathing party. The privilege of leaving the Camp on parole for sea-bathing was withdrawn permanently.

In late 1944 the Camp Theatre, situated in the South Compound, was closed by the Germans for several weeks because some damage had been done by the P's/W to a barrack in the South-West Compound.

(t) *Finance.*
About a third of the pay received by each officer from the Germans was deducted in order to support a General Fund. This Fund was used to pay the orderlies and to all other general debts, i.e. charges for damage to German property, theatrical equipment, etc.; also for all items which could be obtained from the Germans for the Canteen. No individual could buy anything from the Germans and all goods were distributed through the P/W Administration.

The officer in charge of the General Fund was 141825 F/Lt. R.L. Myers R.A.F.

When the Camp was about to be evacuated in May, 1945, the balance in the General Fund was distributed amongst the P's/W in accordance with the amounts which had been collected from each individual.

(u) *Courts Martial.*
(i) The following is an extract from the M.I.9/S/P.G. report in respect of 34006 G/C N.W.D. Marwood-Elton R.A.F:

> "From about the middle of April, 1944 until the middle of August I sifted the causes of casualties to British aircraft by interrogating those survivors of the crews, who had been sent to Stalag Luft I (Barth). I collected detailed information of 87 casualties, which I considered would be valuable to Air Ministry. I briefed all the P's/W who were to be repatriated and each had to learn the information he was to report on arrival in the United Kingdom. Adequate security precautions were taken.
>
> "During my subsequent trial by Courts Martial, part of the evidence against me was the briefing of these P's/W.
>
> "About 14th August, 1944 I completed the preparation of a very full Agenda for the visit of the Protecting Power Representative, who was due to visit Stalag Luft I (Barth) on 22nd August. About the same time I issued an order to all Allied P's/W to the effect that two Allied Parades would be held daily and that the Germans could use these Parades for the purpose of roll call. Each Parade would be followed by 10 minutes P.T. I stated that if the Germans interfered with the Parade it would cease to be an Allied Parade, but become a German Parade, and each individual would then be

166

responsible for his own discipline. As I had a cold I decided to remain in bed for a few days.

"On the following morning's Parade there was a miscount by the Germans and they ordered a re-count. During the re-count the P's/W did not deport themselves as they did on Allied Parades.

"The Camp Kommandant sent for me and I sent a message to the effect that I was in bed and not fit to be seen. The Kommandant then ordered that I was to be medically examined. The British M.O., accompanied by a German medical orderly, examined me and it was agreed that I should remain in bed for another two days.

"On 17th August, the first day I was out of bed, the Kommandant again sent for me and Major Pritchard, who acted as my interpreter. I was taken to the German Medical Quarters, where I was examined.

"I was taken to the Kommandant's office and questioned by the Kommandant about an order which I had written about saluting. I had issued an order to Barrack Commanders to the effect that P's/W did not have to acknowledge "Heil Hitler" salute, but would salute German officers in the fashion of the individual's Service. I told the Kommandant that this order was legal and correct, and that it had not been intended for German eyes. The Kommandant stated that I was to be arrested and tried by Courts Martial for incitement to mutiny. I asked for permission to hand over my duties as Senior British Officer to W/Cdr. Hilton and this was granted.

"I was not allowed to return to my Compound, but W/Cdr Hilton was brought to me. In the presence of two German Officers I told him all that was necessary about the forthcoming visit of the Protecting Power Representative. I also told him to state my case. I told W/Cdr. Hilton that I would not make any attempt to escape in any circumstances, and that if I were reported shot he would know whom should be held responsible.

"Some of my personal effects were brought to me and I was taken by car to the Naval Detention Barracks, Stralsund, where I was placed in a cell. I saw the name 'W/Cdr Ferrers' on some papers which were being carried by a German Officer. I applied for daily exercise and W/Cdr Ferrers and I were allowed to exercise together daily, but we were not allowed to talk.

"A few days after my arrival, we were visited by Mr A. Calder, the Protecting Power Representative. On 8th September, we were visited by Mr Christiansen, of the Y.M.C.A. He was very helpful. On 18th September, I was visited by a German Naval Padre.

"On 6th October, Stralsund was attacked, in daylight, by American aircraft. The whole dock area, in which our prison was situated, was very badly damaged. As a result we had very little water and no heat or light.

"On 15th November, W/Cdr. Ferrers and I were taken to a building in Stralsund, where we were tried by Courts Martial. There was no opportunity to state our cases before the trial. My defence advocate, a man of about 70 years of age, could not speak English and I was allowed only about 40 minutes with him before the trial commenced. An interpreter was present.

"When I was taken before the Court I was informed that I was charged under Section 5 of the Special War Order and that the maximum sentence was death. I was charged on two counts (a) Incitement to mutiny (b) Bringing the Wehrmacht into contempt.

"The Court Interpreter, Unteroffizier Elbing, of the Luftwaffe, a native of Hamburg, was very pro-Nazi and definitely opposition. He was an interpreter at Stalag Luft I and I had the impression that he was largely responsible for the charges against me. W/Cdr Ferrers held the same opinion. Uffz. Elbing taught German to the N.C.O's at Stalag Luft I before it became an Officers' Camp.

"Statements by Major Schroeder, Major von Miller zu Aischolz and Hauptmann von Beck were read in court. A verbal statement was made in court by Major Schroeder.

"Dr Saupe, attorney-at-law, with his office in Anklem, was the equivalent of our Judge Advocate General. He drew up the charges. As far as I am aware he was not present at the trial.

"At the close of my trial I was pronounced 'guilty' on both counts and the President of the Court read my sentence of three years imprisonment off a sheet of paper which obviously had been prepared in advance.

"W/Cdr. Ferrers's trial then took place and he was found guilty as charged. We were then returned to the Naval Detention Barracks, where we remained until January, 1945.

"On that day W/Cdr. Ferrers and I were taken by train, under escort of two Naval Officers and two Naval ratings, to a civil prison in the Cracow suburb of Stettin. Officially we were placed in solitary confinement, but we had a certain amount of freedom and were able to visit each other's cells. We were the only Allied prisoners in this prison.

"While I was at the prison I gained the confidence of Herr Lepke, a trusted prisoner who worked in the Prison Office. He abstracted correspondence relating to my case from the file and translated the contents to me. About the beginning of March, 1945 Dr. Saupe visited the prison in order to investigate whether any Luftwaffe personnel could be released in order to fight. Lepke asked him what was to happen to me. Dr. Saupe said 'This is a difficult case. His letters of appeal against his sentence have been lying in the 'pending' tray on Dr. Conrad's (?) desk for the past three months.' Dr. Conrad (?) would appear to have been Dr. Saupe's senior at Anklem.

"Her Lepke lived somewhere East of the Oder, but his mother and two sisters evacuated to the Kiel area just prior to the Russian advance West of the Oder. I knew that he had established contact with them before we were evacuated from Stettin.

"On 14th March W/Cdr. Ferrers was taken away from the prison.

"On 16th March all O.R's were evacuated from the prison as the area was under Russian shell-fire. Four German officers, 16 German O.R's and I remained until 21st March.

"On that day we were evacuated. We travelled by obtaining lifts on military lorries. I spent the night in a civil prison at Anklem. I met W/Cdr. Ferrers there the following morning. We were then moved to Stalag Luft I (Barth) where we were placed in cells. Col. Spicer U.S.A.A.F who had previously been sentenced to death, was there also.

"On 30th April, The Germans evacuated the Camp and we were released by our fellow P's/W. During the previous three weeks we had been very well treated.

"After the evacuation of the Camp by the Germans all the remaining German documents were examined by Allied officers. Some of the documents relating to my case were found. One of those, which had been signed by Hauptmann von Beck and Major von Miller, stated that I was a nuisance, that I was thought to be a Jew, that I was very unpopular with the other P's/W and it was recommended that I should never be allowed to return to a P/W Camp. This document was destroyed, but W/Cdr Hilton should be able to furnish the names of other officers who read it.

"Major von Miller was posted away from Stalag Luft I (Barth) during the time I was in prison. On 20th April, 1945 the day prior to the German evacuation of the Camp, he returned to the Camp and tried to persuade the Senior British Officer G/Cpt. Weir, to accept him as a prisoner. He then came to see me, but I refused to have anything to do with him. On the morning of 30th April, he approached the Senior American Officer, also without success.

169

"He then went to Barth and took over a civil post, wearing civilian clothes. When the Russian forces arrived he was made town policeman.

"Major von Miller was chief of the Abwehr Department of Stalag Luft I (Barth). He maltreated several men, and in one instance ordered an American to be placed in a civil prison."

(ii) The following is an extract from the M.I.9/S/P.G. report in respect of 25038 W/Cdr R.C.M. Ferrers R.A.F.:

"On the afternoon of 20th July, 1944 at 1400 hours the German Radio announced the attempt on Hitler's life. At approximately 1600 hours that afternoon I was informed that two Czech-born R.A.F. Sergeants from my Compound were to proceed to Prague for interrogation. At the evening roll-call at 1900 hours I asked the German officer taking the roll-call Hauptmann Scheinder, for particulars about this proposed move. He could not tell me what they were to be interrogated about, but gave me his solemn assurance that these Sergeants would return to this Camp (Stalag Luft I Barth) probably in five days, but in a week at the latest, and would be brought back by Obergefreiter Vees, who was taking them.

"On approximately 24th July, I was informed by Group Captain Marwood-Elton, Senior British Officer that he had received a written assurance from the Commandant that those Sergeants would return to the Camp.

"About 1600 hours on 24th August, I was informed by Obergefreiter Vees had been seen in the Compound. I accordingly went to find my Sergeants. They were not in my hut, nor in the cook-house, which was their place of duty. After the evening roll-call parade, I went up to Feldwebel Paul, the Senior interpreter at the parade. He was in company with Obergefreiter Schubert, another interpreter, and I asked him: 'Is it true that Obergefreiter Vees is back?' His answer was 'Yes'. I then asked him: 'Where are my Sergeants?'

"He said that he thought they were at Stalag Luft III (Sagen).

"I then said remembering the order we had read out on parade: 'Sagen! I suppose that means they have been shot! You can tell Obergefreiter Vees with my compliments, that if anything happens to my Sergeants, and Germany loose the war, I shall make it my personal responsibility to see that he is also shot. Yes, and his wife and children sent to Russia!'

"This warning of mine was made subject of a charge and Court Martial, in which I was accused of 'Threatening a Superior Officer in the Execution of his Duty.'

"My defence of this charge was that I gave a warning and not a threat and that Vees was not my superior officer.

"At approximately 2300 hours on 16th August a German search party burst into the hut in which I lived and turned us out into the corridor. I went to the lavatory, and on coming out said to the American officer who was with me: 'I am looking forward to the day when we have arms again and can turn these people out of their homes.'

"The air raid alarm had either just gone or went at this moment, and he replied: 'Don't worry the R.A.F. will do it for us, and probably not leave them any houses to go back to.'

"I said that's O.K. by me. 'I hope these people get bombed till all Germans have to live in pigsties like these.'

"These remarks were made a subject of a second charge of my Court Martial, i.e. 'Causing discontent amongst my comrades in a matter of duty.'

"My line of defence was firstly that my comrades, in this case American Officers, only owed a duty to the American Government, and therefore in my submission, only an Allied Court had jurisdiction to try me for this offence. Secondly, that propaganda was a legitimate weapon of war, and as a senior officer it was both my right and duty to make my junior officers discontented with their conditions and treatment as prisoners, thereby ensuring that they would carry out their duty of attempting to escape.

"I was arrested on 17th August and sent to Naval Prison Stralsund where I was placed in solitary confinement in an Other Ranks' Prison. I was given one hour's exercise each morning, there were no laundry facilities, and I was made to do my own laundry in the shower room in sight of, and seen by, German Other Ranks.

"On 15th November, I appeared before a Court Martial, and was found guilty on the first charge. I was sentenced to nine months imprisonment. I was found 'Not Guilty' on the second charge. I appealed to the Protecting Power against my conviction. My appeal was mainly on the grounds of my defence being prejudiced by not allowed to see my Counsel, Herr Langemark, before my trial.

"On 3rd January, 1945 I was transferred to an Army Prison at Vermiltzbstrasse, Stettin. On 16th March I was taken to Anklem to be re-tried on 20th March.

"At my re-trial I was again tried on both charges, and found guilty on both. I was sentenced to six months on the first charge and one year on the second. The total punishment to be seventeen months.

"On 21st March I was returned from Anklem to Stalag Luft I (Barth) where I was left in solitary confinement till midnight on 20th April, when the German guard withdrew. The Russian forces arrived on 1st May.

(u) *Trial of P's/W by P/W Administration.*
The following is an extract from the M.I.9/S/P.G. report in respect of 32195 W/Cdr. F.W. Hilton R.A.F:

"In February, 1944 I made representation to the Camp Commandant at Stalag Luft I (Barth) requesting the provision of batmen. Later that month a party of approximately sixty R.A.F. N.C.O's arrived from Stalag Luft VI (Heydekrug).

"I informed the party that I did not want N.C.O's as batmen as it was degrading for them and that I had asked for Privates. That if they had been misled by the Germans, and did not wish to carry out the duties of batmen, I would not force them to work, but would endeavour to have them sent back to Stalag Luft VI (Heydekrug). A large proportion of the N.C.O's expressed willingness to remain at Stalag Luft I (Barth) and carry out the duties assigned to them, i.e. labour details for Camp duties. Some of the N.C.O's refused to do any work.

"At an interview with the Camp Commandant I pointed out that some of these N.C.O's had been brought to the Camp under false pretences and I requested that these individuals should be returned to Stalag Luft VI (Heydekrug) at once. The Commandant refused to accede to this request and stated that all these N.C.O's had volunteered.

"At a later interview with the Commandant I pointed out that the dissatisfied N.C.O's were having a bad effect on those who were willing to work. Then he agreed to take action. I pointed out at this interview and at subsequent interviews that I required Privates or Airmen for Camp duties and that N.C.O's should be transferred to an N.C.O's Camp.

"About the end of February, 1944 Sgt. O'Brien, S.A.S. approached me and asked whether he could be placed in charge of tunnelling activities in the Camp. I pointed out that we had an experienced officer, a prisoner with four years experience, in charge of such undertakings, but that any assistance which he cared to give in a part-time way would be welcome.

"Sgt. Greenhalgh (?), R.A.F. approached me about the same time and asked for a position on the Escape Committee. I pointed out that all necessary positions were already filled by experienced P's/W but that any help which he would give to the Committee would be appreciated. He then adopted a very truculent and un-service-like attitude.

"I told both these N/C/O's that I was running the Camp on Service lines and that they would accept my decisions without question or argument.

"O'Brien, Greenhalgh and seven other N.C.O's who were the disgruntled party under the leadership of O'Brien lived in one room in a Barrack commanded by Capt. Button, U.S.A.A.F. Their behaviour was generally unco-operative and un-Service-like.

"In March, owing to body lice in the Compound, I organised a de-lousing parade for all personnel. The personnel in the various barracks were ordered to parade under their Barrack Commanders at the gate of the Compound at stated times, with all their body hair shaved off.

"All personnel paraded according to orders, with the exception of the nine N.C.O's led by O'Brien. These N.C.O's refused to obey the orders of Capt. Button, their Barrack Commander, who reported the matter to me. I gave him a written order signed by me, ordering all British personnel in the interests of Camp health to shave off all body hair and present themselves for de-lousing within three hours.

"At the end of the three hours Capt. Button came to me and reported that of the nine N.C.O's, three had complied with the order and six still refused. Col. Hatcher, who was with me at the time, said that he would see these six N.C.O's. He did so and on returning said that they had agreed to comply with the order. However they did not do so.

"Later that day, I instructed S/Ldr. Harris, R.A.F. to place these six N.C.O's, O'Brien, Greenhalgh (?), and four others (names forgotten), on a charge of refusing to obey orders. I decided to deal with the matter summarily.

"These N.C.O's were brought before me on this charge and I found them guilty as charged. I sentenced them to be reduced to the ranks.

173

"That evening on roll call Greenhalgh (?) and one other (name forgotten) pretended to be insane. This was a disgusting exhibition in front of three thousand P's/W mainly American. They were examined by Capt. Nichols, R.A.M.C. who stated that both men were perfectly sane. The second man was retained in Sick Quarters for 48 hours for further observation and then discharged as being fit.

"On the morning following the roll call incident O'Brien accompanied by another N.C.O. (name forgotten) R.A.F. a man of about 6 feet 3 inches in height, requested a private interview with me. This was granted. In threatening language, O'Brien stated that he personally was holding me responsible for the sanity of the N.C.O's whom I had reduced to the ranks. He remarked that he had been an officer in the Kings African Rifles and had been cashiered for having been involved in a murder charge and that it would not be the last murder in which he would be involved.

"After the termination of the interview I informed W/Cdr. Lee-Evans and W/Cdr. Robinson of the threats which O'Brien had just made. The other N.C.O had not taken part in the proceedings.

"A few days later the disgruntled N.C.O's and a few others were taken back to Stalag Luft VI (Heydekrug) by the Germans in response to my earlier representations.

"A complete record of all the above was kept and a copy posted to Air Ministry with German agreement. I left Stalag Luft I (Barth) before the general evacuation of the Camp following liberation by the Russians and I understood that the Camp records were to be brought to the U.K. and handed over to the Air Ministry.

(ii) The following is an extract from the M.I.9/S/P.G. report in respect of 515182 W.O. Greenhalgh, R.H., R.A.F.:

"In February, 1944 when at Stalag Luft VI (Heydekrug) W.O. Alexander, R.J., R.A.F., the Chief of the Escape Committee, asked me as whether I would be willing to go to Stalag Luft I (Barth) in the guise of a volunteer batman, in order to assist the escape activities of the officers in this newly opened Officers Camp. It was planned that samples of various documents would be sent with me. I agreed to this suggestion and my name was placed on the list of volunteers. I hid the documents in my accordion.

"A few days later during the train journey to Stalag Luft I (Barth) Sgt. O'Brien, S.A.S., W.O. Fraser, D., R.A.F., W.O. Arnold, R.A.F., and several others (names unknown) cut a panel out of the side of the goodswagon in which we were traveling. There were six or eight German guards in the wagon. I played my accordion in order to cover up the noise of this operation. When the work was almost completed, a W.O. (name unknown) R.A.F., who had been informed previously by Sgt O'Brien that an organised attempt was to be made by him, escaped from the next wagon by climbing through the ventilator slit. The train was stationary at the time and he was seen and recaptured at once. This resulted in all wagons being searched thoroughly and the escape panel made by Sgt. O'Brien and his party was discovered. We were compelled to lie flat on the floor for the remainder of the journey with a German guard standing over us with a tommy-gun. The panel had been boarded up.

"On arrival at Stalag Luft I, I passed through the search successfully and in accordance with W.O. Alexander's instructions made contact with W.O. Kerr, R.A.F., who was in charge of the Escape Committee at Stalag Luft I. I had a letter of introduction from W.O. Alexander which I handed to W.O. Kerr. He read it and took it to W/Cdr. Lee-Evans. He returned and informed me that W/Cdr. Lee-Evans would see me at 1500 hours the following day. Later that day W.O. Kerr was taken from Stalag Luft I en route for Stalag Luft VI.

"I saw W/Cdr. Lee-Evans as arranged and showed him some of the documents which I   had brought from Stalag Luft VI. And told him the rough outline of the Escape Organisation in that Camp. He told me to report to the Security Committee later that day.

"I reported as instructed and offered all the documents to S/Ldr. Kilgallin, R.A.F. Regiment. He refused to accept them stating that he had no safe hiding place for them. He instructed me to retain them for the time being. I gave him a rough outline of the Escape Organisation at Stalag Luft VI.

"On the following morning a runner told me to report to W/Cdr Lee-Evans. I did so and he informed me that I would be charged as follows: He then read a charge from written notes which was to the effect that I had exposed the following documents to the Security Committee without having ascertained that this was in fact the Security Committee. A list of the documents followed. I demanded that the written notes should be destroyed immediately. I pointed out that if these should be found by the Germans I would be in a very precarious position. I also pointed out that the Germans would realise that I had brought the documents from Stalag Luft VI and would result in intensive searches there. W/Cdr. Lee-Evans informed me that he would not destroy these notes, then I was dismissed.

175

"On my return to my barracks I informed Sgt. O'Brien, S.A.S., W.O. James, H. R.A.F., W.O. Fraser (navigator) R.A.F. and several other N.C.O's that I had brought certain documents for escape purposes from Stalag Luft VI and that I had just been told that I would be court-martialled for having shown them to the Security Committee without having first identified them as such. Later that day we decided that we would try to get back to Stalag Luft VI.

"We approached the Officer i/c Batmen, S/Ldr. Samuels, R.A.F. with this object in view. He informed us that if we refused to work the Germans would send us back. We decided to refuse to work and maintained this attitude for the remainder of the time we were in the Camp.

"About the end of February, 1944 the Senior British Officer issued an order to the effect that all personnel must remove all hair from their bodies within a specified time in order to combat suspected outbreak of meningitis. In the barrack in which Sgt. O'Brien, S.A.S. W.O.'s James, Arnold, Fraser, Leading Airman Lancaster, N.A.A. and I were living there were about 60 personnel, mostly Americans. I believe that there was only one razor blade for the whole Barrack. The above named and two other R.A.F. N.C.O's (names forgotten) refused to shave unless we were issued with a new razor blade each. We informed the Barrack Commander, Capt. (name unknown) U.S.A.A.F. of our refusal and the reasons for it. A few hours later he brought a typewritten order which stated that we must remove our hair. He stated that no new razor blades were available.

"The following day, without any further warning, the eight of us were instructed to assemble in Headquarters Barrack to appear before a Board of Officers for a Court Martial.

"The eight of us reported as instructed about an hour later. Leading Airman Lancaster, F.A.A. was the first to be admitted to the room. The remaining seven of us were told to wait outside. A few minutes later he came out again and said that he had been demoted, but that he considered that only the Admiralty had such authority. All the others were taken into the room singly. I cannot remember in what order. I believe that I was third or fourth to be dealt with.

"When I was taken into the room I saw the following Officers assembled: W/Cdr. Hilton, R.A.F., S/Ldr. Kilgallin, R.A.F. Regiment, and about ten other officers (names unknown). W/Cdr Hilton read the collective charges against us. I cannot remember the exact wording but I think they were: (a) Refusing to remove the hair from their bodies when ordered to do so by W/Cdr. Hilton, the Senior British Officer; (b) Refusing to remove the hair from their bodies when ordered to do so by Col. Hatchett, the Senior Allied Officer; (c) (Details uncertain).

"W/Cdr Hilton asked me whether I had anything to say. I replied by asking whether there was any officer in the Camp qualified to act as my legal advisor. No answer was given. I then asked under which section of the Air Force Act I was being charged. A section (details forgotten) was quoted by one of the officers present.

"I then stated that I had nothing to say in answer to the charges. The Board of Officers did not concur and W/Cdr. Hilton told me that I was sentenced to be reduced to the ranks with consequent stoppage of pay with effect from that day. I informed W/Cdr. Hilton that I would not let the matter drop on my return to England. I was then dismissed. I joined those who had already been tried and we waited until the whole eight of us had been dealt with.

"We then returned to our room and discussed what had occurred. On my suggestion we decided to apply for copies of the charge sheet, as I intended to raise the matter on my return to the U.K. On the following day we went singly to the Camp Adjutant, S/Ldr. (name forgotten) and asked for a copy of the charge sheet. This was supplied to each of us and I still have my copy, which bears a note written in ink, to the effect that it is a certified true copy. All the names of the others charged with me appear on it.

"A day or two later W.O. Arnold started screaming on parade and then run away from the parade and began to climb the Compound gate. Some American officers left the parade and grabbed him. They took him to the Sick Quarters where he remained for several days.

"Later that day Sgt. O'Brien told myself and the other occupants of our room that he had gone with W.O. Fraser, to W/Cdr. Hilton after the parade mentioned above and told W/Cdr. Hilton that he would hold him personally responsible for W.O. Arnold's sanity.

"I believe that the eight of us were issued with new razor blades after the court-martial and we removed all the hair from our bodies. We were supplied with an ointment to apply to the shaved parts. Later that day I discovered that the parts to which I had applied the ointment had become inflamed and blistered. I informed the Barrack Commander and he examined the burns. He then sent for the Medical officer (name forgotten), who examined me and stated that I was a good actor. He refused to give me any treatment. This was witnessed by Lt. Turner (U.S.A.A.F) whose address I can supply if required.

"About this time we learned that F/Lt. Mitchell R.A.F. was an Administrative Officer. I approached him and told him what had occurred at the court-martial. He stated that he would be willing to act for us.

"Shortly after the court-martial W/Cdr. Lee-Evans sent for me and asked me to hand over the documents which I had brought from Stalag Luft VI. In view of his previous statement that I would be court-martialled for having shown them to the Security Committee, and the fact that it had been made obvious to me that no help was wanted from me in connection with escape matters, I refused to comply with his request.

"Soon afterwards the Senior Allied Officer, Col Hatchett, U.S.A.A.F. sent for me and asked me to hand the documents to him. I respectfully declined to do so, and he gave me a direct order to hand them over to him at once. I stated that I would comply with his order under strong protest. I went to my Barrack and whilst I was in the act of removing the documents from the inside of my accordion two officers (names unknown) entered my room and demanded that I hand the documents to them. I refused to do so and took them to Col. Hatchett as he had instructed.

"About this time, I cannot be certain of the date, I learned that an order had been read in all barracks by the respective Barrack Commanders which was to the effect that I was not to be trusted and no matters affected by security were to be made known to me, or discussed in my presence. I approached my Barrack Commander with a view to ascertaining the source of this order and if possible to try to obtain a copy of it. I was referred to the Senior Allied Officer Col. Hatchett, who instructed me to raise the matter with my Barrack Commander. On going back to him he told me that no action could be taken by him. All my endeavours to investigate the matter were brought to an end by my transfer to Stalag Luft VI, together with the other seven N.C.O's who had also been court-martialled, about a week after the court-martial.

"On arrival at Stalag Luft VI, I reported the full details of the incidents at Stalag Luft I to the Camp Leader W.O. Deans, J.A.G., R.A.F. and the Chief of the Escape Committee, W.O. Alexander, R.J., R.A.F.,

"W.O. Deans informed me that he would endeavour to get a message to G/Capt. Massey, the Senior British Officer at Stalag Luft III, explaining what had occurred".

Chapter 18

Escape Organisation and Escape Materials

3. CONTROL BY CAMP AUTHORITIES

The North Compound, which was occupied by American personnel only, is not dealt with in this Volume, but where necessary specific references are made to it. The Escape Organisation dealt with in this Chapter covered the requirements of the South, West and South-West Compounds.

Throughout the period under review all attempts to escape, including tunnel construction, were controlled by the Escape Committee.

The Escape and Security Organisations were responsible to the Senior British Officer, who selected his executives.

When the N.C.O's, who had occupied the Camp during the period dealt with in Part III of this Volume, were transferred to Stalag Luft VI (Heydekrug) in November, 1943, a certain number volunteered to remain behind to assist the officer P's/W who were known to be arriving. Amongst this number were two members of the N.C.O's Escape Committee:

968327	W.O. Kerr, W.E.	R.A.F.
964794	W.O. Olliver, R.B.	R.A.F.

The abovenamed N.C.O's dealt with all escape matters until the officers formed their own Escape Committee in December, 1943. After that date they acted in an advisory capacity, until they were transferred to Stalag Luft VI in February, 1944.

The Americans and British set up separate Escape Committees in December, 1943. To begin with, the British organisation was similar to that developed by the N.C.O's during the preceding period. It's title was 'X.Y.Z' and was composed of three members:

179

63074 W/Cdr. J.A. Lee-Evans R.A.F.
103829 S/Ldr. D.J. Kilgallin R.A.F. Regt.
49939 Major T.A.G. Pritchard Parachute Regiment

Lee-Evans was responsible for all escape matters – 'X'. Kilgallin was in charge of all security – 'Y'. Pritchard was in charge of all intelligence – 'Z'. Each of these officers had a small staff of Assistants.

Almost immediately the 'Z' Section was detached from the others and from then onwards it operated as a separate unit directly responsible to the Senior British Officer.

Shortly afterwards 'Y' Section was detached in the same way and from this time onwards the 'X' Section functioned as the Escape Committee.

In early January, 1944 the British and American Escape Committees were amalgamated under the Chairmanship of 63074 W/Cdr. J.A. Lee-Evans R.A.F. The other members of the Committee were:

Lt. B.B. Chase	U.S.A.A.C.
136698 F/Lt. W.J. Needham	R.A.F.
83287 F/Lt. D. Ogilvie	R.A.F.
43479 F/Lt. D.I. Pike	R.A.F.
134580 F/Lt. P.H. Spencer	R.A.F.
103482 F/Lt. W.H. Young	R.A.F.

Their functions were: Chase – clothing; Needham – maps; Ogilvie – aircraft details; Pike – tunnels; Spencer – forged documents and escape information; Young – food and equipment. During the next few months the proportion of American P's/W became much greater and it became desirable to have a large American interest in the Escape Committee. In the late Spring of 1944 the Committee was re-organised as follows:

Lt. B.B. Chase	U.S.A.A.C.
158986 F/Lt. J.R. Lake	R.A.F.
63074 W/Cdr. J.A. Lee-Evans	R.A.F.
89763 S/Ldr. A.I. McRitchie	R.A.F.
136698 F/Lt. W.J. Needham	R.A.F.
83287 F/Lt. D. Ogilvie	R.A.F.
43479 F/Lt. D.I. Pike	R.A.F.
Lt. C.E. Shaugnessey	U.S.A.A.C.
134580 F/Lt. P.H. Spencer	R.A.F.
Capt M.P. Ward	U.S.A.A.C.
103482 F/Lt. W.H. Young	R.A.F.

Their functions were as follows: Chase – clothing; Lake – tunnels; Lee-Evans – Chairman of the Committee; McRitchie – tools and electrical equipment; Needham – maps; Ogilvie – aircraft details; Pike – tunnels; Shaugnessey – 'trading'; Spencer – forged documents and information; Ward – food; Young – equipment. Their work is described in the later Sections of this Chapter.

Just prior to this re-organisation it had been found that interest in escape had increased amongst the P's/W as the weather improved. The result was that the Escape Committee was spending a great deal of time listening to schemes, put forward by enthusiasts, which might not be put into operation for a variety of reasons.

When the re-organisation took place it was decided to appoint two Interviewing Officers to interview all intending escapers. They were:

> 100622 S/Ldr. P.R. Goodwin   R.A.F.
> Capt. D.A. Van Epps   U.S.A.A.C.

From this time onwards they listened to all schemes, vetted them, suggested improvements, and when detailed plans were ready submitted them to the Escape Committee.

When it became known in early 1944 that a large number of American personnel were to be accommodated in the North Compound, then under construction, a number of American officers were instructed in the various functions of the Escape Committee. When the North Compound was opened these officers were transferred there as part of the P/W administrative staff. Maps and other escape equipment was transferred to enable the personnel in that Compound to begin activities at once.

In September 1944 the Senior British Officer issued an order forbidding further attempts to escape and the Escape Committee ceased to function.

4. PLANNING

The policy of the Escape Committee was to aid and advise all intending escapers and only to forbid an attempt when it jeopardised another which had been arranged previously.

From December, 1943 onwards all new arrivals were informed, after their bona fides had been checked, and informed that if they wished to make an attempt to escape they must first approach the Leader of their barrack, who would get in touch with the Escape Committee.

For the first few months all schemes were submitted to the Escape Committee direct. If the plan was considered to be feasible it was discussed with the individual, or individuals, and advice and assistance given. From the Spring of 1944 onwards decisions regarding feasibility were made by the Interviewing Officers as related above.

During the period under review no escapes were planned by the Escape Committee. Personnel who wished to attempt to escape devised their own schemes.

5. SECURITY

Adequate security was considered by the Senior British Officer to be the most important factor in connection with subversive activities. In December, 1943 a Security Section, known as 'Y' was set up under the direction of 103829 S/Ldr. D.J. Kilgallin R.A.F. Regt. He was responsible to the Senior British Officer. He appointed Security Representatives in each barrack of the rank of Flight Lieutenant or Captain and it was their duty to ensure that the Camp Security Orders were obeyed. The most important points stressed in these orders were:

(i)There must be no contact with the Germans except by personnel approved by the Security Officer.

(ii) There must be no talking to Germans, except by those officially approved, i.e. 'traders', personnel dealing with Red Cross parcels etc.

(iii) There must be no entertaining of Germans by P's/W without the sanction of the Security Officer.

(iv) In the event of any P/W being sent for by the Germans he must, before complying with the order, report to his Barrack Leader. On return to the Compound he must again report to his Barrack Leader.

(v) There must be no talking on Service matters or Camp activities (a) After "lock-up" [or] (b) Within possible hearing of a German during the hours of daylight.

(vi) No escape must be attempted without reference to the proper authorities.

(vii) No diaries are to be kept.

In addition to being read out to all personnel once each month, the salient points in the above orders were stressed periodically at the end of the daily news bulletin.

In the Spring of 1944, under the direction of Kilgallin, security posters were manufactured in the Camp and placed at every conceivable vantage point. The original design of the poster was obtained from a German one depicting a figure clothed in black with the letters 'P.S.T.' written underneath. The Germans did not object to these posters and allowed them to remain throughout the remainder of this period.

However, they did object to a second poster produced by the Security Section. This was a twisted version of another poster depicting a German guard receiving a bribe from a P/W, with an appropriate warning underneath. This second poster was torn down by the Germans.

The P's/W in the South Compound usually were able to discern when a search was about to take place, by observing the movements of the Germans in the Vorlager. When such activity was noticed, a pre-arranged signal was placed in a window which was visible in the West and South-West Compounds. In addition, P's/W engaged on work in the Parcel Store and elsewhere often learned of impending searches from the Germans with whom they came into contact. As soon as a warning was received that a search was imminent, all personnel engaged on subversive activities were advised and all forbidden materials were hidden.

When the Security Section was organised a system of 'watchers' was inaugurated to guard against the discovery of subversive activities. The Security Officer always was informed when any such activity was about to take place and it was his responsibility to give adequate warning of the approach of any German. As a rule the 'watchers' did not know what they were guarding, but it was stressed that they must report the movements of all Germans in the area and ensure that no German could enter the 'danger' zone without prior warning being given.

In May, 1944 American Security was taken over by Lt. Col. Mackenzie U.S.A.A.C. Kilgallin then became British Security Officer and he and Mackenzie worked in close co-operation.

The possibility that the Germans might have installed microphones in the barracks was taken into consideration. The Security Section carried out a thorough search of all barracks, but no microphones were found. However, traces of the existence of microphones at an earlier date were discovered.

The following British personnel were most active in enforcing the Camp Security Orders:

42742	F/Lt. J.E. Bridger	R.A.F.
925696	W.O. Drummond, R.R.	R.A.F.
120448	F/Lt. T.C. Graham	R.A.F.
144443	F/Lt. N.H. Haley	R.A.F.
J.12814	F/Lt. W.R. Jackson	R.C.A.F.
132174	F/Lt. H.R. Phillips	R.A.F.

It is interesting to observe that German documents, which were examined by the P's/W after the Germans had evacuated the Camp, record that it was difficult to obtain any information from the British owing to their good security; nor was the Abwehr Department ever able to track down the illegal radio receiver operating in the Camp although many intensive searches were made. The German files showed that the Abwehr Officer was keenly conscious of the P/W Intelligence and Security measures. It would appear that all the information which the Germans obtained from the British was derived from two sources: (a) Letters; (b) From the systematic eavesdropping of conversations between the P's/W.

6. CLOTHING

In December, 1943 a Clothing Repair Section was set up under the direction of 136698 F/Lt. W.J. Needham R.A.F. The primary purpose of this Department was the repair of P/W clothing and alteration of new uniforms, but clothing was prepared for intending escapers, mainly from uniforms and greatcoats. The Camp system of 'watchers' was used when escape clothing was being made. The chief workers in this Section, in addition to Needham, were:

| 100235 | L.A.C.Gill, N.S. | R.A.F. |
| 120448 | F/Lt. T.C. Graham | R.A.F. |

Clothing for escape purposes was acquired by 'trading' and other means. The officer responsible for the supply of clothing to intending escapers was Lt. B.B. Chase U.S.A.A.C., who was a member of the Escape Committee. All clothing of this type was passed to him for safe custody until required. Most of it was buried in the Camp. Small items such as German uniform insignia were hidden in dried-milk tins fitted with false bottoms.

7. FORGERY

A Forgery Section was organised in December, 1943 under the direction of 134580 F/Lt. D.H. Spencer R.A.F., who was a member of the Escape Committee. His chief assistant was 926282 W/O. Kilminster, A.R., R.A.F., who had volunteered to remain behind when the majority of N.C.O's were transferred to Stalag Luft VI in November, 1943. This N.C.O was a skilled forger, due largely to the experience he had gained during the period dealt with [earlier] of this volume. Other members of the Forgery Section were J.14507 F/O L.E. Aspinall R.C.A.F. [and] 135487 F/O E.B. Overton R.A.F.

(a) *Papers.*

(i) Hand forgery. Under Spencer's direction excellent

reproductions were made by hand of camp passes, identification papers for foreign workers, labour cards for foreign workers, travel permits, letters authorising a change of employment and domicile, and ration cards. The methods of production were by hand and by means of the jelly duplicator. It was never intended to produce a complete set of identity papers, for which sufficient information, facilities and material were lacking, but only to give intending escapers a fair chance of avoiding summary arrest and to enable them to travel by train.

The standard of forgery was high and can be judged by the following: Three Americans who attempted to escape disguised as Germans and in possession of a forged gate pass were apprehended at the gate. The forgery was considered to be so good that the Camp Commandant at once caused new gate passes to be printed with an elaborate scroll design on the reverse side. The new pass was reproduced by the Forgery Section within a short time.

One unusual document which was produced by the Section was a Safe Conduct Pass. Only one was made and the wording was in English and German. It was made to look like an official document issued by the Air Ministry, with a space for the photograph of the holder. It was couched in careful terms asserting that the bearer had assisted British P's/W. No German was ever issued with such a document, but it was used by the 'traders' to persuade Germans to supply forbidden items: this was very effective.

Documents for copying were obtained from the following sources: (1) Copies of all documents reproduced during the period dealt with in Part III, were retained by Kilminster; (2) P's/W returned to the Camp from the hospital at Neubrandenburg brought original documents obtained from the Polish orderlies there; (3) Copies of the documents produced by the Forgery section of the Escape Organisation at Stalag Luft VI were brought to this Camp by 515182 W.O. Greenhalgh, R.H., R.A.F.; (4) Original documents for copying were obtained from Germans and foreign workers by the 'trading' Section; (5) Printed forgeries of identity cards were received from I.S.9.

(ii) Photographic reproduction.

In the Summer of 1944 a parcel containing a camera and photographic materials was received from I.S.9. From then onwards a number of documents were made by photographic reproduction. The photographer was 926282 W/O. Kilminster, A.R., R.A.F. The following methods were used for the reproduction of documents: (1) The camera was focussed so that the photograph was the same dimensions as the original; (2) In some cases where the original document was not suitable for direct reproduction through being in bad condition, or printed on dark paper, it was drawn by hand and then photographed. The drawings were made double the size of the original so that when the camera was focussed to obtain a photograph of the same dimensions as the original document, the quality of the lettering was improved; (3) An alternative to method 2 was to cut words and letters out of German magazine and paste them on a sheet of paper to form the desired wording. This was photographed as in method 2 and slight faults corrected by re-touching the negative.

In all cases contact prints were made, then dyed the required colour. After trimming, the documents were ready for completion by filling in the written details and affixing the photograph of the persons who were to use them.

The following difficulties were encountered in making spurious documents by photographic means: (1) The photographic printing paper supplied by I.S.9 was not sufficiently large. This paper was very difficult to obtain from other sources and when it was acquired it was not of the required contrast, thus giving inferior results; (2) When photographing documents which were printed on coloured paper it was necessary to use panchromatic film. This made the work difficult under the conditions imposed by the equipment which was available.

(b) *Photographs.*
For the first six months of this period no camera was available in the Camp and the re-touching and altering of photographs for affixing to forged documents was done by 926282 W/O. Kilminster, A.R., R.A.F. After the receipt of the camera sent by I.S.9 normal identity photographs were taken of the individuals who were to use the spurious documents.

(c) *Rubber stamps.*
Reproduction of the impression created by rubber stamps were made by the methods described in Part III. The work was done by 926282 W/O. Kilminster, A.R., R.A.F.. In early 1944 he made stamps which gave satisfactory results by etching the required design on pieces of aluminium with the aid of hydrochloric acid. The aluminium was obtained from cooking utensils. The resist for the design was the chief difficulty to be overcome. At first boot polish was used, then candle grease, and finally cellulose paint.

(d) *Security*.
Two copies were made of all documents which were acquired. This work was completed as soon as possible and the two copies were hidden in separate places. The chief hiding places which were used were: (i) Drawers fitted with false bottoms; (ii) Hollow cupboard doors; (iii) The double walls and roofs of barracks; (iv) The straw of palliasses; (v) Tins buried two or three feet deep in gardens in the Compound; (vi) The covers of books in the Camp Library and elsewhere.

The equipment made for use in connection with photographic reproduction was so designed that when dismantled it gave no indication of its purpose and could be left in full view without danger.

For example, the printing frame when not in use was hung on the wall of a barrack and used as a picture frame. The camera was the only item which had to be hidden. A brick was removed from the corner of a chimney in a barrack and a wooden box, slightly shorter and narrower than the brick, was cemented into the space. A thin slice of the original brick was affixed to each of the two exposed faces of the box. The box was constructed in such a way that the end, to which one of the slices of brick had been attached, was removable. The camera and films were hidden in this cavity and were never discovered by the Germans.

8. FOOD
The officer responsible for the supply of food to intending escapers was 103482 F/Lt. W.H. Young R.A.F., a member of the Escape Committee. He received advice on the type of food which should be supplied from Captain Nicholls R.A.M.C., the Camp Medical Officer.

The scale of rations which was issued to each escaper was: One tin of corned beef, one tin of Spam, two bars of American 'D' ration chocolate, a tin of a mixture of butter, cocoa and sugar, fifty cigarettes and two boxes of matches.

The abovementioned items were drawn from the Camp Red Cross Food Stores by the Parcels Officer, when needed, at the request of the Escape Committee. The food was not issued to the intending escaper until just before he was due to make his attempt.

9. MAPS
(a) *General*.
In December, 1943 a Mapping Section was set up under the direction of 136698 F/Lt. W.J. Needham R.A.F., who was a member of the Escape Committee. The map makers were:

187

J.14507 F/Lt. L.E. Aspinal   R.C.A.F.
126827 F/Lt. I.D. Bolton   R.A.F.
970053 W.O. Everson, J.E.   R.A.F.
N.Z.404362 F/Lt. R.B. Hesselyn   R.N.Z.A.F.
158986 F/Lt. J.R. Lake   R.A.F.
C.1359 S/Ldr. L.E. Logan   R.C.A.F.
155175 F/Lt. P.A. Spencer   R.A.F.

At first there were no maps in the Camp, but gradually a number were acquired from various sources including the 'Trading' Section, new P's/W and I.S.9.

At the end of December, 1943 a very useful 1:100,000 map was obtained of the district surrounding the Camp. Although this was in pieces the Mapping Section was able to make a copy. The Peninsula area was scaled up from it and this map, which was used for briefing intending escapers, was annotated whenever further information was obtained.

Silk maps of Germany, which were received from I.S.9. and new P's/W were copied, but this was very difficult as the silk became distorted in the process. Such maps were of little use as the scale was about 1:2,000,000.

In May, 1944 a quantity of 1:500,000 maps were received from I.S.9. These were invaluable as they covered the Northern Coast of Germany from Holland to Danzig.

(b) *Methods of Production.*
The most suitable paper which was available for use in connection with copying maps was supplied to the Camp by the Germans on parole. As this would not be used, thicker and less transparent paper had to be used. This was rendered less opaque by smearing it with margarine. This was suitable for use provided that a supply of good Indian ink was available.

When suitable ink could not be obtained the paper was not treated with margarine, but was spread over the map and copied on a sheet of glass with a strong light underneath.

During the summer of 1944, when the demand for maps was greatest, they were reproduced in quantity, by means of a jelly duplicator. The jelly base was made of table jellies and the 'master' copy of the map to be reproduced was drawn in duplicator ink. Each 'master' copy produced from twenty to twenty-five duplicates.

(c) *Security.*
As soon as an original map was received a very careful copy was made. This was placed in a sealed tin and buried. The Mapping Officer held a

set of large maps for use by the Escape Committee when an intending escaper was briefed. These were difficult to hide and on several occasions they were placed on a rubbish dump during searches of the barracks by the Germans: they were never discovered.

Maps were not supplied to intending escapers until just before they were due to make their attempts. The Mapping Officer handed them to the Chairman of the Escape Committee, who in turn handed them to the escaper. In this way the escaper did not know who produced the maps, nor did the Mapping Officer know who was about to attempt to escape.

Maps which were not likely to be required at short notice were hidden in the roof of a barrack by a P/W of very small stature. This hiding place was inaccessible to a person of normal stature.

The Mapping Officer kept a number of maps on his person so that they should be available at short notice if required. For this purpose he had special pockets sewn into the crutch of his trousers and in the waistband at the back. When he was subjected to a personal search these hiding places were not discovered.

10. COMPASSES

For the first six months the main sources of the supply of compasses was new P's/W, many of whom had succeeded in concealing their escape compasses during the various personal searches following capture. During the period a certain number of compasses were manufactured out of razor blades by 926282 W.O. Kilminster, A.R., R.A.F., using the method described in Part III.

In the early Summer of 1944 compasses were received in parcels from I.S.9. Throughout the greater part of the period under review compasses of various types were obtained from Germans by the 'Trading' Section.

11. ESCAPE INTELLIGENCE

Escape information was obtained from the undermentioned sources and collated by the Chairman of the Escape Committee. All intending escapers were briefed by him before making their attempt.

(a) *Contacts.*

All information which was obtained by the members of the 'Trading' Section was passed to the officer in charge, 103829 S/Ldr. D.J. Kilgallin R.A.F. Regiment. He conveyed the escape information to the Chairman of the Escape Committee.

(b) *Journeys outside Camp.*

Specially selected members of the 'Trading' Section were included in the parties of P's/W which were taken to Barth Railway Station, under escort, to collect parcels, etc. During these visits information was gathered by personal observation and through conversations with Germans and foreign workers. The most active P/W in this connection was 134580 F/LT. D.H. Spencer R.A.F. Personnel sent for treatment to hospitals at Neubrandenburg and Stralsund were able to supply useful information to the Escape Committee when they returned to the Camp.

(c) *Recaptured escapers.*
All recaptured escapers were interrogated by a member of the Escape Committee as soon as they returned to the Camp after their terms in cells. However, very few P's/W were able to get outside the Camp during the period under review and these were unable to supply much information which was useful to other escapers.

(d) *New P's/W.*
All new arrivals in the Camp were interrogated. Escape information was passed to the Chairman of the Escape Committee.

(e) *From I.S.9.*
A number of messages were received from I.S.9. by means of the P/W code, but the escape information they contained was both vague and out-of-date. It was found that the code messages embodied in the radio broadcast known as "The Voice of America" were far more useful and important than the encoded messages sent by I.S.9 in letters.

A request for details of conditions in German was despatched to I.S.9. by means of the P/W code, but no reply was received.

A message was received from I.S.9. by code-letter which gave details about Swedish ships and the flags flown by them. Most of this information proved to be inaccurate.

Another message was received which stated that if a pair of blue trousers were hung on a line on the Swedish ferry at Rostock it would be safe for a P/W to board the ship. The veracity of this was doubted very strongly.

12. SUPPLIES
The escape material which was obtained from the undermentioned sources was controlled by the Escape Committee and used for escape activities at the discretion of this body.
(a) *Contacts.*
In December, 1943 a 'Trading' Section was formed under the direction and control of the Security Officer 108329 S/Ldr. D.J. Kilgallin R.A.F.

Regiment. Specially selected P's/W were appointed by him to 'trade' with Germans, foreign workers, etc., for the purpose of obtaining escape material, escape and military information, and goods for the general welfare of the P's/W which were unobtainable through normal channels. At the same time orders were issued to all P's/W in the Camp that all 'trading' by unauthorised personnel was forbidden, and that no P/W was permitted to converse with a German without special permission from the Security Officer.

A 'trader' was appointed in each barrack and he was responsible for obtaining as much of the material in the welfare category as possible, within the requirements of the occupants of his barrack. In addition, a number of 'traders' were appointed to deal with the requirements of the Escape Organisation, but both types of 'trader' worked in close collaboration.

This 'trading' was strictly controlled and only those Germans and foreign workers who proved their worth by supplying useful information and items for which they been asked, were rewarded with cigarettes. A scale of prices was fixed for all items and this was based on the risk which would be taken by the 'contact', availability, etc. If difficulty was experienced in obtaining an item urgently required, a ban was placed on all 'trading' until it was supplied. This method was employed frequently during the last nine months before the end of hostilities, when 'trading' was confined almost exclusively to dry batteries for the secret Camp radio receiver.

Blackmail methods were not used to induce 'contacts' to supply forbidden items, but advantage was taken of the German propaganda about "The Soviet Menace". If a 'contact' showed that he was concerned about the treatment he might receive after the collapse of German resistance, he was shown the 'Safe Conduct Pass'. In most cases this produced the desired effect and the 'contact' became co-operative.

In early 1944 a most fruitful source of escape equipment and information was established by P.0788 F/Lt. B.A. De Large R.A.F. He learned that there were Polish orderlies in the hospital at Neubrandenburg to which P's/W from the Camp was sent for treatment. He feigned illness and was sent there. As he was Polish he was able to make arrangements with two of his fellow countrymen and 30191 Lt. Sorel French Army,for the supply of information and equipment to himself and to other P's/W from the Camp who should be sent there in the future. This system operated for several months and much valuable equipment and information was obtained. Every P/W who went to this hospital was specially briefed about how to establish contact with these helpers without arousing suspicion. Sorel was able to

191

supply information which he obtained from French workers in a factory in the Barth area.

Apart from items such as cigarette lighter flints and fuel, pencils, penknives, etc., which were distributed amongst the P's/W, the following were the chief items obtained by the 'trading' Section: Inks, clothing dyes, paper, German money, firearms and ammunition, radio parts, dry batteries, tools of all kinds, maps, original passes and documents for copying, German uniforms and insignia, civilian clothes, etc. Military and escape information was acquired also.

13. 'TRADING' CAPITAL

During the first few weeks the cigarettes which were used by the 'Trading' Section for bribing 'contacts' were obtained from the communal cigarettes supplied by the Red Cross.

In early 1944, The Senior British Officer Wing Commander Hilton, ordered that each P/W should contribute five cigarettes to a Fund which would be used for acquiring items for the common welfare. This order was very unpopular with the P's/W and after a short time it was arranged that a percentage of the profits of 'foodacco' should sustain this fund. This system remained in operation until early 1945.

Throughout the whole of the period under review, cigarettes for bribing 'contacts' to supply escape equipment and items of a similar nature were obtained from the communal stock supplied by the Red Cross.

All trading capital was controlled by the 'Trading' Officer.

14. 'TRADERS'

(a) The chief 'traders', all of whom could speak German, were:

0-432253	Lt. H. Angevines	U.S.A.A.C.
P-0788	F/Lt. B.A. De Large	R.A.F.
100145	F/Lt. E.J. Mitchell	R.A.F.
108583	F/Lt. T. Mitchell	R.A.F.
155900	F/O W.J. Morgan	R.A.F.
0-800775	Lt. M.M. Schorborne	U.S.A.A.C.
0-807937	Lt. C.E. Shaugnessy	U.S.A.A.C.
134580	F/Lt. D.H. Spencer	R.A.F.
331734	W.O. Arnold, J.F	R.A.F.
903431	W.O. Culley, J.M.	R.A.F.
970434	W.O. Eames, J.J.W.	R.A.F.
970053	W.O. Everson, J.E.	R.A.F.
925696	W.O. Drummond, R.R.	R.A.F.

5179986	Pte. May, G.E.	Glos. Regt.
24431	W.O. Mlodzik, A.	R.A.F.
745334	W.O. Read, L.R.	R.A.F.
550365	W.O. Smith, W.G.	R.A.F.

(b) *Camp resources.*
The main items acquired from Camp resources, apart from 'trading' with Germans and others were: (i) Bed boards for shoring tunnels; (ii) Tools stolen from German workmen, etc; (iii) French and Polish uniforms stolen from the Clothing Store situated in the Vorlager; (iv) Tinfoil for use in connection with secret Camp radio receiver; (v) Empty food tins for use as digging implements in tunnel construction; (vi) Service uniforms used for the manufacture of escape clothing.

(c) *New P's/W.*
Maps, compasses and hacksaw blades were obtained from new P's / W arriving in the Camp, as a number of personnel were able to conceal these items which had been issued to them in the U.K., during the various personal searches following capture. The compasses and hacksaw blades were of great value, but the maps were of little use as the scale was too small.

(d) *Parcels from I.S.9.*
Parcels containing escape aids began to arrive in the Camp at the end of 1943, but the majority of these were from American sources. As far as can be ascertained only eight parcels were received from I.S.9 during the period under review. Two of these were discovered by the Germans and the contents confiscated. The contents of the other parcels included a camera, photographic materials, clothing dyes, inks, mapping pens, maps, compasses, hacksaw blades, and a few printed forgeries of identity cards.

15. CARPENTRY
There was no organisation for the manufacture of articles of wood for use in connection with escape activities. Any items of this description which were required were made by the personnel who wanted them. Comparatively little shoring was used in tunnel construction and where necessary this was done by the personnel engaged in tunnelling.

16. METAL WORK
During the first few months of this period, several pairs of wire-cutters were made out of ice-skates by 50365 W.O. Smith, W.G., R.A.F. When completed these were passed to the Escape Committee.

About April, 1944 the manufacture of wire-cutters from ice-skates was organised on a large scale by 89763 S/Ldr. A.I. McRitchie R.A.F. He directed the efforts of between twenty and thirty P's/W and during the next three months about forty pairs of wire-cutters of high quality were produced. As these were completed they were passed to the Escape Committee.

17. LEATHER WORK

No section was organised for the manufacture of articles of leather, but a certain amount of work of this kind was performed by 550365 W.O. Smith, W.G., R.A.F. He made a holster, containing a dummy pistol, from a pair of boxing gloves. This was used by an American officer in an attempted escape. He constructed a hollow in the sole and heel of a boot, into which a miniature pair of wire-cutters was fitted. This boot was supplied to an officer who proposed to attempt to escape whilst in transit to another Camp.

18. TOOLS

At the beginning of this period the only tools in the Camp were three metal files. When the Escape Committee was organised in December, 1943, one of its members was made responsible for equipment, mainly tools. He was 103482 F/Lt. W.H. Young R.A.F.

During the ensuing months a good stock of tools was built up including: Pliers, steel drills, saws, chisels for wood and iron, screwdrivers, metal files, etc. Electric torches and lanterns were acquired also. These items were obtained through the 'Trading' Section and by stealing them from German workmen, etc.

When not being used, all tools were hidden. The chief hiding places were: In palliases, in the double walls of barracks, and buried in gardens where they could be recovered without arousing suspicion. When tools were being used, the Camp 'watching' system was in operation.

19. GADGETS

The only gadgets which were made during this period were air-pumps for tunnels. These were of the 'bellows' type and were made with canvas kit-bags and wood. This work was done by 108583 F/Lt. T. Mitchell R.A.F.

20. TUNNELS

(a) *General.*

All tunnelling activities were controlled by the Escape Committee, chiefly because it was considered that any attempt executed without their knowledge might jeopardise another project. The members of the Committee who were in charge of tunnelling acted in an advisory capacity and organised assistance, e.g. supply of materials, etc.

Personnel who were interested in tunnel construction formed themselves into groups and approached the Escape Committee with details of their schemes. The proposed sites were inspected by the Tunnelling Officer. If he considered a site to be unsuitable, or likely to interfere with another project, the proposers were advised accordingly. Each group appointed its own leader and he allocated the duties of the others.

(b) *Engineering.*

During this period approximately sixty tunnels were started in the Camp. Two of them reached beyond the perimeter fence, but in both cases the first two men to emerge were apprehended by the German guards. None of these tunnels contained any special feature.

The most active British personnel in connection with tunnel construction were:

615517	S/Ldr. A. Abels	R.A.F.
135626	F/Lt. A.E. Ansfield	R.A.F.
47762	F/O R. Atkinson	R.A.F.
126827	F/Lt. I.D. Bolton	R.A.F.
133408	F/O D.J.H. Cheal	R.A.F.
25038	W/Cdr. R.C.M. Ferrers	R.A.F.
120448	F/Lt. T.C. Graham	R.A.F.
103829	S/Ldr. D.J. Kilgallin	R.A.F. Regiment
157305	F/O D.E.A. Lander	R.A.F.
47785V	Lt. E.D. Lugg	S.A.A.F.
34006	G/C N.W. Marwood-Elton	R.A.F.
136698	F/Lt. W.J. Needham	R.A.F.
206392V	Lt. C.M.D. Reitz	S.A.A.F.
130656	F/Lt. R.D. Truscott	R.A.F.
331734	W.O. Arnold, J.F.	R.A.F.
970286	W.O. Atkinson, R.	R.A.F.
548508	W.O. Johnson, H.G.	R.A.F.
920228	W.O. Lee, G.H.	R.A.F.
649279	W.O. Luke, G.	R.A.F.
1340507	A.C.1. Marshall, A.B.	R.A.F.

In this Camp the ideal site from which to start a tunnel was considered to be under a barrack situated close to the perimeter fence. In most cases the trap-door, which was made in the floor of the barrack, was located in such a position that it could not be seen from outside the barrack. Under a bed was a favourite place.

If there was a space between the floor of the barrack and the ground, a trapdoor was fitted over the vertical shaft of the tunnel. When work was not in progress this trapdoor was covered with a thick layer of soil of the same colour as the surrounding area.

The vertical shafts usually were about three feet square and boxed with timber to prevent collapse. They were sunk to below water level, about five or six feet below the surface in most parts of the Camp.

The lateral shafts were excavated just above water level and direction was maintained with the aid of a compass. The tunnels were just large enough to enable a man lying on his stomach to elbow his way along. They were elliptical in shape and very little shoring was needed because of the adhesive properties of the sub-soil.

Sledges were used to haul the sand from the working 'face' to the bottom of the vertical shaft. The 'face' worker filled the sledge as he excavated and this was hauled to the bottom of the vertical shaft by means of a rope. When it was emptied by the man stationed there, the 'face' worker hauled it back. One of the advantages of this system was that an elaborate air-pump was not necessary as only one man had to be supplied with air.

In the Autumn of 1944, after the Senior British Officer had banned all attempts to escape, permission was obtained for the construction of a tunnel for use in the event of an emergency. This tunnel extended to a point beyond the perimeter fence. It was never used, nor was it discovered by the Germans. Its construction was organised by Captain Agar U.S.A.A.C.

The Tunnelling Officers, who were members of the Escape Committee were 43479 F/Lt. D.I. Pike R.A.F.[and] 158986 F/Lt. J.R. Lake R.A.F. Pike held this position from December 1943 until May, 1944, when Lake assumed his duties. Pike continued to act in an advisory capacity.

(c) *Dispersal.*

The greatest difficulty which had to be overcome in connection with tunnelling was the dispersal of the excavated sand. The Abwehr Staff were very expert at detecting freshly dug sand and when this happened intensive searches were conducted until the tunnel was located.

Another difficulty which was encountered was that whatever method was adopted for dispersal, the output of the tunnellers was greater than the dispersers could handle. This was because efficient dispersal was a slow process. In order to deal with the output of sand, dispersal often was hurried and liable to be noticed by an observant German. The following were the methods adopted for dispersal:

(i) The sand was carried in pails from the barrack, in which the tunnel entrance was situated, to the nearest wash-house/lavatory. This was a normal procedure as slops were disposed of in this way and the suspicions of the Germans were not aroused. The sand was dumped into the cess-pool and was not visible. This was the most efficient method, but it was slow as too many trips of this kind from one barrack would have been suspicious.

(ii) The sand was carried in boxes etc. from the barrack, in which the tunnel entrance was situated, to a vegetable plot which was screened from observation by Germans, then it was mixed with the soil of the plot. This method was very slow due to the movements of Germans.

(iii) In some cases the sand was spread under the floor of the barrack from which the tunnel was being constructed. This was possible only when there was a clearance between the floor of the barrack and the ground. This method enabled dispersal to be effected quickly, but the Abwehr Staff invariably detected this within a short time and searched until the tunnel was found.

(iv) An excellent method from the security standpoint was to have a large number of P's/W walk across the football field with their pockets filled with the sand. When scattered this was soon mixed with the loose sand forming the surface. The chief drawback of this method was its slowness.

(d) *Supplies.*

Each group of tunnellers was responsible for obtaining the equipment they required, but the Escape Committee rendered assistance in this respect when necessary. The chief items which were used were: (i) Bed boards for trapdoors, shoring, sledges, etc.; (ii) Digging implements made out of empty food tins; (iii) Empty food tins for use as an air-line in conjunction with the type of air-pump described [earlier]; (iv) String or rope for handling sledges; (v) Illumination at the tunnel 'face' was provided by 'duck lamps' made out of empty food tins, using margarine for fuel and pyjama cord or brace material as a wick, also electric torches and lanterns.

(e) *Security.*

Good security was considered by the Escape Committee to be a major essential in connection with tunnel construction. All personnel engaged on this work were warned of the necessity for exercising the utmost care.

The main points of security in connection with tunnels were: (i) Careful watch to ensure that no P/W was apprehended whilst at work. This duty was performed by 'watchers' under the Camp Security System; (ii) Adequate concealment of the tunnel entrance; (iii) Dispersal of the excavated sand in such a way that the Germans did not suspect that tunnel construction was in progress; (iv) The concealment of sand-impregnated garments worn by tunnellers whilst at work. As a rule these were left just inside the lateral shaft.

(f) *Comments.*

Although no successful tunnels were constructed during this period the activities of the P's/W in this direction served a double purpose:
    (i) It helped to maintain the morale of the P's/W.
    (ii) It caused a great deal of trouble to the Germans, causing them to increase the number of boundary lights and to place sentries in sentry towers which had not been manned previously. The Abwehr Staff were forced to spend much of their time looking for tunnels, thus diverting their attention from other activities within the Camp. It is considered that the main reasons for the failure to construct a successful tunnel were: (1) During the previous occupation of the Camp by Air Force personnel, a very large number of tunnels had been started from every conceivable vantage point. This applied to the South and West Compounds, which were the first to be occupied during this period. Often it happened that old shafts and tunnels were encountered during the construction of a tunnel, which caused large falls of sand. This delayed and sometimes stopped operations; (2) The German anti-tunnelling measures were very efficient; (3) Inadequate security, i.e. inefficient dispersal of sand, inadequate concealment of tunnel entrances, careless talk amongst P's/W after 'lock-up', etc.

21. GATE WALK-OUT SCHEMES
The only attempt which was made during this period by a British P/W to escape by walking through the gates was carried out in June, 1944 by 63074 W/Cdr. J.A. Lee-Evans R.A.F. He was wearing Luftwaffe fatigue dress, consisting of a white jacket, filed-grey trousers and field-service cap. He carried a cloth bag containing food, a torch and cigarettes. He was in possession of a map and German money.

By arrangement, he hid beneath a pile of clothing which was being conveyed from the West Compound to the North Compound on a hand-wagon. This was pushed by a party of P's/W, but they were accompanied by a guard as the Vorlager had to be traversed. On the way the P's/W engaged the guard in conversation and when in the Vorlager, at a moment when the wagon was not being observed by any German, Lee-Evans rolled off upon receipt of a signal from one of the P's/W pushing the wagon.

His disguise enabled Lee-Evans to walk through the Vorlager gate into the woods nearby: this was about 1100 hours. He walked through the woods until he came to a wire fence, over which he was climbing when a German appeared. Lee-Evans dropped back into some undergrowth until the German had gone, then decided to wait until nightfall before making another attempt to climb over the fence. As he had not seen anyone during the day, he made a second attempt during the evening. He was seen by a member of the Camp Staff and recaptured.

22. WIRE SCHEMES
(a) *First attempt.*
In early December, 1943 an attempt was made to cut through the perimeter fence, under cover of darkness, by C.1452 F/Lt. J.R. Bryan R.C.A.F. He was apprehended before he got outside the Camp.

(b) *Second attempt.*
On about 16th January, 1944 an attempt to escape by cutting through two fences was made by C.1452 F/Lt. J.R. Bryan R.C.A.F. [and] 968327 W.O. Kerr, W.E., R.A.F. Bryan claimed to be able to fly a Ju.52 and it was their intention to endeavour to steal an aircraft of this type from the aerodrome situated a few kilometres from the Camp. They were wearing R.A.F. battledress, Luftwaffe field-service caps made in the Camp, and were in possession of forged Luftwaffe Paybooks and sufficient food for two days. Kerr had a pair of wirecutters.

Before dusk they hid under the stage of the Camp Theatre, which was out-of-bounds after dark, and stayed there until the P's/W had been locked in their barracks. At 1630 hours they crawled from under the theatre to a position which was partly screened by a potato clamp from the only sentry tower having a view of the spot. Bryan kept watch while Kerr cut through the nearby double fence into an enclosure round the cook-house portion of the cook-house/theatre building. At this time the lights on the perimeter fence had not been switched on.

It was necessary for Bryan and Kerr to be clear of the Camp before 1800 hours as they were certain to be missed during roll call which took place at that hour.

Owing to the intense cold Kerr was forced to stop cutting before he got through this fence, in order to have his hands massaged by Bryan. While this was being done the lights on the fence were switched on. Kerr returned to the fence and resumed cutting, succeeding in getting through the first part of the fence.

He saw two guards accompanied by a dog approaching for the usual nightly search of the theatre. He returned to where Bryan was keeping watch in the shadow of the potato clamp. The Germans inspected the door of the clamp, then entered the theatre. The dog sniffed at Bryan and Kerr, but did not bark; the Germans had the utmost difficulty in calling him away. After the Germans had completed the inspection of the theatre they went away. Kerr resumed cutting through the second part of the fence.

The delay caused by Kerr's hands becoming too cold for work and the incident of the two guards meant that he would have to work at very high speed if they were to get clear of the Camp before 1800 hours, when the alarm was certain to be raised by their absence from roll call.

When Kerr had made a sufficiently large gap in the second part of the fence, he clambered through and signalled for Bryan to follow. In doing so Bryn injured his eye. They crawled to the second fence which separated the cook-house from the unoccupied South-West Compound, in which barracks were being constructed. This was guarded by one patrolling sentry only.

When they reached this double fence, Kerr noticed that the guards had entered the West Compound for the roll call. He decided to risk being seen in order to cut through the fence more quickly. To do this he worked in a kneeling position instead of lying flat. He had cut through the first part of the fence and the entanglements, and was at work on the second part of the fence when a guard saw him. The area was illuminated by a lamp situated about twenty yards distant.

The guard shouted and ran towards Kerr, who, in the meantime had buried all his escape equipment. Bryan had not seen the guard owing to his eye injury. The guard held them until the arrival of the Abwehr Officer.

(c) *Third attempt.*

On 22nd January, 1944 a partly successful escape was effected by N.Z.404362 F/Lt. R.B. Hesselyn R.N.Z.A.F. [and] 964794 W.O. Oliver, R.B., R.A.F. Hesselyn was wearing a civilian jacket made in the Camp from a blanket, R.A.F. trousers and a Camp-made cloth cap. He had maps, German money and a compass, but no identity papers. Olliver was wearing R.A.F. battledress and had maps, a compass, German money and a forged identity card. Both carried chocolate, biscuits, etc. in their pockets.

At about 1630 hours they hid in the roof of the Camp Theatre and remained there until about 1900 hours, when they crawled through a ventilator on to the roof. They crawled along the roof and dropped to the ground near the gate leading into the South-West Compound, which was unoccupied. They avoided two patrolling sentries and climbed over the gate under cover of darkness and heavy rain. They crawled across the South-West Compound to the Western perimeter fence and climbed over a temporary gate, which was about half-way between two sentry towers fitted with searchlights.

As soon as they were clear of the Camp area they walked South across country. About 0800 hours the following morning they arrived at the outskirts of Velgast and hid in a small wood until 1200 hours. They left the wood and walked to the railway marshalling yard, where they were arrested by four policemen as they attempted to enter. Later that day they were returned to the Camp.

(d) *Fourth attempt.*
On 12th March, 1944 an attempt to cut through the fence was made by:

	Lt. Brown	U.S.A.A.C.
25038	W/Cdr. R.C.M. Ferrers	R.A.F.
	Lt. Patterson	U.S.A.A.C.
	Lt. Stukas	U.S.A.A.C.

The party was led by Ferrers and this attempt was made at about 2300 hours. The party hid under a barrack in the West Compound, which is marked '26' on [Plate 1}. The South end of this barrack was situated about five yards from the fence separating the West Compound from the South-West Compound. The latter was unoccupied as the erection of barracks had not been completed at this time.

After ascertaining that there were no Germans in the vicinity, Ferrers crawled to the fence, which was illuminated, and was about to start cutting through it when he received a warning from Stukas that a dog was in the vicinity. The whole party attempted to get back under the barrack, but they were discovered by the dog and arrested by the guards accompanying it.

(e) *Fifth attempt.*
On 22nd May, 1944 an attempt to escape by cutting through several fences was made by 5460 2/Lt. J. Helland R.A.F. [and] 34006 G/C

N.W.D. Marwood-Elton R.A.F. In preparation for the attempt Marwood-Elton spent about two months learning German phrases from Helland, who was a Norwegian. They were supplied by the Escape Committee with airmen's greatcoats altered and dyed black, black corduroy trousers, French berets and forged identity papers indicating that they were Danish workmen, German money and two pairs of wirecutters made from ice-skates. For several weeks they studied the locations of guards at night, timing of dog patrols, effectiveness of the boundary lighting etc.

They formulated the following plan: To make the attempt from the barrack nearest the gate of the West Compound, as this had a trapdoor in the floor which led into a tunnel about twenty feet in length, which in turn led into the inspection trench running underneath the whole length of the barrack. To crawl from the South end of this inspection trench, which was nearest to the gate leading into the Vorlager, to the gate, a distance of about twenty yards, then to cut through the gate. This fence was patrolled by a guard, but he was not stationed at the gate: this fence was illuminated by arc lamps. To crawl across the Vorlager and cut through the fence surrounding the shower-baths building. Then to cut through the North perimeter fence of the Vorlager, the assumption being that the guards in the sentry towers around the Vorlager would have their attention focussed on the Russian Compound, which was adjacent to the shower-baths enclosure, and on the P's/W Compounds.

They briefed several men to act as watchers during the initial stages of the attempt and arranged a series of signals which were knocks on the wooden floor of the barrack.

At 0100 hours on 22nd May they got into the tunnel under the barrack. A few minutes later they heard the air-raid alarm signal and realised that the guards would be doubled and the light extinguished. They heard the re-call signal as they had not planned to make the attempt during an air-raid alarm period. They discussed the position and decided to ignore the re-call signal and continue with the attempt. After a lapse of about five minutes they emerged from under the barrack and crawled to the gate: the lights had been extinguished.

Marwood-Elton cut through the gate and crawled across the Vorlager followed by Helland. The former cut through the fence surrounding the shower-baths building and they sheltered at the side of the bath-house. This operation had taken about one hour from the time they left the barrack.

Almost at once they heard an air-raid 'All Clear' signal and discussed the advisability of waiting until the lights were switched on before attempting to cut through the perimeter fence. They reasoned that if they were cutting through the fence when the lights were switched on, they would be dazzled. They decided to wait and about ten minutes later the local 'All Clear' was sounded and the lights were switched on. They were blinded temporarily by their brilliance. Then they watched the extra guards returning to the guardroom.

Marwood-Elton left Helland in the shadow of the bath-house and crawled towards the perimeter fence to a point about twenty yards from the sentry tower marked '17' on [Plate 1] which was fitted with a search-light and machine-gun. When near the fence he discovered that he had lost his wirecutters in the long grass and as he failed to find them he returned to where he had left Helland. He got Helland's wirecutterrs and again crawled towards the fence. When he got close to it he realised that it would not be possible to carry on with the scheme as it was almost dawn, and a clear patch of ground had to be crossed outside the fence. The time taken had been much longer than anticipated.

Marwood-Elton crawled back to Helland and they discussed the possibility of hiding in the bath-house during that day and cutting through the outer fence the following night, but decided that this would not be practical. They hid their escape aids, which were recovered about a month later; and ate as much as possible of the food they had with them. At 0500 hours they gave themselves up to the sentry in the sentry tower.

23. WALL SCHEMES
Not applicable.

24. TRANSPORT SCHEME
The only attempt which was made by British personnel to escape by means of being transported through the gate was carried out on 20th March, 1944 by C.1359 S/Ldr. L.E. Logan R.C.A.F. He attached a number of empty food tins to a sack so as to cover one side of it and was placed inside by some fellow P's/W. The sack was placed in a box used for taking empty tins out of the Compound, which was filled up with empty tins. Shortly afterwards the box was carried out of the Camp by a number of P's/W accompanied by a guard. On arrival at the tin dump the guard's attention was distracted by one of the P's/W while the others emptied the box in such a way that the sack containing Logan was not visible.

Logan intended to remain hidden until dark before attempting to leave the area, but at dusk a German guard searched the dump looking for a tin. He selected one which was attached to the sack and on investigating realised that there was someone hidden in it. He stood on top of Logan and called for assistance. A few minutes later Logan was released from the sack and arrested.

25. MISCELLANEOUS SCHEMES
Not applicable.

26. NUMBER OF ESCAPES
There were no successful escapes from this Camp during the period under review.

27. NUMBER OF ATTEMPTED ESCAPES
No details can be given of attempted escapes made by American personnel, except where they accompanied British personnel, as no records of these are available.

In addition to the sixty tunnels which were started in the Camp by British and American personnel and on which a large number of men were engaged, seven separate attempts to escape were made involving thirteen British and American personnel.

28. MASS ATTEMPTS
It was planned that mass attempts to escape would be made by means of the two partly successful tunnels. In both instances the first two men to emerge were apprehended by the Germans.

29. SUMMARY OF METHODS
(a) *Tunnels.*
Comments on tunnel construction during the period under review are given [elsewhere in] this Chapter.

(b) *Gate Walk-out Scheme.*
This attempt would appear to have failed because the escaper became too impatient to get clear of the Camp area to wait until dark before attempting to climb the last obstacle to freedom. It is pointed out that this escaper was the Chairman of the Escape Committee.

(c) *Wire Schemes.*
The five attempts which were made to escape by negotiating the wire are described [elsewhere in] this Chapter.

Insufficient details are known about the first attempt for comment to be made.

The second attempt was well planned and executed, but it is evident that discovery was due to Bryan's eye injury which impaired his efficiency as a watcher.

The third attempt was successful to the extent that the personnel concerned got clear of the Camp area.

It is evident that the fourth attempt failed through inefficient watching in the preliminary stage.

The fifth attempt was extremely well planned and executed. No comment is necessary.

(d) *Wall Schemes.*
Not applicable.

(e) *Transport scheme.*
This attempt was most ingenious. Logan was most unfortunate in that the German selected a tin which was attached to the sack in which he was hiding.

(f) *Miscellaneous Schemes.*
Nil.

(g) *Mass attempts.*
Nil.

(h) *Comments by I.S.9.*
It is remarkable that although the Escape Organisation was in existence, only seven separate attempts were made to escape by British personnel during the period of ten months when escapes were permitted by the Senior British Officer. In only one instance did the escapers get clear of the Camp area.

30. ESCAPE AIDS RECEIVED FROM I.S.9.
As far as can be ascertained only eight uncamouflaged parcels containing escape aids were received from I.S.9. during this period. Two of these were discovered by the Germans; one, containing Christmas crackers, because it was badly packed, and no advice of its despatch had been received, and the second, containing parts of a camera, because no advice of its despatch had been received. The six parcels which were smuggled past the Germans contained maps, German money, a stove and solid fuel tablets, a camera and photographic materials, radio parts, identity cards, maps and compasses.

It has been established that several parcels containing food and clothing were received from an unknown source. These were addressed to the Senior British Officer, and although no advice was received that they contained escape aids, the contents were examined carefully, but no escape aids were found.

Note: Parcels of this type were despatched by I.S.9. to the Senior British Officer of a number of Camps. Maps and German money was concealed in the tins of condensed milk, which were double-sided. It is understood that no games parcels containing escape aids were received from I.S.9. during this period.

The total number of parcels received from I.S.9. during this period compares very unfavourably with the number received by the Americans from the U.S.A. The Americans received over one hundred parcels of two main types – uncamouflaged and containing gadgets of various kinds in which escape aids were concealed. Beside escape equipment of all kinds, these parcels contained midget radio equipment, receivers and transmitters.

No parcels were received from I.S.9. after September, 1944, but the Americans received parcels containing escape aids until the end of hostilities.

31. REMARKS ON PACKING OF ESCAPE AIDS

The package of escape aids received from I.S.9. was satisfactory with the following exceptions:

(i) The Christmas crackers received at the end of 1943 were very badly packed. As a result one of the crackers fell on the floor in the Parcels Store and one of the German censors picked it up, remarking to the P/W Parcels Officer, "Let us pull this one". They did so and to the amazement of both it was found to contain maps and German money.

(ii) Two of the undisguised parcels of escape aids were packed in gramophone record boxes. The Germans were very strict about examining all gramophone records, and it was due to the quick action of the P's/W in the Parcels Store, who hid them before the German censor saw them, that they were smuggled into the Compound successfully.

32. CONCEALMENT OF ESCAPE AIDS – GADGETS, etc.

All the methods used by I.S.9. for concealing the escape aids which were received during this period were successful, with the exception of that described [elsewhere in] this Chapter. Escape aids concealed in gadgets, i.e. cotton reels, sports equipment, etc., all of which emanated from the

U.S.A., were so cleverly hidden that they passed the German censorship without discovery.

The only parcel which the Germans were suspicious about were those containing Christmas crackers and gramophone records.

33. ACQUIREMENT OF SPECIAL PARCELS

All parcels known to contain escape aids, as advised to the Camp by means of code messages, and all parcels which were suspected of containing escape aids even though no advice had been received were abstracted by the P's/W dealing with parcels in the Parcels Store in the Vorlager. These were conveyed into the Compounds without being censored by the Germans.

34. DANGERS OF STEALING PARCELS

The success of stealing parcels prior to censorship was dependent upon the quick wit and ingenuity of the P's/W handling the parcels in the Parcel Store.

As no individual was apprehended whilst stealing a parcel it is not known whether any special dangers existed. It is considered that if any individual had been caught in the act the punishment would have been a short period in the cells and he would have been debarred from handling parcels thereafter. A stricter control of parcels would have ensued for a time, but this would have relaxed within a few weeks.

35. MATERIAL AVAILABLE/ACQUIRABLE ON THE SPOT

A considerable amount of escape material was available, or acquirable, in the Camp.

36. SUGGESTIONS FOR THE FUTURE

It is suggested that parcels containing escape aids etc., should be addressed to individuals, but before this is done contact must be established with the Camp in order to ensure that conditions are such that parcels would be acquired before censorship could be effected. It is essential that advice of the despatch of such parcels should be set to the Senior Officer, or other competent authority, by means of code messages in duplicate and that care is taken to give ample warning. Such advices should give the number, rank, initials and name of the addressee, an indication of any such markings on the parcel to aid identification, a list of the contents.

The system adopted by the Americans for introducing escape aids, etc., into this Camp was excellent.

Chapter 19

Censorship by Germans

37. METHOD

(a) *Parcels.*

Red Cross food, next-of-kin clothing, games, book, cigarettes and tobacco parcels arrived at Barth Railway Station and Post Office. When the Germans learned of the arrival of a consignment of parcels, they sent a party of P's/W, under escort, with a vehicle to collect them. A member of the German Parcel Censorship staff always accompanied these parties. The parcels were loaded on to the vehicle under the close supervision of the censor and the escorting guards.

When the vehicle arrived in the Camp Vorlager, the parcels were unloaded by the party of P's/W and transferred to the Parcel Store. This was done under the strict supervision of several Germans.

In theory every parcel which reached the Camp was censored by the Germans. When the food parcels were being issued, they were opened by the P/W Parcels Staff in the presence of the German Parcel Censors. All tins, except those containing coffee, were punctured at one end by the Censors. This was the only form of censorship imposed on food.

Cigarette, cigar and tobacco parcels were slit open in the presence of the Censors, but the contents were not emptied out of the wrappings. On occasion a Censor would open a packet and remove a cigarette, or cigar and break it.

Parcels containing books were separated from all other parcels and taken to the German Headquarters for censorship. The book censors had lists of forbidden and permissible books. Books which were banned were those dealing with politics, or propaganda and all works by authors who had written, or spoken against the Nazi regime; also all works by authors of Jewish origin. Books which did not appear on either of the lists referred to above were read by the Censors and passed or rejected by them. Books which were passed by the censorship was distributed by the P/W Librarians.

Next-of-kin clothing and games parcels were sorted into piles for the respective Compounds by the P/W Parcels Staff under German supervision. Then they were opened by the P's/W and passed along a bench to be examined by the Censors. After censorship they were re-tied roughly in their original wrappings and placed in sacks for transfer to the appropriate Compounds. When the P's/W saw parcels which they believed to contain escape aids, etc., they were slit open as though for inspection, then re-tied and placed in one of the sacks containing parcels which had been censored, whilst the attention of the Censors was distracted by one or more members of the P/W Parcels Staff. Certain types of American parcels contained escape aids concealed in gadgets and these were passed through the censorship in the normal way.

Parcels known to contain escape aids, etc., which were addressed to personnel located in the North Compound were taken to that Compound, together with innocuous parcels, and handed over to the responsible American officer there.

Similar parcels which were addressed to personnel in the South, West and South-West Compounds were taken to the rooms occupied by the undermentioned personnel who formed the P/W Parcels Staff. The escape aids were removed from the gadgets known to contain them in sports and clothing parcels from the U.S.A., then these parcels were repacked and handed to the individuals to whom they were addressed. The addressees were unaware that their parcels contained escape aids. The escape aids were passed to the Senior British Officer or the Senior American Officer. All undisguised parcels of escape aids, etc. were passed to them intact.

The P/W in charge of all British and American parcels arriving in the Camp was 100145 F/Lt. E.J. Mitchell R.A.F. His assistants were:

Capt. Birkner	U.S.A.A.C.
69445 F/Lt. P.S. Lester	R.A.F.
132770 F/Lt. I.B. Reid	R.A.F.
Lt. (A) H.R. Spedding	R.N.
Lt. Westerfield	U.S.A.A.C.
970434 W.O. Eames, J.J.W.	R.A.F.

(b) *Mail.*

The censorship of all in-coming and out-going mail was done at Stalag Luft III (Sagan). It is worthy to note that mail from the U.K. was delivered from three to four months after posting, while letters posted in the U.S.A. were delivered within a few weeks.

38. RESULTS

(a) *Parcels.*

In theory, the censorship of all parcels was carried out efficiently by the Germans. In practice, all parcels which were believed by the P's/W to contain escape aids, or other forbidden items were removed from the Parcels Store without the knowledge of the Germans.

(b) *Mail.*

The German censorship of letters arriving in the Camp was reasonably efficient. Obscure phrases, stilted sentences and groups of figures were blacked out. There is some evidence that the existence of a secret means of communication between Allied countries and the P's/W was suspected. At irregular intervals a large proportion of the letters arriving in the Camp showed traces of having been tested for invisible writing by means of acids and alkali. As far as can be ascertained the use of a code was not suspected.

39. OBJECT OF CENSORSHIP

(a) *Parcels.*

The object of censorship was to prevent the P's/W from obtaining forbidden items, or concealed messages. The reason for puncturing tins of food was to ensure that the contents would be consumed within a short time and not hoarded for use in an attempted escape.

(b) *Mail.*

The object of censoring mail was to delete passages which might convey a message, or possible keys to a code; also to discover messages written in invisible ink.

40. PARCEL MARKINGS

(a) *British.*

Parcels containing forbidden items which were received from I.S.9. were not marked in such a way that they could be distinguished from normal parcels without difficulty. The P/W Parcels Staff were not in possession of a list of personnel to whom parcels of this type were being addressed. These factors forced them to rely on their powers of observation to discern any parcels which differed from the normal type of innocuous parcel. This was extremely difficult when it is remembered that thousands of parcels were being handled each week by a small number of P's/W.

Two instances of the discovery by the Germans of parcels containing forbidden items have been related [elsewhere]. If advices have been received in the Camp by means of code messages, these parcels could have been removed from the Parcels Store without difficulty by the method described [elsewhere in] this Chapter.

(b) *American.*

All parcels from the U.S.A. which contained forbidden items bore the postmark 'Alabama'. The Service numbers, ranks and names of all personnel to whom such parcels were addressed were supplied to the American code users in the Camp by means of code messages. A separate message was received for each parcel and these advices arrived well in advance of the parcels. This information was supplied to the P's/W who worked in the Parcels Store and action was taken as outlined [elsewhere in] this Chapter.

It has been established that a small number of undisguised parcels containing escape equipment, etc., which had been despatched form the U.S.A., fell into German hands through the carelessness of an American officer. Although the parcels were marked as indicated above, he overlooked them in the preliminary sorting and they were allowed to pass before the German censors.

41. COMMENT

(a) *Parcels.*

The fact that a very small quantity of escape equipment, radio components, etc. was received from the U.K. in comparison with the amounts supplied from the U.S.A., had an adverse effect on the British personnel who knew the details. They felt that the British were being neglected by the responsible authority in the U.K.

(b) *Mail.*

The British P's/W were unable to understand why mail from the U.K. took so much longer for delivery than that from the U.S.A. It was felt that the difference was due to more efficient organisation on the part of the American Government. This factor had some effect on British morale.

Chapter 20

Code-letter Mail

42. INTRODUCTION

For the first few weeks of this period, all matters connected with code-letters were dealt with by 580309 W.O. May, T.K., R.A.F., who had been in charge of the Coding Section during part of the preceding period. May had volunteered to remain when the N.C.O's were being evacuated, in order to teach the code to the officers when they arrived, should that be necessary.

In December, 1943 an officer who had been taught the code before capture arrived in the Camp and took over from May. He was 126827 F/Lt. I.D. Bolton R.A.F.

Shortly afterwards an officer who had been engaged in despatching code messages from P/W Camps in Italy arrived in the Camp. He was appointed by the Senior British Officer to take charge of all coding and to organise a Coding Section. This officer was 49939 Major T.A.G. Pritchard Parachute Regiment.

43. ORGANISATION

(a) *Sources of information.*

Military information for despatch to the U.K. by means of code messages embodied in letters was obtained from the undermentioned sources:

(i) New P's/W. All new arrivals, British and American, were interviewed at once in order to check their bona fides. A few days later, after checking had been completed, they were interrogated in order to discover whether they had any information of military value. These interrogations covered the cause of loss of aircraft, military targets seen, etc. There were British and American interrogators, each dealing with their own Services. The British interrogators were 925696 W.O. Drummond, R.R., R.A.F., who worked alone from December, 1943 until January, 1944. During

212

the latter month he was joined by 85998 F/Lt. E.R. Inkpen R.A.F., and they worked together until March,1944, when Drummond was transferred to the North (American) Compound to act as liaison between the Senior American Officer and the Senior British Officer; also to aid the American Coding Section in that Compound by interrogating newly arrived American P's/W and teaching an American officer to do this work. Drummond ceased interrogating about August, 1944. When Drummond was transferred to the North Compound, Inkpen was joined by 127235 F/Lt. A.F. Gobbie R.A.F., and they worked together until about May, 1944. During that month the Interrogation Section was re-organised and 156011 F/Lt. G.J. Sleeman R.A.F. was appointed to be in charge. His assistants were Gobbie, Inkpen and N.Z.404362 F/Lt R.B. Hesselyn R.N.Z.A.F. In September, 1944 Gobbie was replaced by 43527 S/Ldr. D.W. Barlow R.A.F. Barlow, Hesselyn, Inkpen and Sleeman worked together until they had dealt with the last batch of new arrivals in the Camp: this was about March, 1945.

(ii) P's/W on journeys outside the Camp. All personnel who went on journeys outside the Camp, e.g. on visits to the town of Barth to collect parcels, to hospitals for treatment, etc. were briefed by the individual in charge of the Coding Section before they left the Camp. They were instructed to observe as much as possible and to report anything of interest upon their return to the Camp. This system was in operation throughout the period under review.

(iii) Contacts. The most important source of military information was the 'Trading' Section. The 'traders' obtained the information from Germans, foreign workmen, etc. who were known as 'contacts'. All information was passed to the officer in charge of the 'Trading' Section, 103829 S/Ldr. D.J. Kilgallin R.A.F. Regiment.

(iv) Recaptured escapers. Recaptured escapers were interrogated by the Chairman of the Escape Committee. As only the British personnel got away from the Camp area, very little military information was obtained from this source.

(b) *Collation.*
Throughout the period under review the military information which was obtained from the sources outlined above was collated by the individual in charge of the Coding Section. An attempt was made to verify all information. The results were passed to the Senior British Officer who indicated what information should be despatched to the U.K. He indicated the requirements of the Escape Committee also.

The Senior British Officer and the Senior American Officer maintained a close liaison in this, as in all matters, and passed important information to one another in encoded messages through the agency of Warrant Officer Drummond.

(c) *Coding Staff.*
The person in charge of the Coding Section showed the messages which had been prepared by the Senior British Officer to the code users, or encoded them personally and embodied them in their letters and postcards to the U.K. Each code user did his own encoding of messages for despatch and decoding of the replies from I.S.9. All messages from I.S.9. were passed to the Head of the Coding Section, who passed them on to the Senior British Officer.

Because of the type of code in use no central organisation was possible for the encoding and decoding of messages.

All messages between the Senior British Officer and the Senior American Officer were encoded and decoded by N.Z.404362 F/Lt. R.B. Hesselyn R.N.Z.A.F. [and] 580309 W.O. May, T.K., R.A.F., who worked for the Senior British Officer. May was repatriated to the U.K. in January, 1945 and from then onwards Hesselyn worked alone.

(d) *Code-letter writers.*
A number of selected officers and N.C.O's were taught the code by:

126827	F/Lt. I.D. Bolton	A.A.F
580309	W.O. May, T.K.	R.A.F.
49939	Major T.A.G. Pritchard	Parachute Regiment

and registered by them as code users in their own messages to I.S.9. However there is no record of any messages being received by I.S.9. from Bolton or May.

Some of the personnel who had been instructed by the abovementioned taught others; on the authority of Pritchard, and registered them as code-users in their own messages to the U.K.

The result of the foregoing was that although Pritchard, who was in charge of the Coding Section, thought he had a staff of over thirty registered code users, I.S.9. were receiving messages only from those whom Pritchard had registered in his own messages, and those who had been registered in turn by them.

The following are the personnel from whom code messages were received by I.S.9.:

39842	F/Lt. G.E. Ball	R.A.F.
391525	F/Lt. E.S. Kelly	R.A.F.
49939	Major T.A.G. Pritchard	Parachute Regiment
542049	W.O. Cumpstey, H.G.	R.A.F.
580078	W.O. Jones, A.E.	R.A.F.
929468	W.O. North-Lewis, W.E.	R.A.F.
564766	W.O. Robson, F.	R.A.F.

The following are the personnel who are known to have despatched code messages to the U.K. but from whom no messages were received by I.S.9.:

131561	F/O. A. Bolton	R.A.F.
126827	F/Lt. I.D. Bolton	R.A.F
134060	F/Lt. D. Bower	R.A.F
N.Z.416469	F/Lt. L.S. Dixon	R.N.Z.A.F.
N.Z.404362	F/Lt. R.B. Hesselyn	R.N.Z.A.F.
141825	F/Lt. R.L. Myers	R.A.F
136698	F/Lt. W.J.C. Needham	R.A.F
135487	F/O. E.B. Overton	R.A.F
139484	F/O. H.E. Peake	R.A.F
43479	F/Lt. D.I. Pike	R.A.F
	Lt. (A) H.R. Spedding	R.N.
109026	F/Lt. F.W.A. Westcott	R.A.F
916491	W.O. Ashmead-Bartlett, R.R.A.F	
903431	W.O. Culley, J.H.	R.A.F
925696	W.O. Drummond, R.R.	R.A.F.
790053	W.O. Everson, J.E.	R.A.F.
905095	W.O. Hurrell, H.L.	R.A.F.
580309	W.O. May, T.K.	R.A.F.

Two messages written in a private code, were despatched to his brother by 962982 W.O. Kilminster, A.R., R.A.F. His brother passed these to the Air Ministry.

(e) *Despatch of messages.*
As a general rule, the correct encoding of all messages despatched to the U.K. was entrusted to the individual code users. The only letters containing code messages which were checked by the Head of the Coding Section were those containing very important information and those written by inexperienced or inefficient code users.

44. SECURITY

It was known generally amongst the P's/W that some means of secret communication existed between the Camp and the U.K., but the method was known to only a small number, apart from the code users.

No special arrangements were made to give warning when code users were at work. Most of this work was done in the barrack rooms after 'lock-up'. Although accommodation was crowded the other occupants of the rooms were unaware of the nature of the work which was being done.

No written message was ever given to a code user for encoding. The message as approved by the Senior British Officer was written on a slip of paper and shown to the code user selected to despatch it, then the paper was burnt by the head of the Coding Section.

No code user was ever discovered at work by a German and as far as can be ascertained the code was never compromised.

45. COMMENTS BY I.S.9

None of the personnel who were taught the code in the Camp should have been used for the despatch of messages until an acknowledgement of their registration was received from I.S.9. All registrations of new code users should have been sent to the U.K. in duplicate.

46. CRITICISMS BY P'S/W

A fair number of messages were received from I.S.9. but these were both vague and out of date. It was found that the messages received in code, broadcast as the 'Voice of America' were far more useful and important than the code messages despatched from the U.K. by letter.

A request was sent to the U.K. by code message asking for details of conditions in Germany. No reply was received.

Information was received by code message from the U.K. about Swedish ships and the flags they were flying, most of which proved to be inaccurate.

Another message which was received stated that if a pair of blue trousers were hung on a line on the Swedish ferry at Rostock, it would be safe for P's/W to board the ship. The veracity of this statement was doubted very strongly.

It was felt that a great deal of information which should have been sent was lacking, such as:

(i) Details of shipping routes in the Baltic.
(ii) Times of regular sailings from the Baltic ports.
(iii) Localities where neutral seamen might be found and their known haunts.

(iv) Accurate details of special markings on neutral ships, including flags flown, the signal hoisted just prior to departure, etc.

(v) Descriptions and details of hiding places on board ships and in dock areas.

(vi) Where known, most likely places where neutral ships and dock guards were located.

The general feeling in the Camp during this period was one of separation from the U.K. in as much as information in code letters was lacking. It was felt that although certain gadgets were being despatched to the Camp by I.S.9., information regarding policy was lacking. Direct advice of a positive nature regarding escape would have been invaluable.

The following is an extract from the M.I.9/S/P.G. report in respect of 126827 F/Lt. I.D. Bolton R.A.F.:

"I was registered as a user of Code 6 at Skellingthorpe by F/Lt. Williams in August, 1942. I sent my first letter containing a code message addressed to Mr. J.C. Bolton, 15, Whitefield Avenue, Cambuslang, Lanarkshire, in January, 1944 from Stalag Luft I (Barth). From January, 1944 until March, 1945 I sent about thirty-six letters containing code messages. These were addressed to my father, as above, or to Mrs. M.E.W. Patterson, 34 Stewarton Drive, Cambuslang, Lanarkshire. Nine of these messages dealt with the registration of new code users, the remainder contained general military information.

"The first letter was sent to F/Lt. Williams by my father as I had stated in the letter, in clear, 'Send this to Bill'. Two other letters addressed to my father, containing code messages contained the same message in clear, i.e. 'Send this to Bill'.

"After my return to the U.K. I made contact with F/Lt. Williams at Skellingthorpe. He informed me that he had decoded the first letter referred to above and sent the message it contained and a covering letter to 5 Group Headquarters. He told me that he had received the second letter passed to him by my father, but that he had not been able to decode it. He did not say what further action he took about it. He did not send the third letter, passed to him by my father, to 5 Group Headquarters as he knew it had been examined already.

"About October, 1944 a C.I.D. officer called upon my parents and asked for all my letters sent from Germany. No explanation was offered and my parents were very worried. The C.I.D. officer left instructions that the C.I.D. were to be informed when subsequent letters arrived. This was done and the letters were collected.

"My parents wrote to F/Lt. Williams and explained what had happened. He replied and told them not to worry about it. Sometime later my parents received a communication from Room 327, Hotel Victoria, signed by H.D. White, Esq., stating that letters received from me were to be sent to that address. A lot of correspondence ensued about a card from me, which had been mislaid: it was forwarded eventually. About three months later my parents were informed by a letter from Room 327 signed by Flt/O. Hampson, that letters need not be forwarded if they were marked with a red tick.

"About the end of June, 1945, I went to Room 327, Hotel Victoria and made enquiries about the correspondence which had taken place between my parents and that address. I was able to speak on the telephone to W/Cdr. Harrison, Air Liaison Officer, M.I.9., who arranged that Flt/O Yarwood should meet me at Hotel Victoria that afternoon.

"Flt/O Yarwood showed me the file of messages received from Stalag Luft I (Barth). It did not contain any messages from me. I noticed that the code word which I was using was not the one entered opposite my name. It appeared as 'Alan' which is the Christian name of F/O A. Bolton, also of Stalag Luft I and also a code user. No letters from this officer appeared in the file. The code word entered opposite this officers name was not the code word I was using.

"I noticed that there were very few messages in the file, and I know that a large number were sent. A list of about twenty-five names appeared in the file from whom no messages had been received. I know that a number of the personnel on this list did send code messages. I know of a number of officers who sent code messages whose names   did not appear on the list.

"The following were registered as code users by me in various letters containing code messages: S/Ldr. A. Abels R.A.F.; F/O D.J.H. Cheal R.A.F.; F/Lt. C.W.(?) Cole R.A.F.; F/Lt. A.P. Gobbie R.A.F.; F/O R.H. Kerr R.C.A.F.; S/Ldr. N.P. Samuels R.A.F."

Chapter 21

Radio and News-Letters

47. INTRODUCTION AND CONSTRUCTION

(a) *First receiver.*
This receiver was not completed until 31st December, 1943. During the process of construction the sizes and measurements of the components were decided by trial and error. As in the preceding period, all the work was done by 905095 W.O. Hurrell, H.L., R.A.F., assisted by 970434 W.O. Eames, J.J.W., R.A.F.

The set was worked off the mains until June, 1944, when it was converted into a battery operated receiver in order to listen to a broadcast at 0230 hours daily, when electric current was not available. Flash-lamp batteries were used from then onwards.

(b) *Second receiver.*
About May, 1944 an A.C. mains, all-wave, four-valve German commercial receiver was obtained by 5179986 Pte. May, G.E., Glos. Regiment, a member of the 'Trading' Section who was working as an orderly in the North (American) Compound at that time. The Americans were unable to get it into working order and offered it to the British. The offer was accepted and it was smuggled into the West Compound inside a large soap box.

It was found that the receiver was intact, except for the rectifying valve. Soon afterwards a suitable valve was obtained by another member of the 'Trading' Section and the set was ready for use.

The overhaul of the set was carried out by the Signals Officer at that time 128385 F/O J. Carter R.A.F.

Shortly after the set was put into operation the Signals Officer installed an earphone instead of the loud-speaker in order to reduce noise. At first the change was not satisfactory, but after various adjustments had been made there was a great improvement in reception.

During the winter of 1944 the set became unserviceable. It was dismantled and a two-valve receiver, capable of being operated on batteries, or the mains, was constructed from the parts, and components sent to the Camp from the U.S.A. This work, which was carried out mainly by the Signals Officer at that time J.10025 F/Lt. A.P. Smith R.C.A.F., assisted by 55036 W.O. Smith, W.G., R.A.F., was completed about January, 1945.

(c) *Third receiver.*
In the Spring of 1944 a large quantity of radio components was obtained by 550365 W.O. Smith, W.G., R.A.F., who was a member of the 'Trading' Section. Much of this material was surplus to requirements and the Signals Officer gave permission to Smith to construct a receiver. Smith was assisted by 521567 W.O. Hurford, G., R.A.F.

They constructed a one-valve battery receiver, but this was not very satisfactory. About two months later, in June, 1944, this set was converted into a mains one-valve receiver. This was operated until October, 1944, when it was converted into a two-valve mains receiver. About a month later the set was dismantled in order to provide replacements for [another] receiver.

(d) *Other receivers.*
A number of radio receivers arrived in the Camp in parcels from the U.S.A. None of these were used until a few weeks before the end of hostilities.

48. OPERATION
Until April, 1944 the Radio Section was controlled by the Security Officer, 103829 S/Ldr. D.J. Kilgallin R.A.F. Regiment. From that date onwards the Section was controlled by a Signals Officer. The successive Signals Officers were:

128385	F/O J. Carter R.A.F.	April – May 1944
J10045	F/Lt. A.P. Smith R.C.A.F.	June 1944 – February 1945
43196	W/Cdr. J.R. Blackburn R.A.F.	February 1945 – May 1945

(a) *First receiver.*
From 31st December, 1943 until June, 1944 this receiver was operated daily at 2100 hours by 905095 W.O. Hurrell, H.L., R.A.F., assisted by 970534 W.O. Eames, J.J.W., R.A.F., for the reception of the B.B.C. news broadcasts. Owing to adverse conditions, these broadcasts were not heard every day. The broadcasts were listened to by 49939 Major T.A.J.

Pritchard Parachute Regiment, who took down the new bulletins verbatim. These notes were transcribed and passed to the Security Officer. The set was converted to a battery receiver in June, 1944. From then onwards it was used for the reception of a special broadcast at 0230 hours daily. During the Winter of 1944 the Camp electricity supply was erratic, also the second receiver became unserviceable, and this set was used for the reception of the B.B.C. news broadcasts as outlined at the beginning of this Section, by the same personnel.

(b) *Second receiver.*
In early June, 1944 this set was brought into use and was operated daily, usually to receive the 1300 hours B.B.C. news broadcasts, by 108583 F/Lt. T. Mitchell R.A.F., assisted by J.20399 F/Lt. D.R. Knight R.C.A.F., Lt. O'Brien U.S.A.A.C., [and] 252991 W.O. Eshelby, R.A., R.A.F. The news bulletins were written down by Mitchell, or Knight, then passed for editing to 49939 Major T.A.G. Pritchard Parachute Regiment. The bulletins finally were passed to the Security Officer. This set became unserviceable during the Winter of 1944 and modifications were not completed until January, 1945. From then until 13th May, 1945 this set was used for the reception of the B.B.C. news broadcasts, by the same personnel as formerly.

(c) *Third receiver.*
This receiver was operated by 550365 W.O. Smith, W.G., R.A.F., assisted by 521567 W.O. Hurford, G., R.A.F., from June, 1944 until November, 1944 for the reception of the B.B.C. News broadcasts at 2100 hours daily. The bulletins were recorded by J.20399 F/Lt. D.R. Knight R.C.A.F., then passed to 49939 Major T.A.G. Pritchard Parachute Regiment for editing. Pritchard passed the final bulletins to the Security Officer. This receiver was dismantled in November, 1944.

(d) *Other receivers.*
These were operated by various American officers during the few weeks prior to the end of hostilities.

49. MAINTENANCE
(a) *First receiver.*
The repair and maintenance of this receiver was done by Hurrell assisted by Eames. From April, 1944 onwards they received advice and assistance from the Signals Officer. At first, Hurrell and Eames made most of the parts they required, but later some of these were obtained through the 'Trading' Section and in parcels from I.S.9. and the U.S.A.

(b) *Second receiver.*
From May until June, 1944 the overhaul, repair and maintenance of this receiver was done by the Signals Officer 128385 F/O J. Carter R.A.F., assisted by 108583 F/Lt. T. Mitchell R.A.F. From June, 1944 onwards this work was done by the Signals Officer of the period assisted by Mitchell and 550365 W.O. Smith, W.G., R.A.F. Spare parts were obtained through the 'Trading' Section, in parcels from I.S.9. and the U.S.A., and by dismantling the third receiver. Parts which were unobtainable were manufactured from scraps of material.

(c) *Third receiver.*
All repairs and maintenance was carried out by 550365 W.O. Smith, W.G., R.A.F., assisted by 21567 W.O. Hurford, G., R.A.F. Smith was in possession of a quantity of radio components which he had acquired from a German by bribery.

(d) *Other receivers.*
No details are known.

50. SECURITY
Throughout the period under review the Security Officer 103829 S/Ldr. D.J. Kilgallin R.A.F. Regiment was responsible to the Senior British Officer for all aspects of security in connection with the various radio receivers. After the appointment of a Signals Officer in April, 1944, Kilgallin delegated the responsibility for the safe custody of the receivers, spare parts, etc. and security in connection with operation of the receivers, to the Signals Officer.

The Signals Officer delegated the responsibility for hiding the receivers and spare parts to the personnel operating the sets.

Technically, the Signals Officer ensured that adequate arrangements were made to give warning of the approach of a German while the receivers were being operated, but in practice the personnel operating the sets made all the arrangements as their own safety depended upon an efficient 'watching' system. No operator was ever apprehended by the Germans, nor was any radio equipment found in the Southern part of the Camp.

(a) *First receiver.*
At first, this receiver was hidden in a cavity in a brick chimney in the room occupied by 985095 W.O. Hurrell, H.L., R.A.F., and other N.C.O's in a barrack in the West Compound. In June, 1944, when this receiver was converted to a battery set, a panel of the wooden double wall of the

barrack was hinged and the various units of the receiver arranged on it in such a way that nothing suspicious was visible when the panel was closed. The panel was locked with an invisible catch. The panel was located behind the head of a bed, and maps and pictures of aircraft were pasted over it. The earphones were hidden in dried milk tins fitted with false bottoms. The set was used after 'lock-up' and watchers were posted to give warning if any attempt should be made to enter the barrack.

(b) *Second receiver.*
When this receiver was conveyed from the North Compound to the Southern part of the Camp, it was taken to the Camp Theatre and concealed in the cavity formed by fitting a false back to the cupboard which formed part of the structure of the building. The set was used during the hours of daylight and watchers were on duty to give warning of the approach of any German. This was simplified by the fact that the theatre was some distance from the gate and other buildings.

(c) *Third receiver.*
It is believed that this receiver was hidden behind a panel, similar to the one described in sub-Section (a) of this Section, in a room in the barrack occupied by 550365 W.O. Smith, W.G., R.A.F., and other N.C.O's in the South-West Compound. The set was used after 'lock-up' and watchers were posted at both ends of the barrack to give warning if any attempt should be made to unlock the doors.

(d) *Other receivers.*
No details are known.

51. DISSEMINATION OF NEWS
(a) *Camp newspaper.*
In December, 1943 a camp newspaper was started by 85998 F/Lt. E.R. Inkpen R.A.F., assisted by 156011 F/Lt. G.J. Sleeman R.A.F., 134580 F/Lt. D.H. Spencer R.A.F., [and] 49939 Major T.A.G. Pritchard Parachute Regiment. This newspaper contained items obtained from German news broadcasts, German newspapers, the interrogations of new arrivals in the Camp. Details of Camp activities were included. This bulletin was issued daily and a sufficient number of copies were made on the office typewriters to enable one to be distributed to each barrack, where it was read at midday by an individual selected for his clarity of speech. The Germans were aware of this activity and approved of it. Its production was continued until the evacuation of the Camp after the end of hostilities.

(b) *'Red Star'*
From 31st December, 1943 until the evacuation of the Camp, all the B.B.C. news broadcasts which were heard on the three radio receivers, dealt with in the preceding Sections of this Chapter, were recorded in longhand and passed to the Security Officer 103829 S/Ldr. D.J. Kilgallin R.A.F. Regiment. When the bulletins were recorded from the 2100 hours B.B.C. news broadcasts they were passed to Kilgallin as soon as the barracks were unlocked the following morning. The 1300 hours bulletins were passed on immediately. In all cases Kilgallin at once placed the sheets of paper into a dried milk tin fitted with a false bottom.

Kilgallin lived in a barrack in the West Compound. He left the 2100 hours bulletins in their place of concealment until after the morning parade then, if no searches by the Germans were in progress in that Compound, he prepared a secret news bulletin known as 'Red Star'. This contained the B.B.C. news broadcasts, followed by any secret instructions from the Senior British Officer, and orders from the Security Officer about security matters, 'trading', etc. When the day's issue of 'Red Star' was completed Kilgallin dictated it to a typist. Firstly one copy of the B.B.C. news bulletin only was made on the smallest possible sheet of the thinnest paper available. This was handed to 925696 W.O. Drummond, R.R., R.A.F., who placed it in his wristlet watch, from which the works had been removed. Drummond then set the hands of the watch to the correct time and proceeded to the North Compound. The Germans permitted this as Drummond was the official liaison between the Senior British Officer and the Senior American Officer. The latter resided in the North Compound.

On arrival in the North Compound Drummond read his copy of the B.B.C. news bulletin to Mr. Lowell Bennett, an American journalist, who edited the North Compound newspaper. Drummond burnt his copy immediately.

As soon as Drummond's copy of the news had been typed, Kilgallin dictated the day's 'Red Star' to two typists, who made sufficient copies to enable one to be distributed to each barrack in the Southern part of the Camp. When completed Kilgallin passed these to the Security Officer in each barrack.

At midday, when all the P's/W were in the barracks for their lunch, the Barrack Security Officers posted watchers to ensure that no German could enter without warning being given, then handed 'Red Star' to the personnel selected to read the Camp newsletter. 'Red Star' was read first because the P's/W were most interested in its contents, and because the 'reader' could switch to the Camp newspaper in the event of a warning being received that a German was approaching.

224

(c) *Security.*

A copy of the American edition of the B.B.C. news bulletin was discovered in the North Compound by the Germans. The B.B.C. news bulletin was read daily to Mr. Lowell Bennett, an American journalist in the North Compound, and the typewritten sheet destroyed immediately afterwards. Bennett, who edited the North Compound newsletter, then re-wrote the B.B.C. news bulletin in American fashion and this was circulated in a similar manner to the British-controlled Compounds.

About August, 1944, the Germans carried out a search of Bennett's room and discovered a copy of the Americanised version of the B.B.C. bulletin. As a result, very intensive searches were conducted by the Germans, mainly in the North Compound, where some radio equipment was found. This convinced them that the radio receiver was being operated in this Compound and from then onwards frequent and intensive searches were carried out there in an endeavour to find it. This served to distract their attention from the Southern part of the Camp where the radio receiver was located.

52. VALUE AND REMARKS

The feeling of being in touch with the outside world through the reception of the B.B.C. news broadcasts was of inestimable value in maintaining morale throughout the period, especially during the Winter of 1944 when it was lowest. The following is an extract from a report by the Signals Officer, 43196 W/Cdr. J.R. Blackburn R.A.F., during the last few months:

"My work was not so much technical as diplomatic. All that was required was someone to put co-operation between 'Traders', Intelligence (English and American), Security and Signals, on a practical basis. It is recommended that when a camp becomes large enough and the Senior Officer sets up a Signals Organisation, that tact be one of the qualities prominent in the personnel selected".

53. W/T COMMUNICATIONS – INTRODUCTION

(a) *British.*

No code messages from British sources were received by radio. In September, 1944 an officer who was being repatriated to the U.K. on medical grounds was given full details of a code to be used for sending messages to the Camp from the U.K. by radio and the suggested wavelength. The Camp wireless receiver was trained on this wavelength at the suggested times for several months afterwards, but no messages was received. The Senior British Officers have stated: "It would appear that messages which are given to repatriated personnel were not getting through to the correct Department in the U.K." The officer who was briefed with the details of the suggested wireless code was 79272 F/Lt. R.H. Lucky R.A.F.

(b) *American.*

In June, 1944 the Senior Allied Officer informed the Senior British Officer that a radio programme, broadcast under the title 'Voice of America' contained encoded messages for P's/W. The Senior British Officer gave instructions to the Signals Officer that this programme was to be picked up and recorded verbatim. It was known that the broadcast took place about 0200 hours daily, and as the Camp electricity supply was cut off at this time, the radio receiver described in Section 1, sub-Section (a) of this Chapter was modified as stated therein. When the modification had been completed, a search of the wavebands was carried out daily from 0200 hours until 0230 hours before the first 'Voice of America' programme was picked up; this was on 13th August, 1944.

54. ORGANISATION – RECEIPT OF MESSAGES

(a) *Operation of receiver.*

From the beginning of July, 1944 until 13th May, 1945 this receiver was operated daily between 0200 hours and 0230 hours for the reception of the first 'Voice of America' programme. The operators throughout this period were 905095 W.O. Hurrell, H.L., R.A.F., [and] 962982 W.O. Kilminster, A.R., R.A.F. Hurrell worked on five nights each week and Kilminster on the other two. The programme was missed on only two or three occasions due to technical faults, or poor conditions for reception.

(b) *Recording of programmes.*

In order to decode the messages in the 'Voice of America' programmes, it was necessary that they should be recorded verbatim. To do this the services of a first-class shorthand writer were needed and action was taken to discover which of the P's/W had this qualification. These were tested and the most efficient was selected. He was 0-797626 Lt. L.V. Trouve U.S.A.A.C. This officer was resident in the South-West Compound at this time, but arrangements were made for his transfer to the West Compound where he was accommodated in the barrack in which the radio receiver was located. From the beginning of July, 1944, when attempts to find 'Voice of America' programme were started, until about October 1944, Trouve was on duty from 0200 hours daily and recorded all the programmes which were received. In the Autumn of

1944 he began to show signs of strain and about October an assistant was appointed. He was J.21192 F/Lt. A. Small R.C.A.F., who was moved into the barrack in which the radio set was located. Trouve and Small recorded the programme, working alternative nights, until the evacuation of the Camp on 13th May, 1945.

When it was known that the 'Voice of America' programme was broadcast at 0200 hours daily the Camp was scoured for an alarm clock to awaken the personnel who would be engaged in its reception. It was discovered that an Army orderly had one, but it was broken. It was handed over to Hurrell who repaired it and muffled the bell so that it could not be heard more than a few feet away. This was used by the wireless operator on duty each night to awaken him before 0200 hours, when he aroused the shorthand writer.

(c) *Decoding, etc.*
The shorthand writers transcribed their notes into longhand before parade each morning and handed these to Lt. Col. Mackenzie U.S.A.A.C, the American Security Officer in the Southern part of the Camp. After parade, Mackenzie decoded the message embodied in the programme and conveyed it to the Senior British Officer. A copy was written on a very small piece of paper and handed to 925696 W.O. Drummond, R.R., R.A.F., who took it to the Senior Allied Officer, in the North Compound. Drummond concealed these messages in his wristlet watch. If the messages in the 'Voice of America' programme contained any news of general interest to the P's/W the Senior British Officer conveyed the information to 103829 S/Ldr. D.J. Kilgallin R.A.F. Regiment for inclusion in that day's issue of 'Red Star' but this seldom applied.

(d) *Security*.
The radio receiver which was used to obtain these broadcasts was concealed in such a way that all outward traces of the set could be hidden in a few seconds, furthermore the operator could work whilst in bed. Because of these factors there was no danger of apprehension whilst the set was in use, as no German could enter the barrack without creating a noise as the door was locked. By the time a German could have reached the room in which the set was kept, both the operator and the shorthand writer would have been in bed feigning sleep, having removed all traces of their activities.

The operation of the receiver and the recording of the programmes was done with lighting provided by electric torches.

Only a few Senior Officers, apart from the operators and shorthand writers, knew about the 'Voice of America' programme.

55. VALUE AND REMARKS.

Although the receipt of the messages contained in the 'Voice of America' programmes was of no value to the general body of P's/W in the Camp, as they did not know of its existence, it was of great help to the Senior Officers in that they felt they were in direct touch with General Eisenhower's Headquarters. No message of particular significance to this Cam was received, but the Senior Officers knew that if such a message were sent, it would be received.

56. TRANSMITTER.

About August, 1944 a power and battery-operated radio receiver and transmitter, consisting of four units, was received in the Camp in parcels from the U.S.A. This set had a fault in the rectifier and was not used as the Senior Officers decided that it should be kept for use in an emergency only. It was kept in the cavity described [above], being concealed by 905095 W.O. Hurrell, H.L., R.A.F. It is believed that the Americans used this transmitter on one occasion after the Germans had evacuated the Camp.

57. NEWS-LETTERS

No news letters were received in this Camp during the period under review.

Chapter 22

Intelligence and Anti-German Propaganda

58. MILITARY INFORMATION
(a) *Methods of collection.*
In certain cases, selected personnel who were about to be repatriated to the U.K. were given detailed information which they had to learn by heart. They were briefed by the Senior British Officer and his Staff and instructed to repeat the message to an Intelligence Officer in the U.K.

(b) *Value of direction from I.S.9.*
From a report compiled by the Senior British Officers and the Chief of the Escape Committee it appears that very little direction in matters of policy was received from the U.K. Messages of a directive nature on matters of policy would have been invaluable to the Senior British Officer and the Escape Committee.

(c) *Adherence to direction from I.S.9.*
Little direction of a positive kind was received from I.S.9. and the Senior British Officer was forced to act on his own initiative without the support of instructions from the U.K.

59. INTERNAL SECURITY
(a) *Organisation.*
In order to guard against the possibility of the Germans introducing a spy into the Camp in the guise of a new P/W, the identity of each new arrival, British and American, was checked. This was done by specially selected P's/. No spy was discovered.

(b) *Peculiarities of Camp.*
The use by the Germans of amplifiers which were attached to the windows of barracks after 'lock-up' in order to listen to conversations

229

between P's/W. The use of an electrical system for indicating the location of vibrations caused by tunnelling as the perimeter fence was approached.

60. ANTI-GERMAN PROPAGANDA: INTRODUCTION

(a) *Conversations.*

At first there was no organised attempt to disseminate anti-German propaganda amongst the Germans. Only certain P's/W were permitted to converse with Germans and during the initial stages they endeavoured to lower the morale of their 'contacts' in order to bribe them to supply forbidden items. This proved to be an excellent method and as the 'Trading' Organisation grew in size and importance, the officer in charge of the 'Trading' Section, 108329 S/Ldr. D.J. Kilgallin R.A.F. Regt., instructed his 'traders' about the form the propaganda should take. It was found that emphasis on the rapid Russian advance was the best method of persuading Germans to be co-operative. In this connection much use was made of the 'Safe Conduct Pass'. Susceptible Germans were told that if they were sufficiently helpful one of these passes would be issued to them at the end of the war, otherwise they would be left to the mercy of the Russians.

(b) *Leaflets.*

In April, 1944 the distribution of anti-German propaganda leaflets was introduced by 34006 G/C N.W.D. Marwood-Elton R.A.F. When this officer arrived in the Camp at the beginning of that month, he noticed that apprehension about the advance of the Russians was growing amongst the Germans and decided to play upon it. He instructed a number of P's/W, who understood German, to translate all German newspaper editorials, Wehrmacht communiques and German news broadcasts heard over the Camp loudspeaker system. From these he compounded anti-German propaganda covering the following points:

(i) Promises made by Hitler and the German High Command which obviously could not be kept.
(ii) The increasing number of day and night raids made on Germany by British and American aircraft.
(iii) The progress of the British and American forces.

This propaganda was written in German on sheets of paper in the form of leaflets and distributed by the Barrack Security Officers. The leaflets were placed in conspicuous places around the Camp just before nightfall so that they would be picked up by the Germans who entered the Compounds at dark for 'lock-up'. In some instances, the leaflets were placed in the pockets of guards without them being aware of the fact at the time.

61. ANTI-GERMAN PROPAGANDA: RESULTS.
(a) *Conversations.*
The results of the anti-German propaganda spread by the 'Trading' Section proved very satisfactory. Towards the end of the war almost any forbidden article was obtainable.

(b) *Leaflets.*
The effect of the propaganda disseminated by the leaflet method can be judged by the fact that the Camp Kommandant made very strong representations to the Senior Officers, as a result of which the practice was stopped in August, 1944.

Chapter 23

Camp Defence

62. ORGANISATION

In order to meet any contingency which might arise with the collapse of Germany, a defence scheme for the whole Camp was drawn up in January, 1945 by the Senior British Officer, 33075 G/C C.T. Weir R.A.F., in conjunction with the Senior Allied Officer, Col. Zemke U.S.A.A.C.

It was anticipated that the Russians might drive across country, skirting Berlin, towards Lubeck, thus cutting the Camp off from contact with British or American forces. The plans which were made provided for this possibility.

The whole Camp was organised into Flights and Squadrons, each under the Command of an appropriate ranking senior officer.

The undermentioned personnel were responsible for organising the two main branches of the Defence Plan – Field Forces and Signals

134060	F/Lt. D. Bower	R.A.F.
69445	F/Lt. P.S. Lester	R.A.F.
89763	S/Ldr. A.I. McRitchie	R.A.F.
62214	Lt. Col. W.D.H. McCardie	Parachute Regiment
748199	W.O. Robinson, A.E.	R.A.F.

McCardie was in charge of all Field Forces and his plans included taking over the Camp from the Germans if that should be necessary, also the taking over of Barth aerodrome, the organisation of food and foraging parties, etc. Lester was his second in command. McRitchie was in charge of the Signals Section which was to be responsible for telephone services within the Camp and for the Field Forces, the generation and supply of electricity in the Camp and at Barth aerodrome, and the supply of water to the Camp. His chief assistants were Bower and Robinson.

63. OPERATION

The Germans evacuated from the Camp and withdrew from the area during the night of 30th April, 1945, and the Senior Allied Officer assumed control immediately. P's/W were detailed for duty as sentries and appropriate parts of the Defence Plan were put into operation. All German documents were examined.

The supply of water and electricity had been cut off by the retreating Germans, but within 24 hours water was supplied to the Camp by means of an auxiliary Diesel engine and electric pumps. This supply was maintained for the next two weeks, despite interference by the Russians. Within three days the Camp was supplied with electricity from two power stations in the surrounding countryside.

From the early hours of 1st May until the arrival of the Russians on 2nd May the whole Barth area, including the aerodrome, was under the control of the Ps'/W. On 1st May parties of P's/W began to clear the aerodrome of mines and bombs in preparation for their anticipated evacuation by air.

During the ensuing days an efficient telephone service was maintained within the Camp and to several points on the Barth Peninsula, including the town of Barth and the aerodrome. Water and electricity was supplied to the P's/W stationed at the aerodrome and to a nearby hospital which housed between 400 and 500 former inmates of a local Concentration Camp. On 12th May ten miles of telephone line was laid by the P's/W to various points between the Camp and the aerodrome, and to control points around the aerodrome.

On 11th May, Group Captain Weir persuaded the local Commander of the Russian forces, a Lieutenant Colonel, to accompany him to Wismar to make contact with the British forces. They travelled by car to Hafenau, where the Russian officer signed a statement to the effect that a 'cease fire' order concerning British and American aircraft would be in operation at stated times on 12th and 13th May. Group Captain Weir returned to Barth, having arranged with the British General at Hagenau for the arrival of 300 transport aircraft at Barth aerodrome at stated times on 12th and 13th May.

When Group Captain Weir returned to the Camp, he gave instructions for the evacuation of the Camp to the aerodrome in two parties. A letter to the Russian Commanding General was prepared informing him of the arrangements which had been made for the evacuation of the Camp. The despatch of this letter was so timed that its delivery to him coincided with the arrival of the first flight of aircraft.

The total evacuation of nearly ten thousand British and American personnel was carried out without incident on 12th and 13th May.

Index of Names

234